FEDERAL BANKING IN BRAZIL:
POLICIES AND COMPETITIVE ADVANTAGES

FINANCIAL HISTORY

Series Editor: Robert E. Wright

TITLES IN THIS SERIES

1 Slave Agriculture and Financial Markets in Antebellum America: The Bank
of the United States in Mississippi, 1831–1852
Richard Holcombe Kilbourne, Jr

2 The Political Economy of Sentiment: Paper Credit and the Scottish Enlightenment in Early Republic Boston, 1780–1820
Jose R. Torre

3 Baring Brothers and the Birth of Modern Finance
Peter E. Austin

4 Gambling on the American Dream: Atlantic City and the Casino Era
James R. Karmel

5 Government Debts and Financial Markets in Europe
Fausto Piola Caselli (ed.)

6 Virginia and the Panic of 1819: The First Great Depression and the
Commonwealth
Clyde A. Haulman

7 Towards Modern Public Finance: The American War with Mexico,
1846–1848
James W. Cummings

8 The Revenue Imperative: The Union's Financial Policies during the
American Civil War
Jane Flaherty

9 Guilty Money: The City of London in Victorian and Edwardian Culture,
1815–1914
Ranald C. Michie

10 Financial Markets and the Banking Sector: Roles and Responsibilities in a
Global World
Elisabeth Paulet (ed.)

11 Argentina's Parallel Currency: The Economy of the Poor
Georgina M. Gómez

12 The Rise and Fall of the American System: Nationalism and the Development of the American Economy, 1790–1837
Songho Ha

13 Convergence and Divergence of National Financial Systems: Evidence from
the Gold Standards, 1871–1971
Patrice Baubeau and Anders Ögren (eds)

14 Benjamin Franklin and the Invention of Microfinance
Bruce Yenawine, ed. Michele Costello

15 The Development of International Insurance
Robin Pearson (ed.)

Forthcoming Titles

The Development of the Art Market in England: Money as Muse, 1730–1900
Thomas M. Bayer and John R. Page

Camille Gutt and Postwar International Finance
Jean F. Crombois

FEDERAL BANKING IN BRAZIL:
POLICIES AND COMPETITIVE ADVANTAGES

BY

Kurt E. von Mettenheim

Routledge
Taylor & Francis Group

LONDON AND NEW YORK

First published 2010 by Pickering & Chatto (Publishers) Limited

Published 2016 by Routledge
2 Park Square, Milton Park, Abingdon, Oxfordshire OX14 4RN
711 Third Avenue, New York, NY 10017, USA

First issued in paperback 2015

Routledge is an imprint of the Taylor & Francis Group, an informa business

BRITISH LIBRARY CATALOGUING IN PUBLICATION DATA

Mettenheim, Kurt von, 1957–
Federal banking in Brazil: policies and competitive advantages. – (Financial history)
1. Banco do Brasil. 2. Caixa Economica Federal (Brazil) 3. Banco Nacional de Desenvolvimento Economico e Social (Brazil) 4. Banks and banking, Centra – Brazil. 5. Monetary policy – Brazil.
I. Title II. Series
332.1'1'0981-dc22

ISBN-13: 978-1-138-66136-3 (pbk)
ISBN-13: 978-1-8489-3065-0 (hbk)

Typeset by Pickering & Chatto (Publishers) Limited

CONTENTS

Acknowledgements   ix
List of Figures and Tables   xi

Introduction   1
1 Government Banking Theory   5
2 Bank Change in Brazil   29
3 The Banco do Brasil – *with Maria Antonieta del Tedesco Lins*   59
4 The Caixa Economica Federal (Federal Savings Bank)   101
5 The Banco Nacional de Desenvolvimento Econômico e Social
    (National Bank for Economic and Social Development, BNDES)   145
Conclusion   173

Notes   183
Works Cited   205
Index   219

ACKNOWLEDGEMENTS

This book was written at the Fundação Getulio Vargas Escola de Administração de Empresas de São Paulo (Getulio Vargas Foundation São Paulo Business School, FGV-EAESP) and University of Oxford Centre for Brazilian Studies. Research began in 2002–3 with support from GVpesquisa (FGV-EAESP research fund) and the Fundo de Àmparo a Pesquisa do Estado de São Paulo (São Paulo State Research Fund, FAPESP). Discussions with Lourdes Sola, Moisés Marques, Maria Rita Loureiro and the late Eduardo Kugelmas about the construction of monetary authority helped launch this study. Chapter 4 began as a course on political sociology prepared for the management trainee programme of the Caixa Econômica Federal (Federal Savings Bank, Caixa). Trainees were keenly aware of crony credit and jobs-for-votes trading at the bank. However, they were also inspired by reforms that sought to shift policies toward bankless Brazilians. Early ideas about savings banks and epistemic communities were presented at meetings of the International Political Science Association Research Committee on Democratisation.

A Lecturership in Brazilian Studies at St Cross College made it possible to convene a workshop on Brazilian federal banks in February 2004 and complete a first draft. Thanks are due Leslie Bethell, Peter Evans, Jenny Corbett, Mariano Laplane, Valpy Fitzgerald, Leonardo Martinez, André Carvalho, Robert Bruce Hall, Albert Fishlow and colleagues and students at the Centre for comments and suggestions. Special thanks are due to Laurence Whitehead and Antonio Barros de Castro. Revisions at EAESP incorporated suggestions from anonymous readers and members of our research group on Banking Democratisation, especially co-author of Chapter 3, Maria Antonieta del Tedesco Lins and research assistants Ivan Salomão, Cesar Mori, Gustavo Martucci, Lívia Tominaga and João Maeda. Colleagues and students in the Graduate Programme in Public Administration and Government and, especially, our research group on state reform and public policy (Fernando Abrucio, Luiz Carlos Bresser Pereira, Maria Rita Loureiro, Regina Pacheco) provided further comments.

An international seminar on public banking convened in São Paulo in August 2006 refined comparative and theoretical perspectives. Support from the Konrad Adenauer Foundation and GV pesquisa helped bring political scientists, financial economists, financial statisticians and executives from international financial institutions and public banks together to assess government banking, development policies and social inclusion in advanced and developing nations. Barbara Stallings, Rogerio Studart, Andreas Hackethal, Frédéric Boccara, Olivier Butzbach and José Mena provided insightful presentations about banking in Europe, Asia and Latin America.

Alkimar Moura, Brasilio Sallum, Carlos Augusto Vidotto, Luiz Carlos Bresser Pereira and Maria Rita Loureiro read the manuscript as submitted for transition to full professor in the chair of political sociology at the EAESP Department of Social and Legal Sciences. The University of Washington Department of Political Science provided office space and access to the Suzallo library during July 2007 for reading in the political economy of banking. Presentations on savings bank modernization delivered to senior Caixa management and staff during 2008 and access to untapped historical materials at Caixa archives in São Paulo and Brasilia helped expand the scope of this study. Finally, Armando Vieira and Natalia Fingermann provided assistance while Daire Carr and staff at Pickering & Chatto ensured timely editing and production.

LIST OF FIGURES AND TABLES

Figure 1.1: Government, Private, and Foreign Bank Lending as percentage of GDP, 1988–2009   8

Figure 1.2: Bad Credit in Government, Private and Foreign Banks, Percentage of Total Loans, 1988–2009   9

Figure 1.3: Four Theories of Government Bank Change   15

Figure 2.1: Government, Private, and Foreign Bank Credit to the Federal Government, 1995–2009   35

Figure 2.2: Bad Credit in Government, Private and Foreign Bank Lending to Federal Government, 1988–2009   36

Figure 2.3: Government, Private and Foreign Bank Credit to State and Municipal Governments, 1995–2009   37

Figure 2.4: Bad Credit in Government, Private and Foreign Banks to State and Municipal Governments, 1988–2009   38

Figure 2.5: Government, Private and Foreign Bank Credit to Industry, 1995–2009   39

Figure 2.6: Bad Credit in Government, Private and Foreign Banks to Industry, 1988–2009   39

Figure 2.7: Government, Private and Foreign Bank Credit for Home Loans and Construction, 1995–2009   40

Figure 2.8: Bad Credit in Government, Private and Foreign Banks for Home Loans and Construction, 1988–2009   41

Figure 2.9: Government, Private and Foreign Bank Rural Credits, 1995–2009   42

Figure 2.10: Bad Credit in Government, Private and Foreign Banks to Rural Entities, 1988–2009   43

Figure 2.11: Government, Private and Foreign Bank Credit to Business, 1995–2009   44

Figure 2.12: Bad Credit in Government, Private and Foreign Banks to Business, 1988–2009   45

Figure 2.13: Public, Private, and Foreign Bank Credit to Consumers, 1995–2009   46

Figure 2.14: Bad Credit in Government, Private and Foreign Bank Credit
     to Consumers, 1988–2009   46
Figure 3.1: Banco do Brasil Share Price, 2000–4   96
Figure 3.2: Banco do Brasil Share Price, 2004–9   96
Figure 4.1: Caixa Market Share of Credit to Public and Private Sector,
     1968–2003   125

Table 1.1: Largest Twenty-Five Banks in Brazil, 2006   6
Table 1.2: Government, Private and Foreign Bank returns in Brazil,
     2000–6   9
Table 1.3: Liberal and Developmental/Coordinated Systems in Political
     Economy   20
Table 1.4: Comparing Funds for Public Policy with and without Govern-
     ment Banks   22
Table 2.1: Comparing Late Loans and Provisions in Banks, 2001–8   54
Table 3.1: Banco do Brasil Balance Sheet Summary, 2002–8, R$ billion   92
Table 3.2: Comparing Banco do Brasil, Itaú and Bradesco, 2002–9   94
Table 4.1: Caixa Deposits, Withdrawals and Balance at Treasury,
     1861–89, $000.   112
Table 4.2: Caixa Deposits compared to Banco do Brasil and Bank System,
     1862–89, million milréis   113
Table 4.3: Balance of Provincial Caixa Operations, 1874–81, $000   114
Table 4.4: São Paulo State Caixa Econômica, 1875–1920   118
Table 4.5: Summary of Caixa Structure and Performance, 1995–2008   134
Table 4.6: Caixa Performance Indicators, 2005–8   136
Table 4.7: Caixa AA-H Credit Classification, 2001–8   138
Table 5.1: BNDES Interbank and Non-Bank Loans, 1995–2008, US$
     Billion   161
Table 5.2: BNDES Loan Approvals by Programme, 1995–2007, R$ Bil-
     lion   162
Table 5.3: BNDES Financial Results, 2002–6   164

INTRODUCTION

The elementary truths of political science and statecraft were first discredited, then forgotten.

Karl Polanyi, *The Great Transformation*
(New York: Farrar and Rinehart, 1944), p. 33

Government banks make sense. As banks, they retain competitive advantages because of greater client confidence and unbeatable brand names such as the Banco do Brasil. As policy instruments, they provide branch offices, automated teller machines and mobile services over cellular phones to reach citizens. Their staff can manage complex information about local needs, measure costs, benefits and risks, and assert contractual control to correct public policies before they run astray. Government banks provide large policy levers for political leaders and social forces. These institutions are often large enough to provide counter-cyclical credit to avert or ameliorate recessions. Federal banks may implement reforms such as privatizations and public sector modernization through 'IMF-like' conditional loans to sub-national governments. In the past, directed credit from government banks drove rapid industrialization in late-developing countries. Such policies continue in many emerging, transition and developing nations. But government banks do much more than direct industrial change. Government *savings* banks have served local communities across Europe, some for centuries, to emerge after liberalization of the industry and monetary union with increased market shares and renewed social mandates. Brazilian federal banks have also emerged from military rule, abuse by traditional elites during prolonged transition, monetary disorder and financial crises to shape development and democracy. Three big banks, a commercial-investment bank, a savings bank and a development bank provide over a third of domestic credit in twenty-first-century Brazil. These institutions are commanding heights, both in the traditional sense of directing large industry and in a new sense. Federal banks have provided a new channel for social inclusion of the bankless (80 per cent of Brazilians in 2000!) and essential policy alternatives for reform and economic management amidst boom and bust cycles.

A problem with government banks is that liberal market economies such as the United States and United Kingdom have none (ignoring support/ownership during crisis and past experiences). Government banks remain dissonant from liberal principles such as free trade and free market equilibrium. Nonetheless, these institutions remain at the centre of political economy in advanced and developing countries. Federal banks in Brazil have persisted because they provide valued policy alternatives and retain competitive advantages over private and foreign banks.

This returns to old ideas about how public banks may steer development and sustain social economies. However, the question is not whether commanding heights can centralize power and policy. This study is about commanding depth, both in a social and a financial sense. From Lenin through Alexandre Gerschenkron, Arthur Lewis and Gunnar Myrdal, central government banks were seen as critical agents for rapid industrialization and modernization. To *command depth* implies decentralization and diffusion to embed government banks in society, politics, firms and markets. Unless government banks are part of the complexity, diversity and contestation involved in citizenship, political parties, interest groups, social movements and transparent government that reflect the separation and diffusion of power true to democracy, then government banks will fall short of their potential. Large-scale lending offends liberal principles and often damages the environment. It also distances decisions from citizens, institutions of representative government and measures of supervision and control that are needed for democracy *and* prudent banking, sound risk analysis and informed decision making about resource allocation.

These claims are grounded in theories of political economy, banking and democratization. However, they differ from neo-liberal theory. The Brazilian case counters the idea of global convergence toward private banking through liberalization and privatizations. This is not an anti-market observation. The Brazilian stock market Bovespa grew from 3 per cent of GDP in 1990 to over 100 per cent of GDP in 2008 (before losing then regaining *half* its value), with a variety of futures markets, mutual funds and financial instruments now available to firms and investors. These advances notwithstanding, government banks still provide over a third of domestic credit. Government banks have not impeded financial development. To the contrary, Brazilian federal banks have led in the creation of new markets and new banking services in Brazil. Case studies describe how these institutions have been central players in the record number of initial public offerings, the unprecedented capitalization of firms on the stock market, policies designed to democratize stock and bond ownership and the creation of futures markets for interest rates, foreign exchange and commodities that have served as bellwethers to approximate public policy and investor confidence. Without government banks, Brazilian financial markets would not be where they are today.

Government banks have not crowded out financial markets. Instead, paraphrasing Polanyi's claim about regulation, government banks and markets have grown together in Brazil. Federal banks have also implemented new social services and family grants through ATM citizenship cards to help reverse severe inequality. This has impaired neither their leadership in credit, finance and capital markets, nor their ability to help adjust the economy and reform the public sector.

Bank change in Brazil thus confirms core ideas in political economy about varieties of capitalism and institutional foundations of competitive advantage. Differences from liberal market economies and neo-liberal theory do not imply dysfunctionality. And Brazil is not an outlier. Government banks remain at the centre of both coordinated market economies across Continental Europe and many emerging and developing nations. This anomaly for liberal theory and market-centred approaches both inspired this study and shaped its course. Research began in 2001 when privatization remained an unshaken principle at international financial institutions and largely accepted as best policy by scholars. Orthodoxy was also adopted by the coalition government led by President Luis Inácio Lula da Silva's Partido dos Trabalhadores (Worker's Party, PT) in 2003 to avert a foreign exchange crisis that would have delegitimized the Brazilian left for a generation. Consensus about neo-liberalism has since given way, but comparative studies, causal analysis and alternative theories remain embryonic. To explain why federal banks remain so important in Brazil, it was necessary to go back to basics in political economy, public policy and banking.

Debates in comparative financial economics about bank-centred versus market-centred financial systems first led me astray. The compelling fit between this dichotomy and Hall and Soskice's varieties of capitalism (liberal and coordinated market economies) seemed to provide the key to explaining why government banks remained so important in Brazil. However, as reference to the booming Brazilian stock market suggests, the dichotomy between bank- and market-centred financial systems is forced and now out of favour. Financial economics now emphasizes the importance of legal systems and the particularity of domestic configurations of banking and finance. The liberalization and deepening of financial markets in traditionally state- and bank-centred systems such as France and Japan (and Brazil, ignoring differences for the moment) also reveals that banks and markets mix better than scholars feared. But the banks versus markets dichotomy tends to obscure a more fundamental reality about Brazil. Advanced political economies tend to have *both* deeply leveraged bank credit and capital markets. Developing nations tend to have *neither*.

This is a study of how federal banks helped bring Brazil out of underdevelopment, military rule and monetary chaos by providing policy options for adjustment, reform and social inclusion. Brazilian federal banks helped buffer shocks, induce reform, reach the bankless and manage the economy. This has involved innovations in electronic banking and information technology, growth more driven by the service sector and popular consumption, second-generation or microeconomic reforms and the organization of a new democracy in a large but underdeveloped emerging economy. Theory and evidence suggest that government banks may steer financial systems toward social inclusion, sustain growth during crises and compete against private and foreign banks.

Since the late 1990s, citizenship cards (110 million), family grants (12.5 million), new simplified bank accounts (9.8 million) and bank correspondents (110,000) have reached an estimated 40 million bankless Brazilians. Social banking has a long history. And micro-credit, finance and insurance have become widely discussed since the United Nations declared 2005 International Year of Microcredit and the 2006 Nobel Peace Prize was rewarded to the Grameen Bank and Muhammad Yunus. Microcredit has profound implications for political economy. A core assumption in theories of both Welfare States and democratic breakdown is that markets constrain political change and limit social policy. This is now only partially correct. Theories of banking and money, information technology and innovations such as ATM citizenship cards suggest that past constraints to change may be circumvented. Not ignored, circumvented. New policies and channels for change are at hand. Advances in monetary theory and policy, central banking, credit risk analysis, more transparent financial reporting standards, basic income policies and client confidence in public institutions suggest that capitalism in the twenty-first century provides different channels for change than the large wage increases and fiscal excesses that fuelled conflict and contributed to democratic breakdown in the past. The microeconomics of social inclusion differ from the macroeconomics of populism. This has fundamental consequences for labour parties, social movements, theories of the state, conceptions of constraints to change and comparative studies of public policy and democratization.

These arguments were not clear in 2001. Nor were they apparent to Brazilian policymakers. Indeed, the intuitive reluctance to privatize federal banks in Brazil illustrates how policymaking differs in developing countries. Instability, uncertainty, complexity, volatility and shifting circumstances mean that policymaking in developing countries is usually closer to Lindblom's description of *muddling through* than derived from theories or ideologies. The centrality of Brazilian federal banks is thus as surprising to participants and observers as it is an anomaly for liberal theory. The structure and content of this book reflect this element of surprise, puzzle in the face of anomaly and search for explanation amidst deeply contested concepts and theories that cross several social science disciplines.

1 GOVERNMENT BANKING THEORY

The Anomaly

This book began when I opened the morning paper in São Paulo on 21 June 2001. Finance Minister Pedro Malan and Central Bank President Arminio Fraga had capitalized Brazilian federal banks to meet Bank for International Settlement (BIS) Basel II Accord guidelines for capital risk. The image of a US-trained economist and advocate of liberalization and privatizations aside a former emerging markets trader at the Soros Fund announcing the capitalization and reform of government banks seemed very odd. Was this another bailout of bureaucrats? Why did reformist President Fernando Henrique Cardoso capitalize rather than privatize these banks after seven years in office, just a year before a decisive campaign to elect his successor? Was this a return to Brazilian statism? Did private banks somehow conspire or acquiesce to keep out foreign competitors (having acquired state government banks and large market shares themselves)? Were Brazilian federal government banks simply too big to fail or too broke to privatize? A mental experiment came to mind. What would a US president do with three big banks? President Andrew Jackson's veto of the Second Bank of the US in 1832 made it hard to imagine a US federal bank (I later learned of Abraham Lincoln's advocacy of a National Bank and the US Postal Bank, 1945–8). But the experiment stuck. It seemed impossible that having three big banks under government ownership and control made no difference for policy and political economy.

Understanding these differences was not easy. A glance at primary materials confirmed that each federal bank has a long history and still-marked place. Founded to finance the Portuguese empire in 1808, the (third) *Banco do Brasil* remains the largest financial conglomerate in Latin America and primary agent in Brazilian capital markets, agriculture and agro-industry, international trade and export finance. Founded as an act of royal philanthropy in 1861, the *Caixa Econômica Federal* (Federal Savings Bank, Caixa) led during most of the twentieth century in terms of popular savings and credit, urban development, sanitation and directed credit for housing while providing social benefits such as pensions, unemployment funds and income grants. Founded in 1952, the *Banco Nacional de Desenvolvimento Econômico e Social* (National Economic and Social Development Bank, BNDES) has since provided long-term credit to infrastructure and strategic economic sectors, coordinated privatizations during the 1990s, and remains a major source of corporate finance, agent for new development strategies, manager of directed credit programmes, export-import bank, leading underwriter of initial public offerings and mergers and acquisitions, the globalization of Brazilian firms and source of liquidity during financial crises, notably during the recent global crisis.[1]

Table 1.1: Largest Twenty-Five Banks in Brazil, 2006.

Bank	Assets	Net Worth	Net Profit	Deposits	Emp.	Br.	Basel	FA/EQ
BANCO DO BRASIL*	136.613.854	9.709.148	1.008.226	74.294.181	107.101	4.048	17.25	14.84
BRADESCO	99.767.507	11.579.412	877.735	39.274.622	70.924	3.018	18.76	48.01
CAIXA*	98.004.132	4.294.887	487.470	56.777.592	104.934	2.428	25.29	19.75
BNDES*	86.597.553	8.929.808	1.409.654	12.253.204	1.855	5	24.71	52.41
ITAÚ	95.957.053	13.193.919	1.572.156	29.112.769	57.989	2.534	18.30	42.18
ABN AMRO	55.734.473	4.952.260	548.288	25.789.623	31.039	1.095	13.76	19.87
SANTANDER -BANESPA	47.767.043	3.730.408	351.965	14.932.317	22.955	1.062	15.37	16.50
UNIBANCO	45.736.733	4.686.155	334.095	17.011.394	25.917	934	15.99	44.85
SAFRA	28.915.032	1.920.519	231.435	6.045.194	5.629	104	12.44	14.33
HSBC	27.252.445	1.923.253	234.119	17.645.040	27.724	935	14.23	34.83
VOTORAN-TIM	26.523.612	2.407.178	310.708	9.186.754	692	10	16.08	1.63
NOSSA CAIXA**	18.390.735	1.215.599	76.507	12.893.481	16.630	539	23.39	19.88
CITIBANK	14.385.030	1.491.466	95.432	2.600.211	4.950	111	12.87	18.33
UBS-PAC-TUAL	9.476.453	679.869	155.805	1.225.867	464	4	16.73	8.76
BANRISUL**	7.342.052	605.414	80.821	4.903.108	10.931	415	20.16	24.04
BBM	5.800.638	311.067	51.299	1.071.975	330	6	16.09	9.10
BNB*	5.836.026	702.689	59.075	1.238.575	10.496	181	18.98	12.23
ALFA	5.180.416	575.503	40.104	1.779.066	1.009	9	16.99	12.69
BNP PARIBAS	4.992.136	428.500	18.732	1.639.454	290	4	19.34	4.88
DEUTSCHE	4.212.961	244.925	55.105	518.355	209	2	20.01	8.88
CREDIT SUISSE	5.056.844	564.159	56.465	1.306.820	81	2	28.21	3.52
JP MORGAN CHASE	3.874.013	696.515	14.753	181.495	326	5	31.57	3.36
FIBRA	3.903.320	206.104	20.576	868.367	316	1	13.56	12.75
BIC	3.426.139	250.306	24.133	1.178.536	683	27	15.16	4.14
BASA*	2.412.966	794.710	60.559	429.956	4.499	102	33.82	16.73

Source: Central Bank of Brazil. Top fifty banks, available at www.bcb.gov.br
Note: * = federal government bank. ** = state government bank. FA/EQ = fixed assets / equity.
Basel = Basel II Accord Index of Capital Adequacy.

Brazilian federal banks remain commanding heights. Not in the sense of Clause IV of the 1918 British Labour Party programme that has come to symbolize unrealized aspirations of European socialism. Nor do they solely pursue rapid industrialization as emphasized by Gerschenkron, Myrdal and Lewis in the 1960s and 70s. There is no single doctrine behind these institutions. They were captured by rent seekers under military rule (1964–85) and traditional elites to feed inertial inflation during the 1980s and early 90s. However, instead of following the theory of financial repression and recommendations from abroad to privatize state enterprises (especially banks) to free markets, Brazilian policy-makers capitalized federal banks and challenged these institutions to reform and develop new strategies for faster growth and social inclusion. Comparisons with private and foreign bank performance in Brazil and three case studies suggest that they have done so, certainly more than the still widespread belief in privatization would expect.

Before we get to the argument, a look at federal banks and banking in Brazil is in order. Table 1.1 reports the US dollar value of assets, net worth, net annual profits and deposits, the number of employees and branch offices and the Basel Index and ratio of fixed assets to equity for the largest twenty-five banks in Brazil at year-end 2006. The Banco do Brasil, Caixa and BNDES remain three of six financial institutions that dominate domestic banking. The global integration of Santander (having acquired São Paulo state bank Banespa) and ABN-Amro (having acquired the Brazilian private bank Real) placed a new foreign bank near the top five. Merger between Itaú and Unibanco in 2009 created the largest private bank in Latin America and bumped Bradesco from second place. In 2008, Banco do Brasil acquisition of Nossa Caixa (São Paulo state savings bank) and purchase of 51 per cent stake in Votorantim Bank reasserted its first place and further concentrated the industry. Banking in Brazil thus centres on three federal banks, two private domestic banks (Bradesco and Itaú-Unibanco) and one new foreign bank (Santander). Six banks thereby increased market share of bank assets in Brazil from 60.6 per cent in 2006 (R$566.7 of R$934.4 billion) to 76.5 per cent in September 2009 (R$1.53 of R$2.0 trillion).[2]

The data also suggest that federal banks are not black holes. Returns on assets, profits, liquidity, measures of capital risk, reserves against losses, level of bad and late loans, efficiency ratings and *many* further indicators presented in this study suggest that the Banco do Brasil, Caixa and BNDES remain competitive financial institutions fifteen years after opening the industry to foreign competition and ten years after privatization of most state government banks. This is the anomaly for neo-liberal theory. Federal banks remain at the top of Brazilian banking fifteen years after price stability, privatizations and opening the industry to foreign competition.

Trends in lending, bad loans and bank returns confirm this anomaly. The trajectory of public, private and foreign bank lending in Brazil as a percentage of

GDP from 1988–2009 suggest that liberalization, privatization of state govern-ment banks and reform of federal banks have transformed the industry. A new division of financial labour has replaced the state-centred system built during the twentieth century under national populism, developmentalism and military rule (see Figure 1.1). From 1988 at the brink of hyperinflation to 2001 (when bad credits were transferred to an asset management entity at Treasury in June), credit from government banks declined from 23.8 to 8.2 per cent of GDP. How-ever, government bank credit almost doubles after 2001 to reach 16.0 per cent of GDP by March 2009. Private bank lending also dropped to 6.0 per cent of GDP under instability by 1990, but surpassed the value of government bank credit during 2001 to reach 26.5 per cent of GDP by 2009. Foreign banks also gradu-ally increased market share from below two per cent of GDP in 1990 to 8.7 per cent by 2009. This data is disaggregated in Chapter 2 and case study chapters.

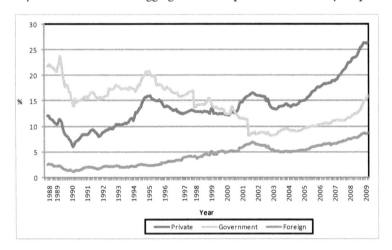

Figure 1.1: Government, Private, and Foreign Bank Lending as percentage of GDP, 1988–2009.
Source: Central Bank of Brazil, Sisbacen, 2009.

Increased credit can simply be bad credit that will never be repaid. Bad credit is thus a standard measure of quality in banking and bank systems. Data from the Central Bank of Brazil suggest that the performance of government banks has converged toward levels of private and foreign banks operating in Brazil (See Figure 1.2). Bad credit in government banks rose during economic instability in the early 1990s (from 12–22 per cent 1989–92) and again during economic crises (14–22 per cent in 1999 and 15–19 per cent in 2003). Early peaks of bad credit in government banks also reflect acquisition of late and non-performing loans from private and public banks assumed by the federal government during the 1995–6 banking crisis (one caused by price stability examined in Chapter 2). Since privatization of state government banks in the late 1990s and cleanup and capitalization of federal banks in 2001, peaks of bad credit in government bank portfolios reflect their counter-cyclical role. Bad credit increases during crisis and downturn. However, the trend is clear. Since economic recovery in 2003, the value of bad credit held by government banks fell under 10 per cent of total credit, breaching the difference between government, private and foreign banks. Government banks have converged toward the performance standards of foreign and private banks operating in Brazil.

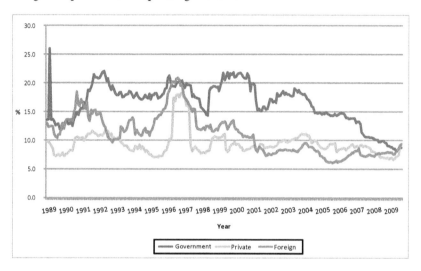

Figure 1.2: Bad Credit in Government, Private and Foreign Banks,
Percentage of Total Loans, 1988–2009.
Source: Central Bank of Brazil, Sisbacen, 2009.

Table 1.2: Government, Private and Foreign Bank returns in Brazil, 2000–6.

		Government		Private		Foreign	
Business Cycle	Semester	RLA	ROA	RLA	ROA	RLA	ROA
Before Capitalization	Dec. 2000	5.5	0.4	9.4	1.1	−6.0	−0.6
	June 2001	−12.0	−0.9	10.5	1.2	−20.4	1.9
During Crisis and Adjustment	Dec. 2001	−3.6	−0.3	10.2	1.2	7.9	0.8
	June 2002	7.6	0.5	8.2	0.9	12.8	1.4
	Dec. 2002	12.3	0.6	20.2	2.0	28.4	3.4
Since Recovery	June 2003	22.2	1.2	19.7	2.2	8.5	1.1
	Dec. 2003	23.5	1.3	16.0	1.7	10.1	1.4
	June 2004	19.9	1.1	19.8	2.2	10.6	1.3
	Dec. 2004	21.5	1.3	26.2	3.0	6.1	0.8
	June 2005	24.9	1.5	24.6	2.8	8.6	1.0
	Dec. 2005	26.5	1.7	25.9	2.9	16.6	1.8
	June 2006	33.7	2.2	27.3	3.0	10.6	1.0

Note: RLA = returns on liquid assets, ROA = returns on assets.
Source: Central Bank of Brazil, *Financial Stability Reports*, 2002–6.

Further evidence that government banks have performed well since capitalization and reform in 2001 can be seen by comparing their returns with private and foreign banks from 2000–6 (see Table 1.2). Transition toward international financial reporting standards at the Central Bank of Brazil breaks the time series after 2006, but case studies and further comparisons confirm this trend through adjustment to the recent financial crisis and recovery during 2008–10.

Losses during 2001–2 reflect the reality that banks confronted 1) an economic shock due to energy shortages, 2) capital flight from Brazil in the wake of the 11 September attacks on the US and 3) perceptions of political risk during 2002 that produced further capital flight, a twofold devaluation of the real against the US dollar, inflationary pressures and the need for tougher adjustment that reduced bank lending. Lower government bank returns during 2001–2 also reflect downsizing from reforms. However, strong returns at government banks since 2001 suggest that these institutions performed *better*, on average, than private domestic banks. And since recovery during 2003, government banks have reported returns *almost double* those of foreign banks. High interest rates and bank spreads, the concentration of the industry, different portfolios and policies and barriers to competition may partially explain these results. But comparison of returns sums with the data on bank size, performance and market shares to introduce our anomaly for liberal theory. Since 2001, federal banks in Brazil have converged towards and often outperformed private and foreign banks.

The Explanation

Our explanation of this anomaly is that Brazilian federal banks provide policy alternatives and retain competitive advantages. This checks preferences for privatization and counters two further bodies of scholarship, critics of government banking in the new political economy and views of politics and statism in Brazil as largely dysfunctional. To counter recent critics of government banking, we return to fundamentals of banking theory and classics in political economy such as Polanyi, Gerschenkron, Shonfield and Zysman. This study also suggests that views of Brazilian politics and policies are dated and biased. There is now gradual recognition that problems after transition from military rule have given way to new developments under democracy. But accounts of Brazil remain biased by idealized views and slippery benchmarks from older democracies and advanced economies.[3] Political development in Brazil was reversed by military coup in 1964. Brazilian politics also proved disappointing during the terribly prolonged transition from military rule (formally 1985, but really 1974–94!). This study examines change after 1994, a better baseline year because it combined the first full national elections after military rule and the Real Plan that restored price stability after a decade of record inertial inflation. Our findings are thus about political development. Because federal banks provided policy options, sustained coalitions for reform and helped implement new social policies able to bypass political machines built under military government to bring social services and basic income to bankless Brazilians, these institutions have contributed to democratization and political development.

This implies that Brazilian *federal* banks differ from *state* government banks responsible for unchecked creation of money during the 1980s and early 90s.[4] The mismanagement of state government banks by traditional regional elites and their role in deepening monetary disorder under military rule and prolonged transition have been widely cited and exceptions noted.[5] However, scholars have also recognized that reforms to improve fiscal discipline, bank supervision, privatizations and financial transparency came from the top-down and centre-out.[6] Federal government reforms were often resisted by entrenched elites in state government banks determined to retain control over jobs and access to easy money. Federal banks also differ from state banks because federal politics differs from state politics. Federal politics is more contested, involves more actors and draws more media attention. It also bears repeating that bad banking increased during military rule and prolonged transition before mechanisms of external control, transparency, bank supervision and international accounting standards were introduced. Democracy cannot be blamed for abuse of government banks in Brazil.[7] Indeed, financial repression (the crowding out of market forces by state allocation of credit and finance) occurred most notably under military rule and during a 'last dance' syndrome[8] wherein traditional elites pillaged state banks while opposition leaders were absorbed with writing a new constitution and learning how to run the federal government.

But disagreements about government banking go beyond Brazil. Government banks inspire fundamental disagreements about the validity of state intervention, the value of banking for development and proper relations between politics, public policy and markets. We suggest that government banks provide advantages in the Brazilian context of underdevelopment, shallow markets, dismal income distribution and volatile business cycles. Government banks provide policy options and powerful means to induce public sector reform. Their branch offices, ATMs and correspondent-banking service points improve access to public goods and banking. Banks, especially government banks, provide more patient capital than equity markets to help firms and households through hard times. As banks, government banks can monitor firms, debts and the economy better where shallow markets fail to provide accurate information and impede efficient pricing. Government banks provide longer time horizons for infrastructure and social investments where private agents remain unwilling to put money. Government banks also provide a powerful fiscal advantage. They produce more public policy for less cash. Government banks can help cover the costs of public policy because they retain competitive advantages over private and foreign banks. Their reputations, organizational breadth and networks that cross politics, branches of government and social forces provide competitive advantage in banking and shape markets. In Brazil, government banks also embody traditions of social economy and solidarity that resonate with the reformist and labour parties that have emerged in the country since transition from military rule. These claims are based on theories from several disciplines.

The Literatures

Explanations of bank change in Brazil are taken from a tradition in political economy that emphasizes how politics and governments shape markets.[9] Specifically, this study focuses on how organized interests, ideas, political parties and epistemic communities shape domestic financial systems.[10] Polanyi's *The Great Transformation* and Shonfield's *Modern Capitalism* remain canons. Polanyi argued that *laissez faire* policies during the nineteenth century generated movements of social self-defence in the form of organized labour, efforts to address the social question (such as savings banks and cooperative banks although he did not mention them) and central banking, the latter created to protect private banks from downturns and currency devaluation under the gold standard. Import tariffs, imperialist rivalries, subsidies to agriculture, military mobilization of large industry and top-down social policies also prevailed over liberalism and free markets, especially after the 1873 financial crisis. In the twentieth century, *politics* continued to dominate economic policy during two world wars and recovery from global depression. After 1945, Shonfield argued that Continental European 'miracles' were engineered by recasting government ownership to meet imperatives of recovery rather than ideology or nationalist design. Necessity and improvisation also place government banking in post-war Europe closer to Lindblom's *muddling-through* than Leninist theories that saw large state banks as means to ideological ends.[11] For Shonfield, government intervention is consistent with liberal and pluralist conceptions of policymaking.[12] And Shonfield places government banking *first* among five factors explaining why rapid growth was sustained in post-war Continental Europe.[13]

Shonfield's treatment of causal relations across politics, public policies and economic growth also remain relevant. Issues such as the importance of improved data, forecasting and transparency for convergence between public policy and investor expectations remain beyond the scope of this study. But his emphasis on improvisation, reacting to circumstances, unexpected consequences and the forging of epistemic communities is essential to explain bank change and the size, shape and importance of federal banks in Brazil. Shonfield's idea of policy *coordination* also remains at the centre of research in political economy, finance and banking. From this perspective, banking and finance have to do less with abstract estimates of optimal equilibrium or efficiency and more to do with social networks and political webs that link public and private sectors, determine the reputations of managers and make or break public and corporate finance. In financial economics, this is described as relational banking.[14] In political economy, this is described as policy coordination.[15] Both point to institutional foundations of competitive advantage. And both often involve government banking.

Since Shonfield, political economy has clarified the virtues and vices of government intervention and ownership. Early comparisons tended to contrast market-centred experiences (usually the UK and US) with state-centred experiences in France and Japan or social corporatism in Germany.[16] Post-World War II growth under Welfare States remains memorable. However, since stagflation in the 1970s, political economists have shifted back and forth in evaluation of government intervention. During the 1980s, scholars tended to describe advanced economies as neo-corporatist and emphasize how business groups and trade unions shaped or constrained policies.[17] During the 1990s, research became more micro, focusing on specific industries and sectors, innovation strategies and developments on factory floors such as flexible production.[18] During the 2000s, the varieties of capitalism approach and studies of finance, money and banking once again returned to the macro level to understand the more profound processes of liberalization across advanced, developing, transition and emerging economies.

Research has thereby returned to core ideas of Polanyi and Shonfield. For Kirschner, because finance and money policies often impact welfare equally and in unpredictable ways, politics determines policy choices and market equilibrium.[19] The politics of building coalitions for economic reforms and adapting policies to domestic markets and institutions have also become central in recent research.[20] Hoffman argues that *political* philosophies periodically recast US banking during critical junctures since independence.[21] Coming closer to our object of inquiry, Laurence, Toya and Amyx argue that *politics* explain the origin, character and implementation of big-bang financial reforms in Great Britain and Japan in the 1980s.[22] Pérez describes how domestic groups shaped banking and finance reforms in Spain,[23] an argument consistent with both Maxfield's analysis of a banker's coalitions in Mexico[24] and Woo-Cummings analysis of politics and finance in Korea.[25]

Maxfield's comparison of banking in Mexico and Brazil through the 1980s suggested that economic internationalization increases dependence on capital flows and, consequently, the power of (private) bankers' coalitions. The evidence from Brazil through the 1980s is consistent with her argument. Because the Brazilian economy remained closed and barriers to competition in banking remained in place until the 1990s, a domestic (private) banker's coalition favouring orthodox policies and independent central banking consistently lost disputes to national-developmentalist networks. Chapter 3 traces a veto coalition and caucus led by Banco do Brasil staff that delayed creation of a central bank until 1965 under military rule.[26] However, liberalization (and privatization of state government banks) opened Brazilian banking and finance to foreign competition in the 1990s. This has indeed reinforced coalitions of private bankers along the lines suggested by Maxfield, Pérez and Woo-Cummings. But here our anomaly arises. The capitalization, reform and competitive advantages of federal banks suggest both a different political logic and more complex division of financial labour. Neither liberal theories of privatization nor the power of a private banker's coalition fully explain bank change in Brazil.

Theories of Government Bank Change

Our explanation of bank change in Brazil is based on one of four broader theories. Figure 1.3 represents these theories along two axes, a vertical axis representing levels of welfare and a horizontal axis the market orientation of domestic banking and finance. The first, most widespread theory of government bank change can be described as modernization. For theories of modernization, privatization increases welfare and produces financial development.[27] Because privatizations increase welfare, the relation between politics and privatizations is positive sum.[28] Privatization of government banks reinforces political groups and leadership by improving corporate governance, reducing waste of resources and eliminating inflationary pressures that arise from bad banking. Replacement of inefficient state-owned banks with more efficient private banks and market forces increases welfare and improves distributive justice. The privatization of government banks is thus part of a broader process of modernization towards a liberal market economy, one with stock markets, shareholders and private banks at the centre of the financial system. This view is widely shared in international financial institutions and the social sciences, despite reassessments since collapse of private banks and markets in the US during 2007. Social science research has also cast doubt on the idea of convergence toward financial market centred economies and private banking.[29]

Critics of government banking also advocate the theory of privatizations as modernization. La Porta, Lopez-de-Silanes and Schleifer argue that 'government control of finance, through its banks or otherwise, politicizes resource allocation for the sake of getting votes or bribes for office holders, softens budget constraints and lowers economic efficiency'.[30] They also argue that this view is 'buttressed by considerable evidence documenting the inefficiency of government enterprises, the political motives behind public provision of services and

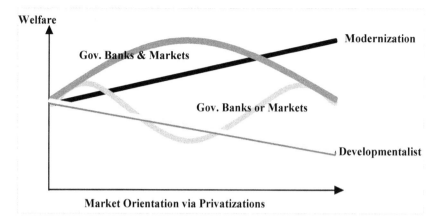

Figure 1.3: Four Theories of Government Bank Change.
Source: Top three from: J. P. Krahnen and R. H. Schmidt (eds), *The German Financial System*
(Oxford: Oxford University Press, 2004), pp. 497–516.

the benefits of privatisation' and, finally, that 'government ownership of banks is higher in countries with less developed financial systems'. Government banks are thus supposedly responsible for moral hazard and financial repression, crowding out free markets and impeding the flow of finance and credit.[31] From this perspective, government banks reproduce underdevelopment, poverty, rent-seeking and bad equilibrium.

This view is wrong for three reasons. First because free markets are presumed to be superior, second because correlations between government ownership and underdevelopment are spurious and third because aggregate patterns in national data tend to conceal how causal relations determine development paths.[32] Statistical analysis of cross-national aggregate data can rarely support such strong claims. Instead, the aggregation of data tends to *conceal* both differences across financial systems and the direction of causal relations. This can be described as the fallacy of aggregation. Given the small number and contested character of government banks, it follows that case studies and small *n* comparisons are required to identify causes and understand consequences.[33] Fortunately, case studies of large banks provide an analytic advantage. Because federal banks provide over a third of credit in Brazil, analysis of corporate governance, financial statements, annual reports and balance sheets, organizational structures and banking phenomena on the micro level reveal consequences that sum to the meso- or macro-level.

This is not to deny the contribution of critics. They describe how government banking can go wrong and provide measures to control for bad banking. But critics fail to consider how government banks may succeed, as banks, as agents of public policy and as essential parts of political and social economies.

Mismanagement of government banks is part of Brazilian history, especially under monarchy, military rule, protracted transition and inertial inflation. But it is not the whole story. Theory, comparisons and three case studies suggest that these institutions cannot be disregarded as corporatist agents of crony credit, fiscal excess, moral hazard, undue rents and inflation, especially since transition to democracy in 1994.

A second theory of bank change is described as 'government banks or markets'. In this theory, welfare can be maximized in *either* bank-centred financial systems *or* market-centred financial systems. The dual peaks in the medium grey line of Figure 1.2 represent two alternative but *incompatible* financial systems. Core functions of finance can be performed by different structures in different ways. Either banks or financial markets can allocate household savings to firms, smooth consumption and corporate investments over time and spread the cost of covering household risk and entrepreneurial innovation. The relation between politics and privatization of government banks from this perspective is zero-sum because of transition costs between financial systems. And the barriers to reform are political. Given the consequences of privatizations and market reforms in the short term such as unemployment and dislocation, leaders will find it difficult to maintain political coalitions and/or office long enough for benefits to appear.[34] Comparative financial economists suggest that bank- and market-centred financial systems may generate similar levels of welfare. If these systems are equal, why then would politicians incur the costs of transition from a (government) bank-centred financial system to a market-centred financial system?

Moreover, Allen and Gale argue that bank- and market-centred financial systems may not be equal. Banks may smooth shocks to domestic economies *better* than markets. Inter-temporal smoothing is a core idea in finance that, in the long term, welfare is higher when adjustment averts greater downturns in business cycles. Allen and Gale note that the oil price shock of 1973 caused the value of stock markets to decline by half from 1972 peaks in paradigmatic market-centred economies (US and UK), causing severe contraction in household incomes, especially pensions based on equities. In contrast, because neither households nor pensions held many equities in the bank-centred systems of Japan, Germany and France, these countries were able to adjust with substantially lower costs.[35] Since the 1980s, booming equity markets often shifted judgements in favour of market-centred financial systems. And even severe downturns are defended by advocates of free markets as 'creative destruction' necessary for modernization. However, the severity of financial market downturns during the 2000s alongside successful adjustment and recovery in countries with paradigmatic bank-centred financial systems such as Germany and Japan suggest that bank-centred financial systems may indeed have once again fared better.

Allen and Gale also estimate *better* equilibrium across generations in an intermediated (bank-centred) financial system compared to a market-based system. In this respect, Allen and Gale concur with the varieties of capitalism approach and reinforce our core argument. Banks are not necessarily culprits of bad equilibrium and slow growth. Banks can monitor firms, provide longer term finance and use local knowledge and information better than liquid equity markets. It follows that bank-centred financial systems may produce stronger, more sustainable growth than economies based exclusively on equity markets. These capacities of banks are critical in a large but still underdeveloped economy like Brazil. And if government banks perform adequately as banks, it is not a slight of hand to insert the adjective 'government' in front of banks or bank-centred financial systems.

King and Levine also suggest that the capacity of banks to work with information (greater incentives for research and analysis, proprietary control, freedom from disclosure) may make banks better than 'atomistic' markets.[36] Banks may also finance innovative firms better than markets because of longer time horizons and more credible commitments and contracts to fund projects when they take off. However, the information advantage of banks may produce distortions. Hellwig and Rajan argue that these advantages can lead banks to extract rent and protect firms rather than finance innovation.[37] Weinstein and Yafeh argue that banking (and regulatory requirements) can induce conservative bank behaviour and impede innovation.[38] Networks of banks on corporate boards can also lead to collusion with firm managers against outside investors to veto innovation.[39] In sum, banks can outperform markets in terms of core functions of finance. However, banking also involves risks that may undercut these advantages.

Our explanation of bank change in Brazil is part of a third group of theories that affirm that *combining* attributes of bank- and market-centred financial systems may maximize welfare. This theory of 'government banks *and* markets' is portrayed in Figure 1.3 with a single peaked dark grey line. From this perspective, market orientation improves welfare up to a certain point, but wholesale privatization of banks and deregulation of financial markets would reduce welfare beyond that point. Liberalization may improve competition. Privatizations may help political leaders shed government banks that are beyond reform or bailing-out. However, because government banks provide policy alternatives and retain competitive advantages over private and foreign banks, complete privatization would, in theory, decrease welfare. Relations between politics and privatizations from this perspective are positive sum, up to a point, and negative sum after optimal equilibrium between government banking and market orientation has been reached.

This third 'government banks and markets' theory of bank change is reinforced by recent research that emphasizes market failures, the importance of legal systems and recognition of the complexity and diversity of domestic finance and banking. Combining government banks and financial markets may maximize welfare because public banks serve as effective intermediaries to overcome information barriers and avert market failures.[40] Allen and Gale also argue that models assuming perfect information and free markets poorly describe financial systems. It follows that privatizations, especially wholesale privatizations, may fail to free market forces and increase growth, especially in developing nations with shallow markets. Banks help overcome information barriers to efficient market pricing. And government banks can fulfil this role.

In a broader sense, recent research in finance is consistent with this third 'government banks and markets' theory of change because scholars no longer set banks against financial markets.[41] This also turns on the fallacy of aggregation. Cross-national statistical analysis has been unable to confirm causal relations between types of domestic financial systems and growth (or industrialization or other measures of financial development).[42] This reinforces perceptions that the particularity of domestic configurations of banking and finance matters. Demirgüç-Kunt and Levine advertise their edited volume suggesting that the evidence 'points not to markets versus banks, but to markets and banks'.[43] If government banks perform well, provide policy alternatives and retain competitive advantages, then a combination of government banks and markets, in theory, can be seen to maximize welfare. Finally, new research from critics of government banks such as La Porta emphasize the importance of legal traditions and relational banking. This also suggests that a division of labour and combination of attributes from bank-centred and market-centred financial systems may produce the highest levels of welfare.[44]

Our theory of government bank change is represented by a single peaked dark grey line indicating a single optimal equilibrium combining banks, government banks and financial markets. Because government banks provide policy options and retain competitive advantages, a single optimal political economic equilibrium obtains. The relation between politics and privatization from this perspective is positive, up to this optimal mix of government banking and liberalization, and negative thereafter. The Brazilian banking system can be said to have approached this peak once the industry was opened to foreign competition and state government banks were privatized.

A fourth group of theories about government bank change critical of privatization can be described as developmentalist. This perspective includes approaches such as the commanding heights tradition, nationalist and developmentalist perspectives, theories of policy coordination in coordinated market economies, Post-Keynesian approaches and critical approaches toward market failures and corporate governance. These different traditions and approaches are represented by the light grey line that indicates a negative relation between privatization, market orientation and welfare. This fourth group of theories about bank change includes a variety of approaches in political economy. For example, Bresser-Pereira reviews errors of liberalization and calls for a new developmentalism.[45] Amsden argues for a return to classic themes about production and government policies in late development.[46] Evans and Chang also argue that most states still embed and underpin economic policies and that market-centrism during the 1980s and 90s has concealed this fundamental insight.[47] These differences about bank change are not new.

Liberal versus Coordinated and Developmental State Economies

The existence of four competing theories about government bank change reflects the essentially contested character of political economy. For the commanding heights tradition, government banks were seen as critical to accelerating industrialization. Critics hold that government banks are among the worst cases of state intervention, impeding more efficient resource allocation and repressing free markets. The global financial crisis has produced reassessment and reinforced state-centred policies and approaches in political economy. Hall and Soskice describe Continental European experiences as coordinated market economies. For these perspectives, government policies and political forces are seen as fundamental for social inclusion, sustainable development and the maintenance of comparative and competitive advantages. For liberal critics, government banks and intervention are grabbing hands that reproduce underdevelopment and bad equilibrium. These debates cross the social sciences. Table 1.3 summarizes the concepts and characteristics associated with what can be described, after Chalmers Johnson, as two fundamentally opposed liberal market and developmental state traditions.

Government banks tap fundamental differences. Comparative financial economists differ about market- and bank-centred systems. Corporate governance studies retain diametrically opposed views about banks, markets and firms summarized in categories of 'outsider' or 'insider' control. Management styles vary accordingly, from the arms-length market for managers reinforced by financial markets and outsider control to the face-to-face management style and insider control of corporate governance found in bank-centred financial systems. Debates about banking involve defenders of free banking and financial markets (that reinforce outsider control and arms-length management) versus defenders of bank-centred systems and public and mixed ownership of banks (that reinforce face-to-face management styles and internal control of corporate governance). Banking is thus at the heart of different varieties of capitalism.[48] Liberal market-economies are driven by equity markets, thrive on public information and spurn coordination. Coordinated market-economies are driven by bank credit, thrive on concealing (limited sharing) of firm strategy with financiers and spurn markets for their excessive volatility. In sum, from a market-centred perspective, neo-institutionalism is nothing but neo-protectionism. From the perspective of coordinated capitalism, excessive financial liberalization and privatizations would simply throw babies (cherished institutions of social policy and domestic control) out with the bathwater.[49]

Table 1.3: Liberal and Developmental/Coordinated Systems in Political Economy.

	Liberal	Developmental/Coordinated
Concepts		
Max Weber	*Verkehrwirtschaft*	*Planwirtschaft*
Ralf Dahrendorf	Market Rationality	Plan Rationality
Ronald Dore	Market-oriented systems	Organization-oriented systems
George Kelly	Rule-governed State	Purpose-governed state
Hall and Soskice	Liberal Market	Coordinated Market
Government Characteristics		
State Type	Regulatory state	Developmental State
Predominant Branch	Legislature	Executive
Legal Tradition	Common Law	Roman Law
Policy Debates	Neo-Classical Economics	Public Goods
Social Characteristics		
Social Structure	Mobile	Hierarchical
Elite Formation	Private Sector	Public Sector/Mixed
Labour	Mobile	Fixed
Labour Union Strategies	External Bargaining	Internal Participation
Educational System	Liberal Arts	Vocational-Technical
Income Equality	Lower	Higher
Finance & Management		
Financial System	Financial Markets	Banks
Corporate Governance	Outsider	Insider
Management Style	Arms Length	Face-to-face
Inter-Firm Relations	Independence	Networks/Cross-shareholding
Banking System	Private	Public/Mixed
Core Ideas		
Normative Bias	Individual Liberty	Collective Good
Core Value	Individual Freedom	Solidarity
Welfare Maximization	via Competition	via Cooperation
International Projections	Convergence	Divergence
Information	Transparency	Proprietary
Core Basis	Economic	Political
Policies		
Pension System	Private/Individual	Public/Universal
Comparative Advantage	Free Markets	Invest in Institutions
Interest Organization	Pluralist	Neo-corporatist
Employment Protection	Lower	Higher

Source: First three lines, Johnson, *Miti and the Japanese Miracle*, p. 18. Subsequent lines, Hall and Soskice (2001), Allen and Gale (2000), Berger (1981), Jackson (2003), Vitols (2003).

These debates frame study of Brazilian banking. However, concepts from advanced economies should not conceal how large but underdeveloped countries like Brazil provide a far different setting. Advanced economies have consolidated institutions and more stable markets embedded in social and political relations. In comparison, households, firms and governments in Brazil and other developing countries face volatile business cycles, shallow markets and less durable ties and networks in society and politics. And politics in Brazil, and other new democracies, are based neither on compelling social pacts, nor on class compromises along the lines of Keynesian policies and Welfare States in Europe. New and often embattled democracies in developing countries also pale in comparison to past experiences with national-populism, state-led development and import substitution industrialization that promoted social inclusion and legitimized regimes. Neo-conservatism and neo-liberalism have largely failed to generate stable partisanships. Politics, policies and banking in developing countries therefore tend to tap fundamental disagreements about markets, institutions, government, law and social justice. Policymaking in developing countries amidst volatility, crises and even catastrophe implies a different type of unsettling statecraft.[50]

Because government banks provide policy alternatives and retain competitive advantages, these institutions are critical for political and economic development. It follows that, instead of insisting on forced dichotomies and antagonistic policy options from advanced economies (whether liberal versus coordinated market economies or banks versus markets), it is more accurate to say that, in Brazil, there is room for all. This reinforces the idea of a positive sum division of financial labour, between capital markets and banks and across private, foreign, government and cooperative institutions. Chapter 2 examines this new division of financial labour after liberalization in Brazil.

The Advantage of Government Banks for Public Policy

Critics argue that government banks are less efficient than private banks. From aggregate, cross-national comparisons or simple measures of bank efficiency it is inferred that privatization would provide benefits. Other economists differ.[51] Comparison of bank performance and three case studies suggest this claim of greater efficiency in private banking is overstated. But comparisons of bank efficiency (basically administrative costs) not only tend to commit the fallacy of aggregation, they also conceal fundamental differences for public policy.

Government banks provide large levers for government. In terms of fiscal cost and government budgets, government banks can do more for less: *ten times more* if one compares the cash needed to directly implement public policy to holding cash in reserve at government banks to secure loans, credit, finance, consortia or sale of stocks or bonds.[52] This is the core of government banking theory.

Government banks can implement public policies at 10 per cent the fiscal cost of cash outlays. From the broader perspectives of politics, public policy and development, a 90 per cent cost advantage more than compensates for the 2–10 per cent higher levels of administrative costs in government banks (compared to private banks) cited by critics.

The advantage of government banking for fiscal accounts and public policy is illustrated in Table 1.4. The first column reports hypothetical annual budget allocations of one million in (any) domestic currency eleven years out from 2000. Each year the government has one million available. The second column sums this hypothetical spending from 2000–10 (total spending = 11.0 million). The third column calculates the advantage of government banking for public policy. Given the same one million allocated per year, it calculates the amount government banks are permitted to lend under Basel II Accord guidelines against capital risk (i.e. ten times reserves, rounding and ignoring risk weighting for the moment). One million in reserve covers ten million in loans. Profits or losses are not counted. According to this exercise, the amount available for governments without banks sums in column two to 10.0 million by 2010. Compare column three. For governments *with* government banks the total value of loans sums to 110.0 million. Government banks cannot perform all tasks of government. However, when they can, they provide a tenfold cost advantage as well as instruments for contractual control and policy supervision.

Table 1.4: Comparing Funds for Public Policy with and without Government Banks.

Year	From same $ Budget		Government Spending without Banks		Value of loans via Government Banks
2000	1,000,000	→	1,000,000	vs	10,000,000
2001	1,000,000	→	2,000,000	vs	20,000,000
2002	1,000,000	→	3,000,000	vs	30,000,000
2003	1,000,000	→	4,000,000	vs	40,000,000
2004	1,000,000	→	5,000,000	vs	50,000,000
2005	1,000,000	→	6,000,000	vs	60,000,000
2006	1,000,000	→	7,000,000	vs	70,000,000
2007	1,000,000	→	8,000,000	vs	80,000,000
2008	1,000,000	→	9,000,000	vs	90,000,000
2009	1,000,000	→	10,000,000	vs	100,000,000
2010	1,000,000	→	11,000,000	vs	110,000,000

Note: Figures based on 10 per cent reserve requirement. If government bank is allocated one dollar, real, or euro, the bank can lend ten times that amount keeping in reserve cash against risk of non-payment of loans. BIS Basel II Accord capital guidelines set this figure at 8 per cent (risk weighted), while Central Bank of Brazil guidelines set this figure at 11 per cent. Ten per cent is used for clarity of calculation. Retained profits or losses not counted.

Banking theory describes banks as multipliers of money. Banks do not create money through magic. To create money they must create assets. More accurately, they must help create assets by providing credit and finance to individuals, firms and other entities public and private. This holds for government banks. Budget allocations to government banks become reserves against loans. These loans multiply the amount of money in the economy. It follows that concerns about banks also apply to government banks. Excessive lending may feed inflation. Banks may create credit bubbles that exacerbate boom-and-bust cycles. Without adequate supervision, crony credit, corruption and waste of resources may occur, whether the bank is private, domestic, foreign, government owned or a cooperative. We control for these risks throughout this study. However, the core and largely unappreciated difference between private and public banking is not the often slight or nonexistent efficiency advantage of private over public banks (an empirical question) but the very large levers that government banks provide policymakers. Even the self-professed Brazilian liberal economist and policymaker Roberto Campos argued for development banking in these terms. For Campos, shifting from cash outlays to government banking (and therefore cost-benefit and credit analysis, and supervision and control during the implementation of projects and programmes) would increase government capacity, improve control, decrease government spending and accelerate economic development during the 1950s.[53]

The Advantages of Government Banks for Social Inclusion

Brazilian federal banks also provide policy options for social inclusion. Debates about these institutions during the 1990s were overshadowed by the risk of inertial inflation, fiscal reforms and the realities of reconstructing monetary authority. During the early 2000s, debates about federal banks turned on their ability to provide counter-cyclical lending to speed recovery from economic shocks and financial crises (this came to the fore once again in 2008–9). However, as markets recovered, foreign capital returned and the pace of growth in Brazil increased during 2004, different questions emerged on the policy agenda. Perhaps the most innovative involve a variety of efforts to accelerate social inclusion. Brazilian federal banks have experimented with new policies designed to expand access to finance, provide micro-credit and use correspondent banking to reach unbanked regions and citizens. Their success counters expectations that opening the industry would broaden banking services through leadership of more efficient private and foreign banks.

Case studies explore how federal banks used competitive advantages to reach bankless Brazilians. From 2000–7, Central Bank data suggest that the number of bank accounts in Brazil has increased from 63.7–112.1 million (from 37.5 to

60.6 per cent of population).[54] From 2000–7, the number of savings accounts increased from 45.8 million to 82.1 million (26.9 to 44.3 per cent of population) and debit cards from 28.0 million to 93.0 million (16.4 to 50.2 per cent of population). These numbers (of bank accounts) overstate change because Central Bank estimates indicate that individuals with bank accounts tend to hold, on average, between 1.5–2.0 bank accounts.

The margin of error is large but cannot conceal the stark level of underdevelopment. Access to banking is a concern in advanced economies where, generally, over 90 per cent of citizens hold bank accounts. If Central Bank estimates of 1.5–2.0 bank accounts per person (from 2006) are accurate for preceding years, then between 18–23 per cent of Brazilians owned bank accounts in 2000. Using the same calculation, new policies have increased the number of Brazilians with bank accounts to between 30 and 40 per cent of the population in 2007. Around 38 million Brazilians have thus been brought into the banking system since 2000. This change is notable, but access to banking in Brazil still remains shockingly low in comparative perspective.

The evidence nonetheless suggests that federal banks have been *by far* the largest agents for providing banking services to the bankless in Brazil. Research at the World Bank suggests that access to banking services has a substantial impact on the alleviation of severe poverty.[55] If World Bank estimates are correct, then the impact of an increase of 48.4 million bank accounts, 36.3 million savings accounts and 65 million bank cards from 2000–7 can be seen as a significant contributing cause to the marked improvement of living standards among the worst off in Brazil that has been reported in government censuses and independent research.

The 2006 National Household Survey (Pesquisa Nacional de Amostra a Domicílios, PNAD) of the Instituto Brasileiro de Geografia e Estatística (Brazilian Institute of Geography and Statistics, IBGE) indicates that 48 million Brazilians (one quarter of population) lived in 11.2 million families with federal government family grants as their exclusive source of income. Family grants distributed through ATM cards have been widely credited with reducing destitution and poverty. Marcelo Neri's studies of PNAD social surveys estimate that family grants are responsible for forty per cent of social improvements recorded since 1994.[56] From 1992–2006, misery in Brazil is estimated to have declined from 36.5–19.2 per cent of population. Extreme poverty is estimated to have fallen from 11.7–4.7 per cent. From 1993–2008, the Gini coefficient is estimated to have declined from 0.62 to 0.52. Family grants and other social services introduced during the 1990s and early 2000s such as school grants, unemployment insurance and pension funds were consolidated into a single *Cartão do Cidadão* (Citizenship Card), an ATM bank card (with the Caixa brand name on it). Citizenship Cards have been distributed to over 110 million Brazilians by the Caixa since 2002 under federal government contract. This provides competitive advantage. The Caixa has requested permission from the Central Bank to transform Citizenship Cards into debit cards. This would more than double the number of bank cards in the country. These policies are examined in the Caixa case study chapter.

Bank change in Brazil provides new perspectives on economic constraints to change. Since abandonment of the electoral road to socialism and the breakdown of democratic regimes in Latin America and other developing nations during the 1960s and 1970s, social scientists have emphasized economic constraints on government policy, limits to popular inclusion and the perverse impact of politics on markets. Przeworski summarizes this structuralist view of constraints to change exemplified by the breakdown of democracy in Chile in 1973.[57] Transitions from authoritarian regimes in Southern Europe, Latin America, Eastern Europe and the former Soviet Union and many developing countries have done little to change the overwhelming sense that markets severely constrain governments and social policies. Meanwhile, neo-conservative politics and neo-liberal policies have dismantled Welfare States and worsened inequalities in many advanced economies. This study reports progress from the periphery. Policies of popular savings and credit have brought large numbers of bankless Brazilians into the economy and reversed forces of impoverishment and exclusion.

Government bank change implies new relations between markets, money and politics. Until recently, the macroeconomics of populism, economic constraints on public policy, capital flight in the face of labour, left or nationalist governments and financial crises in developing and emerging countries all tended to set politics and social inclusion against market efficiency and good policy. To the contrary, recent theory, policy and evidence suggest that inclusion of bankless Brazilians was essential to *improving* the ability of the Central Bank and monetary authorities to manage the economy. Concepts in monetary economics developed during the 1990s such as the credit channel and interest rate channel help describe how banks may pursue policies of social inclusion that do not reduce investment and drag growth. Instead, the relation is positive sum. As bankless Brazilians are brought into the formal economy, tax revenue increases and policies become *more* effective in terms of managing credit flows, interest rates and the pace of economic activity. Advances in the transparency of financial reporting, government accounts and banking supervision reinforce this shift and provide new kinds of data about government policy, market perceptions, bank portfolios, credit risk and social inclusion. This has profound consequences for theories of constraints to change.

The Competitive Advantages of Government Banks in Banking Theory

Banks are institutions that accept deposits and make loans. This is a minimal definition that captures the core characteristics of banks. Banks do many other things such as provide financial services, manage assets and liabilities, pursue business strategies, play important and sometimes dominant roles in financial markets and retain networks and memberships on the boards of large corporations and small firms. Banks make donations to political parties and candidates. They seek to influence agendas and government policies through industry associations, interest groups and lobbying. Banks tend to be *more* political than other enterprises. Large banks symbolize national presence and success in the global economy. Banks are often seen as too important to fail, even by politicians normally disposed to close firms to avert moral hazard. Moreover, other institutions provide many of the same services as banks such as stockbrokers, insurance companies, pension funds, mutual funds, credit cooperatives, mortgage and savings associations and a variety of other entities.

Banking theory provides concepts used herein to examine Brazilian federal banks. However, we start with a warning. Traditonally, economists argued that banks *do not* play an independent causal role in growth and development. Gurley and Shaw described banks as intermediating institutions that respond to policies of monetary authorities on the one hand and non-financial agents on the other.[58] Fama argued that banks simply provide payment services and allocate resources according to the Modigliani-Miller theorem (that describes financial decisions as neutral or irrelevant to economic equilibrium).[59] Neo-classical theories of banking provide a more dynamic view of banks. Tobin argued that 'old views' of banks failed to consider the impact of loan practices and interest rates on the economy.[60] For Tobin, bank assets and liabilities are also determined by the behaviour of banks. Banks seek to maximize returns from lending and interest rates on deposits. Klein extends this organizational conception of banks, suggesting that lending is determined by the marginal returns of assets over the cost of liabilities. This tradition has developed complex microeconomic models of how banks manage reserves, calculate liquidity risk and lend.

Santomero models how banks attempt to maximize returns, an approach used to analyse how banks manage both the asset and liability sides of balance sheets.[61] O'Hara describes how banks perform further functions.[62] For O'Hara, banks are complex organizations that provide brokerage and transform risk, while responding to shareholders and regulatory agencies in the context of uncertainty. This combines views of how banks diversify and value assets with research that emphasizes the function of banks as delegated monitors for the evaluation of risk. O'Hara also emphasizes the importance of liability management and reviews the long line of research on money deposits with banks.

Recently, scholars have explored the behaviour of banks in the context of a still wider range of economic phenomena.[63] Post-Keynesian approaches suggest that banks are an independent causal factor capable of braking or accelerating economic growth, employment, inflation and other economic indicators. For Studart, 'The supply of finance is causally determined by banks: it is banks and not savers, who hold a key position in the process of growth.'[64] Post-Keynesians draw two insights from Keynes; that perceptions of uncertainty are not probabilistic and that banks, and other economic agents, therefore favour liquidity. This informs our claim that federal banks in Brazil have repeatedly provided countercyclical lending to avert crisis and ease adjustment (in contrast to the liquidity preference of private and foreign banks that exacerbates downturns).

Banking theory also focuses on liquidity in another sense. The liquidity of liabilities related to phenomena such as runs on deposits during banking crises.[65] Diamond and Rajan provide a dynamic theory of bank capital based on relations between assets and liabilities, the importance of bank safety and access to refinancing at low cost, and the ability of banks to enforce repayment or liquidate bad loans. They pursue further modelling of strategic positioning by banks and creditors during refinancing.[66] Another claim about Brazilian federal banks is based on these concepts from banking theory. Federal banks retain a significant competitive advantage over private and foreign banks because of greater confidence among depositors. This has proved critical during crises in Brazil since the nineteenth century. For example, private banks and policymakers sought to stem a run on deposits during 1995–6 that threatened to escalate into a full-fledged banking crisis. Meanwhile, the Banco do Brasil and Caixa experienced *inflows* of deposits. Greater client confidence and trust in federal banks provide a competitive advantage over private banks. Clients withdraw deposits from private banks during banking crises. Deposits tend to *increase* at government banks during banking crises. This competitive advantage reinforces the capacity of federal banks to provide counter-cyclical lending.

These matters are critical because revolutions in information and communication technologies are profoundly changing the banking industry. It is argued above that government banks can produce better government for less cost. Government banks can also do more today than in the past because new technologies have reduced the cost of bank transactions an estimated *100-fold.*[67] In the past, bank transactions involved expensive, fully-equipped branch offices and large numbers of white collar staff. Estimates suggest that face to face bank transactions at a teller cost 100 times more than an internet transaction, fifteen times more than an electronic transfer and ten times more than an ATM transaction. The supply curve for banking is shifting to the right. This helps explain the apparent anomaly for liberal theory. Instead of being replaced by more efficient private and foreign banks, government banks use their scale, brand name, reputation and accumulated trust of clients to reposition their operations and realize competitive advantages as the industry adjusts, consolidates and modernizes taking deposits, providing loans and the myriad other activities of banks.

Banking theory views banks as firms that allocate assets, monitor firms and consumers, and balance costs, benefits, risks and returns in the context of depositors, debtors, government regulators and business cycles. Concepts and categories drawn from banking theory in this chapter inform the following comparisons of government, private and foreign banks operating in Brazil and case study chapters. Banking theory clarifies how government banks provide policy alternatives and retain competitive advantages.

2 BANK CHANGE IN BRAZIL

In Chapter 1 it is argued that government banks provide policy alternatives for economic management and social inclusion while retaining competitive advantages over private and foreign banks. This chapter turns to evidence from Brazil since price stability, transition from military rule and liberalization of the industry.[1] In April 1994, the Real Plan ended over a decade of inertial inflation and launched then Finance Minister Cardoso to win the presidency for the coalition between the Partido da Social Democracia Brasileira (Party of Brazilian Social Democracy, PSDB) and Partido da Frente Liberal (Liberal Front Party, PFL) in the first national elections held since transition from military rule. In 1995, President Cardoso's coalition government reduced protection of domestic banking set in the 1988 Constitution, permitted foreign participation in privatization auctions and provided incentives for foreign investment in financial industries. From 1994–2002, foreign investment in banking and finance reached US$19.8 billion (15 per cent of total direct foreign investment). However, instead of leading to the predominance of foreign and private banks, a new division of financial labour emerged. Privatizations reduced the presence of state government banks. Liberalization increased the importance of foreign banks.[2] However, the anomaly for liberal theory is that federal banks 1) were capitalized 2) were challenged to pursue new strategies and policies and 3) have provided policy options and competed successfully since opening the industry.

This chapter explores in turn these elements of anomaly. First, comparison and tracing of policies during the 1990s to save private banks, privatize state government banks and capitalize federal banks help explain the latter. Second, data on market shares and levels of bad credit held by private, foreign and government banks in lending to industry, agriculture, business, consumers, housing and the public sector from 1995–2009 (bad credit from 1988–2009) clarify the policies, performance and new division of labour among banks in Brazil. Third, the competitive advantages of federal banks are explored in terms of organizational breadth, policy experience and leadership in the development and implementation of new services such as correspondent banking and card payment markets. Fourth, comparison of government, private and foreign bank behaviour during crises demonstrates that government banks provide lending of last resort and counter cyclical credit. Finally, a series of control variables such as bad credit, late loans, risk matrices, Basel indexes and stress tests are used to further compare private, foreign and government banks operating in Brazil. The data suggest convergence of government banks and the banking system in Brazil toward, and often beyond, international standards of reporting, transparency and performance.

Somewhat paradoxically, another reason why federal banks have competed successfully since liberalization is that banks modernized in Brazil *before* opening the industry in 1995. Brazilian banks modernized during the 1980s and early 90s because of large gains during inertial inflation. High inflation increased spreads between low interest rates paid on bank deposits and high returns from markets and financial instruments indexed against inflation, largely government paper. As Goldfajn, Hennings and Mori note, this 'induced banks to expand, open new branches, offer "free" bank services and develop a high degree of technological progress, especially aimed at enhancing the speed of transactions'.[3] This helps explain the apparent anomaly for liberal theory. Modernization and adoption of information technology in Brazilian banking began during high inflation in the 1980s and 90s before liberalization (1995), price stability (1994) and privatizations. Timing matters because seemingly minor differences can create enduring competitive advantage.[4] Given the modernization of banks in Brazil *before* opening the industry, foreign banks have failed to exhibit powerful competitive advantages afterward.

PROER, PROES and PROEF

It is also somewhat paradoxical that the end of inertial inflation and price stability in 1994 required three different programmes to rescue banks. From 1995–2001, government programmes were created 1) to save and sell failed private banks, 2) privatize bankrupt state government banks and 3) capitalize and reform federal government banks. These programmes were:

> PROER, 1995–7: Programa de Estímulo à Reestruturação e ao Fortalecimento do Sistema Financeiro Nacional (Programme to Stimulate the Restructuring and Strengthening of the National Financial System),[5]
> PROES, 1996–9: Programa de Incentivo à Redução do Setor Público Estadual na Atividade Bancária (Incentive Programme for Reduction of State Public Sector in Banking Activity)[6]
> PROEF, 1999–2001: Programa de Fortalecimento das Instituições Financeiras (Federal Programme to Strengthen Federal Financial Institutions).

Private banks required attention first because failure of the sixth and eighth largest private banks in Brazil during 1995 produced a run on bank deposits. The

Banco Econômico (August 1995) and Banco Nacional (November 1995) failed because price stability reduced earnings from inertial inflation. An absence of deposit insurance also increased uncertainty and the risk of panic.[7] PROER policies included timely intervention into and resale of the Banco Econômico and Banco Nacional and creation of a new deposit insurance fund. The collapse of private banks revealed the competitive advantages of federal banks. Although private banks suffered withdrawals, deposits at federal banks *increased* from clients in search of security. Greater trust in federal banks helped avert escalation of the banking crisis during 1995–6.

PROES policies for state government banks included intervention into and sale or reorganization of twenty-eight institutions. Emergency measures and politics came first. On 31 December 1994, the Central Bank intervened into BANESPA (São Paulo State Bank), the third largest bank in Brazil and BANERJ (Rio de Janeiro State Bank), the thirteenth largest bank in Brazil. This produced a *fait accompli* for governors taking office the next day.[8] During 1995, the Cardoso administration pursued reforms through a Programme of Assistance for State Fiscal Adjustment (Programa de Apoio à Reestruturação e Ajuste Fiscal dos Estados, PAREFE) that set budget targets for rescue of state governments also unable to adjust to the end of inertial inflation. Federal government refinancing of states was first implemented through conditional loans to state governments made by the Caixa. However, as the Caixa case study chapter reveals, these loans were at odds with the mission and lending guidelines of the federal savings bank and inspired opposition from Caixa management.

In 1996, the PROES programme was designed to either privatize state government banks or replace them with finance agencies. State government bank change under the PROES involved the following privatizations by state governments:

Credireal, Banco de Crédito Real de Minas Gerais S.A. R$123.7 million sale in 1997

Paraiban, Banco do Estado da Paraíba S.A R$30.9 million sale in 1997

Banerj, Banco do Estado de Rio de Janeiro S.A. R$289.1 million sale in 1997

Bandepe, Banco do Estado de Pernambuco S.A. R$153.6 million sale in 1998

Bemge, Banco do Estado de Minas Gerais, S.A. R$511.3 million sale in 1998

Baneb, Bancoc do Estado de Bahia S.A. R$151.2 million sale in 1999

Banestado, Banco do Estado de Paraná S.A. R$960.8 million sale in 2000

And the following privatizations of state government banks by federal government:

Meridional, S.A. (Rio Grande do Sul) R$157.2 million sale in 1997
Banespa, Banco do Estado de São Paulo S.A. R$3.69 billion sale in 2000
BEG, Banco do Estado de Goiás S.A. R$280.3 million sale in 2001
BEA, Banco do Estado de Amazonas S.A. R$80.2 million sale in 2002
BEM, Banco do Estado de Maranhão S.A. R$26.0 million sale in 2004
BEC, Banco do Estado de Ceará S.A. R$700.0 million sale in 2005

And intervention into the following state government banks by federal government:

Banacre, Banco do Estado do Acre S.A.
Banap, Banco do Estado do Amapá S.A.
Bandern, Banco do Estado do Rio Grande do Norte S.A.
BDRN, Banco de Desenvolvimento do Estado do Rio Grande do Norte
    S.A.
Bemat, Banco do Estado do Mato Grosso S.A
Beron, Banco do Estado de Rondônia S.A.
Minascaixa, Caixa Econômica do Estado de Minas Gerais
Produban, Banco do Estado de Alagoas S.A.
Baner, Banco do Estado de Roraima S.A. (liquidated)

And state government banks capitalized and reformed by state governments:

Banese, Banco do Estado de Sergipe S.A.
Banestes, Banco do Estado de Espírito Santo S.A.
Banpará, Banco do Estado de Para S.A.
Banrisul Banco do Estado do Rio Grande do Sul S.A.
NCNB, Nossa Caixa Nossa Banco S.A.
BEP, Banco do Estado de Piaui S.A. (acquired by Banco do Brasil in
    2008, value not revealed)
BESC, Banco do Estado de Santa Catarina S.A. (acquired by Banco do
    Brasil in 2008, value not revealed)

While two state government Banks remained outside the PROES programme, suffering no intervention:

Bandes, Banco de Desenvolvimento de Espírito Santo S.A.
BRB, Banco Regional de Brasília S.A.

The privatization of state government banks generated over R$6.45 billion for Treasury and remains emblematic of fiscal recentralization after transition from military rule in Latin America.[9] Provisional decree 1.514 of August 1996 defined the terms for federal government interventions. State governments were offered credit to reorganize state banks into development agencies, sell them at privatization auctions or transfer control to the federal government. PROES policies were consistent with the theory of privatization as modernization. Privatization and liberalization were seen as necessary to reduce financial repression and free market development.[10] PROES privatizations also suggest agreement between policymakers in Brazil and World Bank recommendations to reduce state presence in banking.

PROEF: Capitalization and Reform of Federal Government Banks

Policies for federal banks differed. Privatization of Brazilian federal banks was recommended by the World Bank, a position reiterated provocatively during financial crises by International Monetary Fund (IMF) President Michel Camdessus (in 1999) and Goldman Sachs representative Paulo Leme (in 2001).[11] Vidotto traces the emergence of alternative policies.[12] In 1991, a legislative proposal from the opposition (by then PT Federal Deputy José Fortunati) sought to increase the accountability of federal government banks along three dimensions; their performance as commercial banks, their fiscal impact, and special accountability for their use of funds from official savings programmes. In 1993, the presidency created a Management Committee of Federal Public Financial Institutions (Comitê Gerencial das Instituições Financeiras Públicas Federais, COMIF) at the Ministry of Finance to coordinate policies across the six federal government banks. In 1993, the Plano de Ação Imediato (Immediate Action Plan) under Finance Minister Cardoso also included plans for 'rigid control and supervision' of state government banks and, in distinction, 'cleanup' (*saneamento*) of federal government banks. These plans were influenced by Eduardo Lundberg's policy paper that argued, somewhat differently, for separate consideration of the development roles of federal government banks (involving fiscal, budgetary and policy matters) from their performance as commercial and investment banks (involving monetary and central bank supervision).[13] The importance of federal banks to ensure competition was also emphasized. In sum, state government banks gained widespread condemnation. But even liberal economists such as Fraga and Sérgio Werlang argued that coordination could mitigate problems with federal banks.[14]

Debate about federal banks shifted further away from privatization in 1995 when Finance Ministry Technical Note 20 circulated in the executive and legislature.[15] Prepared by Finance Ministry Secretary Parente and endorsed by Minister Malan, this paper advocated reform of federal banks for reasons of 'strategic security'.[16] Private banking and capital markets were seen as unable to replace BNDES long term finance or credit flows from other federal banks, especially for agriculture, agro industry, housing, construction, sanitation and regional and urban development programmes. Analysis of federal banks was also commissioned from Booz Allen-Hamilton and the University of São Paulo Foundation for Economic Research and posted on the Finance Ministry website during 2000. [17] This report presented alternatives for reform based on a typology of public banks from abroad (commercial banks, banks for popular access, urban development agencies, agricultural development agencies and development banks).

Debate ended in June 2001 when, as mentioned at the outset of this study, the Cardoso administration announced capitalization of federal banks within BIS and Central Bank of Brazil capital risk guidelines. Thereafter, no legal or regulatory grounds would exist for Central Bank intervention into federal banks. Bad credits were transferred to a new asset management entity (Empresa Gestora de Ativos, Emgea) at the Finance Ministry. Low interest paying assets were swapped for new paper from Treasury earning (high) market interest rates.[18] Capital was injected into three of six federal banks. The cost for Treasury during 2001 has been estimated at R$12.5 billion, while R$62.4 billion in government bonds were issued to pay for assets transferred to Emgea. This brought federal banks well above Basel II Accord capital guidelines (8 per cent capital reserves weighted by risk) and tougher requirements set by Brazilian Central Bank resolution 2.682/99 for provisions against risk (11 per cent capital reserves weighted by risk).

The cost of saving private banks (0.88 per cent GDP) and privatizing state government banks (5.68 per cent GDP) sum to 6.5 per cent of Brazilian GDP. This was expensive, but well below the average cost of domestic banking crises during the 1980s and 90s in developing economies (17 per cent GDP) and advanced economies (12 per cent GDP).[19] The cost of capitalizing federal banks is more difficult to estimate. Government accounts suggest that R$12.5 billion was spent during 2001, while losses since then at Emgea (the balance of capital injections and asset and liability swaps since 2001) sum below R$13.0 billion. The cost of capitalizing federal banks can thus be estimated at R$25.5 billion, or 2.1 per cent of 2001 GDP (R$1,185.0 billion). Again, was it worth it? Do the policy alternatives provided by and competitive advantages retained by these institutions justify this cost?

Government, Private and Foreign Bank Lending, 1995–2009

To address these questions, this section first turns to aggregate data on government bank performance and market shares. Comparison of government, private and foreign bank credit market shares (1995–2009) and levels of bad credit (1988–2009) in lending across economic sectors (the federal and sub-national government, industry, home loans, rural entities, business and consumers) helps identify competitive advantages and controls for mismanagement of banks. The data suggest a substantial decline of bank lending to the public sector (until the 2008 credit crisis), convergent trends in public and private bank lending to industry and leadership of private banks in lending to business and consumers. Government banks predominate in lending for housing and agriculture. Breaks in the data from the late 1990s are largely related to stuffing federal bank portfolios with bad credit from private and public banks that were acquired by the Central Bank for resale or privatization. Breaks in the data largely end upon capitalization of federal banks in June 2001 (except for an upturn of government bank lending in 2008–9 that suggests counter cyclical lending). Government banks have converged toward private and foreign banks in terms of bad credit.

The Public Sector

The first sector to be examined is lending to federal, state and municipal governments. Government bank lending to the federal government (not counting state owned enterprises) declined by half from levels between R$8.0–R$10.0 billion in 1995–6 to under R$4.0 billion by 2004 and remained low until the credit crunch and financial crisis hit in 2008. This suggests convergence of government banks toward private bank lending practices (the latter also providing less than R$4.0 billion to the federal government since 2004). The increase of government bank lending to the public sector to over R$8.3 billion during 2008–9 reflects the countercyclical strategies of President Lula's administration in reaction to financial crisis and sharp downturn of the economy (industrial production fell over 7 per cent in 2009). Case studies trace a variety of capital transfers to federal banks during the recent crisis.

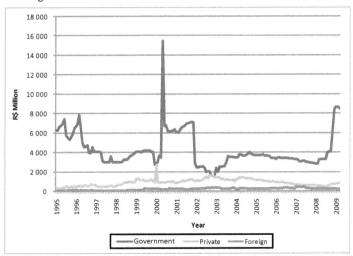

Figure 2.1: Government, Private, and Foreign Bank Credit to the Federal Government, 1995–2009.

Source: Central Bank of Brazil, 2009.

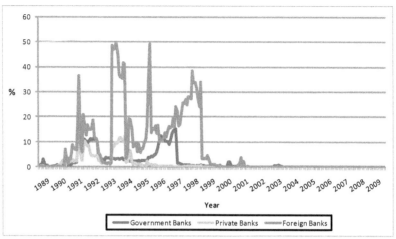

Figure 2.2: Bad Credit in Government, Private and Foreign Bank Lending to
Federal Government, 1988–2009.
Source: Central Bank of Brazil, 2009.

Liberalization of Brazil's state centred financial system has left sub-national governments starved for capital and largely without access to finance. From 1998
until the 2008 crisis, banks failed to lend significant amounts to the public sector.
Instead, the renegotiation of sub-national government debts during 1997 and the
Fiscal Responsibility Law (Lei de Responsibilidade Fiscal, LRF) in 2000 froze
state and municipal government debt (at 9 per cent interest rates!). Thereafter,
bank lending to the federal government from 2004–7 remained below R$6.0 bil-
lion, while credit to state and municipal governments remained below R$12.0
billion (below 0.5 and 1.0 per cent GDP respectively). This has changed only
incrementally. Capital starvation of state and local governments continues,
despite rules from the Central Bank, Senate, and Treasury in August 2006 to free
municipalities to finance up to 120 per cent of liquid receipts. Few of Brazil's
5,565 municipal governments took on bank loans until the 2008 financial crisis
cut federal government transfers and produced budget shortfalls. In partial compensation, government banks provided counter cyclical lending.

The lopsided curve of government bank lending to state and municipal governments from 1995–7 reflects emergency lending by the Caixa for sub-national
governments to meet obligations after the end of high inflation (see Figure 2.3).
Government bank lending to state and municipal governments increased from
around R$20.0–R$52.0 billion from 1995 to year-end 1997. From 1998 until
crisis in 2008, government bank lending to state and municipal governments
declined to roughly R$10.0 billion per year. Foreign banks lent only R$491.0
million to state and municipal governments. Bank lending to state and local governments in March 2009 thereby remained R$17.9 billion or 1.4 per cent of total

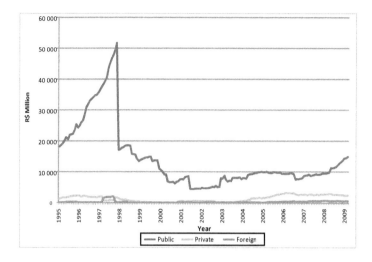

Figure 2.3: Government, Private and Foreign Bank Credit to State and
Municipal Governments, 1995–2009.
Source: Central Bank of Brazil, 2009.

bank credit. The lack of sub-national government finance suggests more capital starvation of the public sector than financial repression of the private sector.

From renegotiation of sub-national debts in December 1997[20] until the crisis in 2008, government bank lending to state and municipal governments remained below R$3.0 billion. Much ado has been made about fiscal misman-agement and debt from sub-national governments in Brazil. The data suggest otherwise. State and municipal finance was largely limited to lending for adjust-ment to price stability rather than a repeated or structural feature of Brazilian federalism or local government. From 1997–2006, sub-national governments were largely prohibited from financing operations or investments. And despite procedures introduced in 2006 to permit municipal finance up to 120 per cent of liquid receipts, few municipal governments have done so. Municipal finance remains starkly underdeveloped in Brazil. Far from the long term bond markets that serve as safe havens for investors and permit local and state governments to tap capital markets and shape development, public finance in Brazil remains shal-low and centralized, largely confined to federal government bond issues. Despite the profound capitalization of the Bovespa stock market and improved terms for federal government bond issues, municipal and state governments remain pro-hibited, by law, from capitalizing on the remarkable transition in Brazil from the state centred financial system to a market oriented financial system. Although beyond the scope of this study, the prohibition of public finance in Brazil is another consequence of liberal hegemony and bias against the public sector.

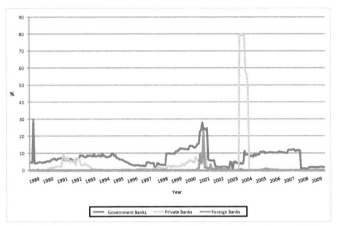

Figure 2.4: Bad Credit in Government, Private and Foreign Banks to State and Municipal
Governments, 1988–2009.
Source: Central Bank of Brazil, 2009.

Data on bad credit suggest that government bank lending to state and municipal governments has improved, even amidst increases during 2008–9 to counter
financial crisis. Levels of bad credit to state and municipal governments in government, private and foreign banks have largely converged during the 2000s (See
Figure 2.4). From 1995 through June 2001, surges in bad credit reflect the use of
federal banks to take on bad credits from private and state government banks and
clean up portfolios for privatizations. After transfer of non-performing loans to the
Emgea asset management entity in 2001, bad credit to sub-national governments
at government banks remained low until 2004, increased to around 10 per cent
before converging in 2008 to levels reported by private banks operating in Brazil.
A peak of 80 per cent bad credit in this sector at private banks during 2004 is an
anomaly due to the low value of private bank loans to sub-national governments.

Industry

In terms of credit to industry, the data suggest a predominance of private and
government bank lending and significant increases in credit flows to industry
since liberalization in 1995, a trend that lasted until financial crisis abroad produced a credit crunch during 2008 (See Figure 2.5). Government bank lending
since price stability (1994), liberalization (1995) and capitalization of federal
banks (2001) increased largely apace with and in a very similar trajectory to private bank lending. Moreover, while credit from private banks to industry stalled
during crisis in 2002–4 (and once again in 2008), the curve of government banks
suggests a slower but more sustained pace of expansion since capitalization and
reform of these institutions in 2001. Public and private banks have converged

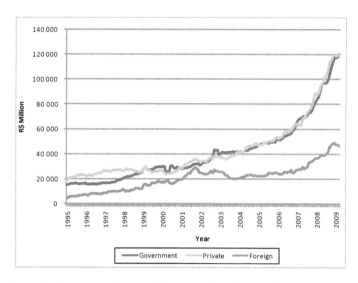

Figure 2.5: Government, Private and Foreign Bank Credit to Industry, 1995–2009.
Source: Central Bank of Brazil, 2009.

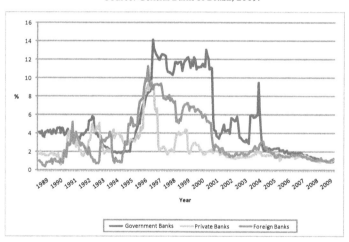

Figure 2.6: Bad Credit in Government, Private and Foreign Banks to Industry, 1988–2009.
Source: Central Bank of Brazil, 2009.

to increase lending to industry from R$39.1 billion in January 1995 to R$90.4 billion in December 2001 and R$287.1 billion at year end 2008. Government banks also appear to continue to provide counter-cyclical credit during downturns, a policy advantage explored further below and in case studies.

The value of late and non-paying loans to industry suggests improvement in government bank management and convergence toward standards of private and foreign banks operating in Brazil. Bad loans to industry in government bank

portfolios peaked at 14 per cent of loans during 1996, but declined thereafter to
1 per cent in August 2007, breaching levels of bad credit in private bank lending
to industry. Bad loans to industry in private banks also peaked during 1996 at 10
per cent of total loans, but declined thereafter to 1 per cent by 2005. That government banks have approached levels of private and foreign bank performance
is incompatible with the type of politicization of credit ascribed to government
banking by critics in the new political economy.

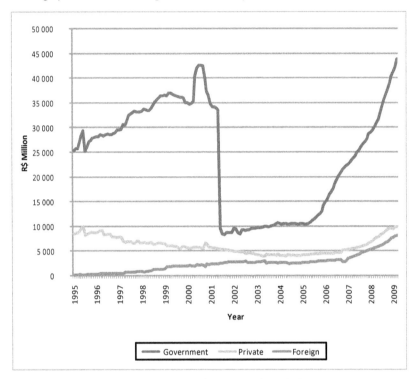

Figure 2.7: Government, Private and Foreign Bank Credit for Home Loans
and Construction, 1995–2009.
Source: Central Bank of Brazil, 2009.

Home Loans and Construction

Comparison of government, private and foreign bank lending of mortgages and
home construction loans suggests a significant competitive advantage of government banks and converging standards of performance (See Figures 2.7 and 2.8).
Trends suggest three periods. First, the higher value of home loans in government bank portfolios from 1995–2001 reflect the realities of 15–20 per cent bad
credit in contracts originating from the Sistema Financeiro de Habitação, (Home
Finance System, SFH)[21] and Banco Nacional de Habitação (National Housing

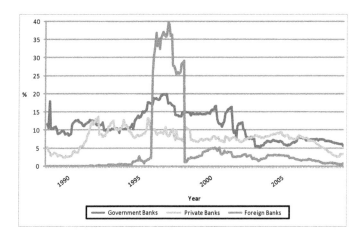

Figure 2.8: Bad Credit in Government, Private and Foreign Banks for Home Loans
and Construction, 1988–2009.
Source: Central Bank of Brazil, 2009.

Bank, BNH) created under military government in 1965 and assumed by government banks in 1986 (discussed in case study chapters).[22] Once the BNH portfolio was transferred to the Emgea asset management entity and non-performing home loans from the period of military rule were written off in June 2001, bad home loans at government banks dropped from over R$40.0 billion to under R$10.0 billion. Private banks also experienced high levels of non-performing mortgage loans from 1996–9, reaching 40 per cent of loans of private banks to the sector during 1997. A new Sistema de Financiamento Imobiliário (Mortgage Finance System, SFI) was created in 1997 with new prerogatives for lenders and securitization of mortgages, the latter receiving further incentives in 2003.

Lending for home loans and construction stagnated until 2005. Since design of the regulatory framework and recovery during 2005, government banks have led both in new directed credit programmes for lower income housing and newly regulated mortgage markets. Government bank lending for home purchase and construction increased from approximately R$10.0 billion (from 2001–5) to over R$40.0 billion in 2009. In comparison, private and foreign bank lending in this sector increased at a significantly slower pace from under R$5.0 billion from 2002–7 to remain below R$10.0 billion each in 2009. Once again, bad credit in government banks from loans for home purchase or construction has converged toward levels reported by private and foreign banks. This suggests the modernization of government bank management toward international banking standards.

Government banks have realized significant competitive advantage over private and foreign banks in directed home credit *and* newly regulated markets for home mortgages while averting past problems with non-paying loans in this sector. The Caixa case study chapter takes a closer look at change since new regulations (1997) and rules for securitization (2003) improved lending in this sector. Policies of liberalization, new regulatory frameworks, and dual markets for directed and free credits for home construction and capitalization of firms on the stock market transformed this sector into a major driver of economic growth in Brazil.

Agriculture and Agro-Industry

Data on bank lending to rural entities suggest a predominance of government banks and improvement in performance in terms of bad credit since 2001. From 1995–2002, public bank credit to rural entities remained between R$15.0 and R$20.0 billion. Downturns in lending reflect federal government intervention into state government banks during 1996–7 and reform of federal government banks in 2001. During 2003–4 public bank credits to the rural sector increased from R$17.0–R$28.0 billion. However, private bank lending also increased from R$10.0 billion in first quarter 2002 to R$17.0 billion in first quarter 2004. Again, liberalization has not produced displacement of public for private credit nor, apparently, crowded private lending out through directed credit or government banking. In agriculture and agro-industry, increased lending and decreased bad credit suggest a more positive-sum division of labour between government and private banks since price stability and democratization.

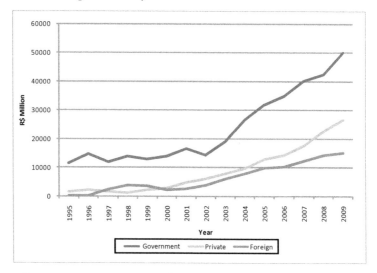

Figure 2.9: Government, Private and Foreign Bank Rural Credits, 1995–2009.
Source: Central Bank of Brazil, 2009.

This ignores periodic refinancing of farm and agro industry debts by the federal government. For example, civil disobedience and lobbying by farm and rural business organizations during 2006 led President Lula's PT coalition government to set aside R$70.0 billion for renegotiation of farm loans. Subsidized farm credit policies and debt rescheduling involves both federal and private banks. The following case study chapter traces Banco do Brasil dominance in rural, agricultural and agro industry lending and finance during transition from past systems of directed credit to new frameworks that introduce market pricing but retain subsidies through periodic renegotiation of debts.

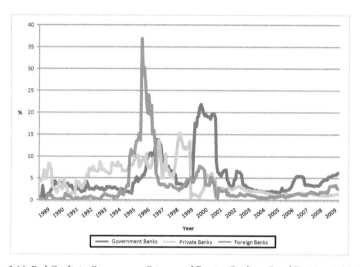

Figure 2.10: Bad Credit in Government, Private and Foreign Banks to Rural Entities, 1988–2009.
Source: Central Bank of Brazil, 2009.

Data on bad credit to rural entities suggest improvement from the very high levels of non-performing loans during the 1990s and early 2000s, but continued differences between private, foreign and government banks. Private and foreign banks reduced non-paying loans to rural entities from past peaks of 36.7 and 15.0 per cent respectively, to below 3 per cent since the mid 2000s. Since the mid 2000s, government banks retained twice the value of bad loans to rural entities in their portfolios. The Banco do Brasil case study chapter further explores this transition in rural credit.

Non-Financial Business

Central Bank data on credit to business from 1995–2009 suggests leadership from private banks, convergence of government bank performance since 2001 and counter-cyclical lending from the latter during the 2008 financial crisis. Private bank lending to business remained at around R$10.0 billion from 1995–2000, increased to R$20.0 billion by 2004 and surpassed R$50.0 billion in 2008 before the global crisis hit Brazil. From 1995–2008, foreign banks and government banks followed this trend, albeit at half the value of credit from private banks. However, foreign bank lending declined substantially during 2008, while government banks continued to produce real increases in lending (both through acquisition of private banks in trouble and counter cyclical lending policies). Private banks provide half of credit to business in Brazil, while foreign and government banks share the other half.

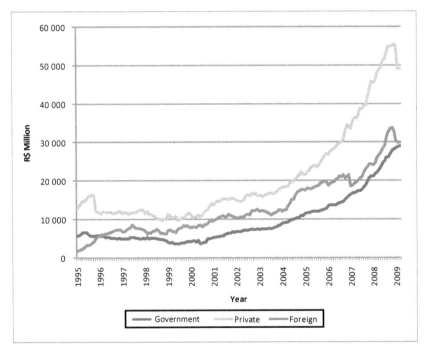

Figure 2.11: Government, Private and Foreign Bank Credit to Business, 1995–2009.
Source: Central Bank of Brazil, 2009.

Peaks of bad credit recorded by private banks during the banking crisis of 1996–7 and at government banks from 1997–2001 have not recurred since 2001. Since 2001, bad loans to industry at government banks since 2001 have converged toward levels reported by private and foreign banks operating in the country. In sum, liberalization appears to have increased private, foreign and government bank lending to industry and produced convergence in performance standards.

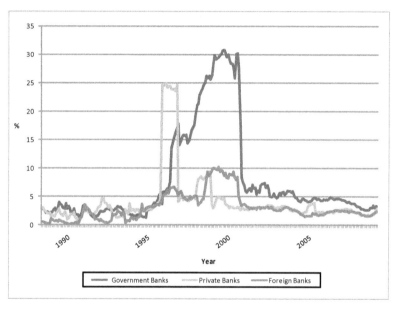

Figure 2.12: Bad Credit in Government, Private and Foreign Banks to Business, 1988–2009.
Source: Central Bank of Brazil, 2009.

Consumers

Similar trends appear in consumer credit. From 1995–2009, private bank lending to consumers predominates, while government and foreign banks share smaller market shares. Again, peaks of bad credit during 1996–7 in private and foreign banks (and at government banks during 2001) have not recurred. Since 2001, bad credit at government banks has converged toward levels in private and foreign banks, especially since 2005. Lending to consumers from private banks remained below R$20.0 billion from 1995–2000, increased to around R$40.0 billion through 2003, then doubled to R$80.0 billion by 2005 and reached R$120.0 billion in 2007 and R$190.0 billion before financial crisis in 2008. Crisis abroad produced a sharp downturn in industrial production and credit to industry in Brazil. Credit to consumers levelled off but did not collapse. This confirms the importance of consumption and popular inclusion in the Brazilian economy, characteristics that help explain the combination of sharp declines in industrial exports in 2008–9 and consumer led recovery during 2009.

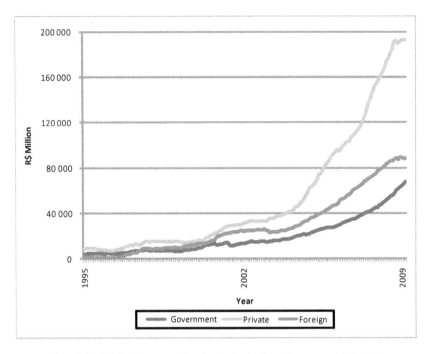

Figure 2.13: Public, Private, and Foreign Bank Credit to Consumers, 1995–2009.
Source: Central Bank of Brazil, 2009.

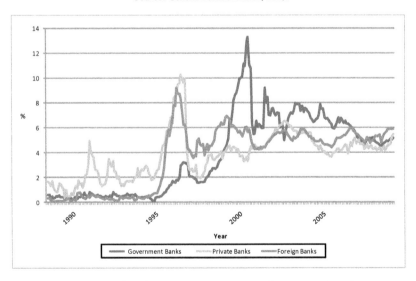

Figure 2.14: Bad Credit in Government, Private and Foreign Bank Credit
to Consumers, 1988–2009.
Source: Central Bank of Brazil, 2009.

Consumer credit retains a market structure similar to that of lending to industry. Private banks retain over half of the consumer credit market while foreign and government banks retain 25 per cent market shares. Although private and foreign bank lending to consumers levelled off during 2008, government bank lending to consumers continued to increase at paces recorded since 2005. Central Bank data on bad credit to consumers also suggest that the performance of government banks has converged toward levels reported by private and foreign banks operating in Brazil.

In sum, liberalization, modernization and transition to market allocation of credit has not led to the elimination of government banks but to competition and coexistence between private, federal and foreign banks.[23] The trajectory of credit (1995–2009) and bad credit (1988–2009) in private, foreign and government banks suggest a new distribution of financial labour in Brazil. Price stability and opening the Brazilian banking industry to new foreign competition has deepened credit markets. Bank credit increased from 29.7 to over 50 per cent of Brazilian GDP from 1989–2008. But private banks have not replaced government banks. Government banks have improved performance and realized competitive advantages, the latter especially in home loans and credit to agriculture and agro-industry. Government, private and foreign banks cohabit, compete, cooperate and complement policies and practices.

Convergence has thus occurred in terms of organizational imitation rather than transition to private banking through privatizations. Bad credit in government banks has declined from peaks during adjustment, instability and banking crisis in the 1990s toward levels reported by private and foreign banks. Government banks have reformed, cut costs, downsized operations, outsourced inputs and increasingly adopted market criteria and tighter procedures for risk analysis and loan approval. Bank change in Brazil thus reflects modernization and adaptation to price stability amidst a series of shocks and financial crises from 1994–2003, followed by four years of growth interrupted by financial crisis abroad in 2008.

Institutional Foundations of Competitive Advantages at Federal Banks

The competitive advantages of federal banks can be measured in terms of organizational structure. Banking studies suggest that networks of branch offices, organizational presence in local communities and relations with firms, social networks and political webs provide competitive advantage. As noted, Caravelli argues that the excessive consolidation of private banks in England and the US have placed their banking systems at a *disadvantage* in comparison to Continental Europe, where banks retain a larger number of branch offices and presence in local communities to better serve small enterprises and local needs. From this perspective, management strategies that pursue downsizing and cost reductions by closing branches and cutting staff may improve aggregate measures of efficiency but hurt bank performance. Downsizing may improve balance sheets and efficiency ratings. However, aggregate improvements may conceal the deterioration of institutional foundations of competitive advantage.

Data on government bank branch offices in Brazil suggest two phases, the first a period of downsizing federal banks to reduce the large number of political appointments inherited from military rule and delayed transition, then a second a period of organic bank growth since 2001. Federal government bank branch offices declined during the 1990s from a total of 7,232 to 5,611. The decline of state government bank branch offices from 1,863 to 1,884 (1995–2001) also reflects the impact of privatizations, mirrored by the increase of foreign bank branches from 91 to 3,799 (1995–2001). This indicates the liberalization and internationalization of the state-centred Brazilian banking system during the 1990s.

Since capitalization of federal banks in 2001, these institutions have expanded their networks of branch offices. From 2001–6, Banco do Brasil branch offices increased from 3,068 to 4,046. Caixa branch offices increased from 1,689 to 1,981. This is consistent with data from private and foreign banks and credit cooperatives. Although beyond the scope of this study, it is of note that credit cooperative branch offices also increased apace. From 2001–6, SICREDI (Sistema de Crédito Cooperativo, Credit Cooperative System) increased branch offices from 718 to 914 and UNICRED (Confederação Nacional das Cooperativas Centrais, National Confederation of Central Cooperatives) from 274 to 358.

Again, in this respect, the BNDES is different. The BNDES retains a single headquarter in Rio de Janeiro and four regional offices with 1,855 employees (top-six banks retain between 50,000–100,000 employees). Furthermore, according to a strict definition of commercial banks as deposit taking institutions, the BNDES is *not* a bank because it does not accept deposits from the general public. Indeed, reliance of the BNDES on government pension funds and other official savings funds (and, for example, transfer of R$100.0 billion from Treasury in 2009 to provide lending of last resport) has attracted criticism from private banks and liberal economists. We return to this competitive advantage of low administrative costs and access to cheap funds in the BNDES case study chapter. However, the point here is that we relax the strict definition of commercial banking to include the BNDES. The BNDES lacks organizational breadth that embeds savings banks and commercial banks in Brazilian society and political economy. However, the centralized organizational structure of the BNDES nonetheless provides a powerful competitive advantage for pricing. The 'per-loan' cost at the BNDES is far below that of banks that maintain nation- or region-wide branch networks. The centralized structure of the BNDES is typical of development banks. Access to official savings as a deposit base and small administrative structure provides a powerful competitive advantage that lets the BNDES provide below market interest rates on long term loans *and* produce strong returns.

Branch offices provide institutional foundation of competitive advantage in banking. However, recent bank strategies to reach clients and provide services involve new technologies such as automated teller machines (ATMs), bank outposts, correspondent banking (i.e. agreements with businesses or non-governmental organizations to provide banking services) and electronic payment services via debit and credit cards or mobile banking on cellular phones or the internet. The number of bank branch offices in Brazil actually declined from 17,400 in 1994 to 16,189 in 1999 because of mergers, acquisitions, privatizations, reforms and downsizing. The number of fully staffed mini-branches (*pontos de atendimento bancário*, PAB) also remained largely stable in 2000–7. In contrast, alternative banking service points in Brazil have increased exponentially. ATMs in Brazil increased from 3,446 to 22,428 in 1994–2002, reaching 34,790 (in shared networks) and 84,894 proprietary ATMs by 2007. Internet banking remains restricted to upmarket clients. Mobile banking via cellular phones has just begun to emerge in Brazil, despite the acquisition of cellular phones by an estimated half of 193 million Brazilians.

Federal banks have realized competitive advantages to establish large market shares in new banking practices. Federal banks have outpaced private and foreign banks in correspondent banking. Central Bank of Brazil resolution 2.640 (1999) freed banks to contract 'correspondent' institutions to provide basic banking services. By 2002, 16,453 correspondent banking points of service were installed (8,961 Caixa concession lottery shops). By 2005, bank correspondents had increased to 40,411 and reached an estimated 110,000 in 2008. Correspondent banking reduced the number of Brazilian municipalities with no bank service points from 1679 in 1999 to zero in 2003, thereby beginning to provide banking services across the vast interior of the country.[24] This reverts to our anomaly for liberal theory. Opening the industry, foreign bank acquisitions of domestic institutions and modernization of federal banks have expanded access to banking services. However, to date, correspondent banking has proved substantially more able to reach distant areas and, apparently, citizens largely excluded from the banking system than other technologies such as ATMs or mobile banking. Data reported in a World Bank study of correspondent banking in Brazil confirms the competitive advantages of government banks in correspondent banking agreements.[25] Competitive advantages of federal banks have provided policy alternatives for the federal government. Meanwhile, foreign and private banks in Brazil cherry picked the best urban and upmarket areas to avoid incurring the greater cost of reaching clients in sparsely populated and poor areas of the interior.

Creation of *contas simplificadas* (simplified bank accounts) has also contributed to the inclusion of bankless Brazilians. The number of simplified bank accounts opened by July 2005 reached over six million (4.75 million remained active). By year-end 2008, 9.87 million accounts had been open (5.77 million remained active).[26] Microcredit programmes normally involve expensive face-to-face lending. The large number and anonymous character of microcredit in Brazil suggests a different experience. For example, the creation of 6.8 million new accounts for bankless Brazilians at the Caixa since 2003 (with *no* credit analysis and *no* information supplied by client beyond a Brazilian identification card) suggests a different strategy for financial inclusion. The Caixa case study chapter further examines competitive advantages of this government savings bank for social inclusion.

In sum, since price stability and opening the industry to foreign competition in the 1990s, Brazilian federal banks have used their networks of branch offices, reputations as public and social policy agents, and brand names to expand banking services to the interior of the country and 'downmarket' to reach bankless Brazilians with new technologies such as ATM bank cards, simplified accounts and correspondent banking. Institutional foundations of competitive advantage help explain why private and foreign banks have largely failed to create substantial numbers of simplified bank accounts and remain behind federal banks in these new markets for banking services and products.

Government Banks during Crisis and Recovery

Comparison of government, private and foreign bank behaviour during cycles of crisis, adjustment and recovery suggests that Brazilian federal banks provide counter-cyclical credit and finance. For example, in second-semester 2002, risk aversion, capital flight and evaporation of even traditional (foreign government guaranteed) sources of export finance produced a credit crunch. Benchmark JP Morgan Emerging Market Bond Index premia on Brazilian sovereign issues reached 2,400 points (24 per cent) above interest rates on US Federal Reserve bonds, reflecting both a general aversion to risk and perceptions of political risk from PT government among international investors. Despite a sudden stop of foreign finance, domestic credit *increased* 7.8 per cent during second semester 2002 due to counter-cyclical lending from federal banks. From June to December 2002, government banks *increased* credit 14.5 per cent and their share of total domestic credit by 2.3 per cent. By December 2002, government banks provided 39.8 per cent of domestic credit (private banks, 35.4 per cent; foreign banks, 24.8 per cent).

The Bovespa stock market also collapsed, further increasing the importance of counter cyclical credit from and stock holding by federal banks. Of R$1.23

billion in stocks on the Bovespa market at year-end 2002, government banks held 44.6 per cent. Domestic private banks held 32.8 per cent of stocks and foreign banks 22.6 per cent. Like the practice of holding bonds for term rather than trading (that increases the cost and worsens terms of public debt during crises), government bank holding of stocks provides another counter-cyclical cushion in the Brazilian financial system. Federal banks are under less pressure to unload stocks during downturns. And their shareholdings reinforce networks to provide market leadership and power.

Evidence of counter-cyclical lending from government banks can also be seen in data on credit leverage. Credit leverage (the proportion of credit/assets) indicates the extent to which banks lend compared to other asset allocations. The credit leverage of government banks declined from 10.32–6.65 from 1994–9, but increased thereafter to 8.68 by 2000.[27] In comparison, the credit leverage of foreign banks increased from 2.33–3.11 from 1994–8, then declined to 2.25 (1999) and 2.47 (2000). Meanwhile, the credit leverage of private domestic banks decreased from 8.98–5.54 from 1994–9, increasing thereafter to 6.24 by 2000. Government, private and foreign banks retain different policies and strategies. Foreign banks apply resources to credit at less than one third levels reported by government banks and less than half levels reported by domestic private banks. BIS capital risk guidelines first reinforced this bias of foreign and private banks away from riskier credit allocation toward government paper because the latter was classified as zero risk (later altered). Data on credit leverage confirm that federal banks remain critical agents for counter-cyclical credit in Brazil.

Central Bank of Brazil data on whether banks hold or trade Treasury bonds indicate another dimension of counter-cyclical policies at federal banks in financial markets.[28] At government banks, roughly half of Treasury bonds were held 'until term', that is to say, not traded (53.6 per cent traded, 46.4 per cent 'held' in 2004, similar levels in 2006). At domestic private banks, 82.9 per cent of Treasury bonds were traded during 2004 (83.5 per cent in 2006). At foreign banks, 79.9 per cent of Treasury bonds were traded in 2004 (91.7 per cent 2006). Holding government bonds to term at federal banks reduced market pressures that would have further increased the cost and shorten the terms of public debt during financial crises.

In sum, government banks provide more loans *per capita* and more counter-cyclical credit to help firms and households through economic downturns. In Brazil, government banks hold stocks longer-term and treasury bonds *for the term* rather than seek short-term gains from trading that often erodes the working capital of firms and increases government debt during crises. Counter-cyclical policies expose government banks to late and non-payment of loans during economic downturns. This reduces profits. Longer-term strategies to 'hold' government securities also reduce profits. Nonetheless, data presented at the outset of this study indicates that government banks have reported *stronger* returns than private and foreign banks since capitalization in 2001.

It should also be noted that banking in Brazil generally records higher returns than other large Latin American countries and other referent and emerging economies. The returns and profits recorded by Brazilian government banks from 2003–6 far exceed levels reported by the bank systems of other Latin American and other reference countries (except for Australia).[29] High returns reflect high spreads and interest rates in Brazil. A variety of explanations for high spreads and interest rates have been cited by the Central Bank of Brazil, World Bank, and economists and banking specialists in academic journals and public debate. None cite government banks as a contributing cause. To the contrary, research and debate reinforce the core argument of this study. Brazilian federal banks are seen to retain (some say unfair) competitive advantages that make them able to apply pressure on private and foreign banks by cutting commercial and consumer interest rates. President Lula once again challenged federal banks in late 2008 and early 2009 to cut interest rates to help avert recession and reverse the credit shortage. Resignation of Banco do Brasil President Antonio Francisco Lima Neto in April 2009 turned on this issue. We examine these tensions between market performance, shareholder returns and the counter-cyclical policies in case study chapters.

Controlling for Bad Banking: Bank Solidity, 2002–8

Countercyclical lending increases the exposure of banks to bad credit and decreases revenue during economic downturns. Under international accounting and Central Bank regulations, bad loans must be written off as losses or assumed by second party guarantor. This reduces the risk of passing on losses to others through fiscal accounts or the money supply. Data from the Central Bank of Brazil make it possible to control for these risks and compare bank performance in terms of Basel Indexes, bad credit, late loans and stress tests that estimate impacts of hypothetical shocks to bank portfolios. Basel Indexes reported by government, domestic and foreign banks from 2002–6 suggest that (during this business cycle of crisis, recovery and growth) government banks remained capitalized well above Central Bank of Brazil guidelines (11.0 per cent since 1999).[30] The BIS requires a minimum of 8.0 per cent of reserves against losses in lending and finance. From 2002–6, the average Basel Index for Brazilian government banks increased from 16.7–19.7 per cent, remaining *twice* levels recommended by the BIS. In comparison, the average Basel Index for private banks operating in Brazil increased from 15.1–17.0 per cent from 2002–6, while foreign banks, on average, reported Basel Indexes of 15.2 in 2002, reaching 15.4 in 2006. Government banks in Brazil retain sufficient reserves against risks arising from bad credit or losses in financial markets.

This provides a cushion for counter-cyclical lending. Private and foreign banks adopted more cautious strategies and provided less credit during the downturn of 2002. These institutions thereby maintained higher reserves. The average Basel index for the domestic financial system at year end 2002 remained increased only 0.6 per cent over the 16.2 level reported for June. However, this average conceals an *increase* of 2.1 per cent in the Basel Index for private banks (meaning they chose to hold low risk rated government paper) and a *decline* of 2.3 per cent in the Basel Index for government banks (meaning they incurred risks to lend during downturn and adjustment).

Two trends suggest that government banks provided counter cyclical credit without endangering bank solidity. First, the Central Bank of Brazil requires banks to maintain a Basel Index of 11.0 per cent, 3 per cent above the 8.0 per cent minimum required by the 1988 Basel Accord. Brazilian banks thus set aside almost half again more in reserves than determined by BIS regulations. Second, the different Basel Index ratings of government and private banks reflects the greater weight of credit, and therefore credit risk, faced by government banks. In this respect, data presented above on bad and late loans since 2001 suggest that brief increases in the average Basel Indexes reported by government banks *do not* reflect broader deterioration of portfolios.

Banks operating in Brazil, and especially government banks, tend to be more conservative than institutions abroad. Banks in Brazil set aside a full *50 per cent* of deposits in the form of compulsory reserves at the Central Bank (seen as one reason for high interest rates and bank spreads and the competitive advantage of the BNDES that remains exempt). However, banks in Brazil also retain large reserves in house against bad loans and losses. Data compiled by the Central Bank of Brazil from the IMF and Bankscope suggest that Brazilian banks tend to set aside considerably larger reserves against bad loans and losses. Of eight countries reported by the IMF and Central Bank of Brazil (four from Latin America, four for reference), Brazil retained substantially larger reserves against bad loans than any country (except Spain in 2007).[31] Banking in Brazil thus involves higher operating costs, lower levels of operating efficiency, larger reserves and provisions against losses, and still very expensive credit (40 per cent annual interest rates on premium consumer and business loans in 2009).

The convergence of bad credit at government banks toward levels reported by private and foreign banks introduced this study. Government banks retain higher levels of bad and late loans in specific sectors (especially home loans). However, the value of late loans as a percentage of total loans in government banks fell *below* levels reported by private and foreign banks during 2008. Loans over twelve months past due in government banks decreased from R$37.2 billion–R$14.9 billion from year end 2001–June 2006. This placed the value of bad credit in government banks *below* the value found in private and foreign banks. Bad credit in private banks increased from R$17.3 billion in 2001 to peak at R$25.5 billion during 2003, declining to R$18.0 billion in 2006. Foreign banks also reported increases in bad credit, from R$12.3 billion in 2001 to R$14.1 billion in 2003, thereafter declining to R$13.0 billion in 2006. In 2001, late loans remained 8.5 per cent of total loans in government banks (above 7.5 per cent in private and 6.5 per cent in foreign banks). However, by 2008 the rank is reversed. In 2008, late loans at government banks declined to *3.2 per cent* of total loans, while remaining at 3.7 per cent in private banks and 4.5 per cent in foreign banks.

Government banks in Brazil also set aside greater provisions against bad and late loans than private or foreign banks. In 2004, government banks retained 8.6 per cent of the value of total loans in provision against losses from non-paying loans, while private banks retained 6.0 per cent and foreign banks 5.1 per cent. In 2008, provisions at government banks had declined, on average, to 6.8 per cent, but still remained above the levels of 5.2 and 5.1 per cent recorded at private and foreign banks.

Table 2.1: Comparing Late Loans and Provisions in Banks, 2001–8.

	Government Banks			Private Banks			Foreign Banks		
	R$bi >12m	% Late	% Prov.	R$bi >12m	% Late	% Prov.	R$bi >12m	% Late	% Prov.
2001	37.2	8.5		17.3	7.5		12.3	6.5	
2002	39.4	5.5		20.2	7.3		14.1	6.0	
2003	32.6	7.0		25.5	7.4		15.9	6.6	
2004	13.3	3.5	8.6	16.0	3.1	6.0	10.2	3.2	5.1
2005	13.4	3.9	8.1	16.3	3.5	5.9	10.7	3.5	4.8
2006	14.9	4.2	6.8	18.0	4.4	6.6	13.0	4.5	5.3
2007		3.5	7.5		3.7	5.5		4.3	5.0
2008		3.2	6.8		3.7	5.2		4.5	5.1

Note: R$bi >12m = loans past due over 12 months. % Late = percentage of total loans >120 days overdue. % Prov. = percentage of total loan value set aside as reserves against losses. Empty cells reflect lack of data because of changing reporting standards at Central Bank.

Source: Central Bank of Brazil. *Financial Stability Report*, November 2008, p. 56 (and 2002–6 reports).

Unless late loans are renegotiated, they must be either written off as losses on balance sheets or placed under guarantee and co-obligation to permit resumption of payments. Data from 2003–8 suggests that government banks also compare favourably with private and foreign banks operating in Brazil in this respect.[32]

The value of loans less than 12 months overdue at government banks increased from R$5.3 billion–R$7.7 billion from 2003–8. However, the value of loans less than twelve months overdue at private banks increased from R$5.4–R$10.5 billion, and at foreign banks from R$3.1–R$6.2 billion; this while the percentage of credit less than twelve months overdue *decreased* from 3.8–2.4 per cent of total credit in the country. The substantial reduction of credit between 13–48 months overdue indicates improvement in Brazilian banking and at government banks. The value of credit between 13–48 months overdue at government banks declined from R$22.4–R$12.2 billion from 2003–8. Meanwhile, the value of credit overdue between 13–48 months at private and foreign banks *increased* from R$9.6–13.8 billion and R$6.8–7.5 billion.

Data on the value of loans under guarantee and in co-obligation provide further control for abuses at government banks. While the value of loans under guarantee at government banks increased from R$6.2–R$23.0 billion from 2003–8, private banks recorded increases from R$21.7–R$69.7 billion, and foreign banks from R$16.2 billion–R$36.6 billion. These trends reflect the deepening of Brazilian credit markets. The average value of credit falling under guarantee clauses remained at moderate levels of 11.9 per cent and 12.2 per cent. The value of co-obligations is even less relevant, but nonetheless provides further control for bad banking practices in government banks.

In comparative perspective, Brazilian banking tends to run on more expensive credit, higher returns and profits, higher levels of late and bad loans, and higher administrative and personnel costs. Banks in Brazil also tend to set aside more generous reserves and provisions against losses. Data reported by the World Bank confirm these characteristics. [33] From 2001–5, administrative costs as a percentage of bank assets in Brazil declined from 6.9 per cent to 5.8 per cent, but remained significantly above levels reported from Chile (3.0–2.7 per cent) Mexico (4.7–4.6 per cent), and reference countries such as Australia, Canada and Spain (1.6, 3.6, and 1.1 per cent in 2005 respectively). [34] Although time series impede comparisons after 2005, administrative costs as a percentage of assets in Brazilian banks decline from 5.8–4.2 by 2008.

Large and underdeveloped markets in Brazil seem to shape these characteristics. A glance at the size and composition of bank assets and credit markets in Brazil and Latin American neighbours clarifies this difference. In 2005, bank assets in Chile summed over 95 per cent of GDP – well over the 74 per cent recorded for Brazil. However, the dollar value of bank assets in Chile (US$211 billion) remained less than a third of bank assets in Brazil (US$684 billion). [35] The larger size and underdeveloped character of markets in Brazil provide a different context for bank policies and performance.

Comparative data also confirm the capital starvation of the public sector in Brazil. In 2005, 17 per cent of credit in Mexico and 48 per cent of credit in

Argentina was to the public sector. In Brazil, only 4 per cent of credit went to the public sector. Again, sovereign issues at home and abroad have provided significant finance to the Brazilian federal government. Since President Lula took office in 2003, federal government debt fell from 56–36 per cent of GDP in 2008 before the financial crisis hit. That the Banco do Brasil and Caixa retain approximately 20 per cent of federal government bonds suggests that these institutions have also exercised leadership in bond markets. They have also acted to broaden the base of bond holders. For example, the Banco do Brasil and Caixa are first and third ranked institutions in terms of individual investors registered for direct purchase of government bonds, the number of which has increased from 34,413 in January 2005 to 153,723 by March 2009.

Stress Testing Government, Private and Foreign Banks

A final comparison of bank solidity is taken from Central Bank estimates of how hypothetical shocks to the Brazilian economy would impact banks. Estimates are based on the value-at-risk method proposed by Boudoukh, Richardson and Whitelaw that adapt the original *VaR* calculations of JP Morgan.[36] Central Bank of Brazil estimates suggest that, in a hypothetical scenario of currency devaluation and interest rate shock, government banks would nonetheless remain at (or very slightly below) the 11.0 per cent capital requirements.[37] Given that government bank portfolios include more credit than private banks and, especially, foreign banks, the estimate of a shift to 10.9 in the average Basel Index for government banks during the most severe scenario of a credit shock and foreign exchange shock provides further evidence that these financial institutions are solid and their reserves sufficient. The Basel Index reported for government banks for less severe stress test scenarios (separate shocks from credit crunch or foreign exchange valuation) was 13.5, above the 11.0 Central Bank of Brazil guideline and well above the 8.0 level suggested by the BIS.

Banks in Brazil have repeatedly coped with real shocks since transition to democracy and price stability. During crisis in Mexico in 1994–5, the Central Bank of Brazil increased Selic benchmark overnight interest rates to *42 per cent*. The Asian financial crisis during second semester 1997 led the Central Bank of Brazil to increase interest rates to *43.4 per cent*. In 1998, the declaration of moratorium on foreign debt payments by Russia once again reversed progress in Brazil and forced the Central Bank to increase interest rates to *40 per cent*. The coincidence of crisis in Russia and national elections in October 1998 led the IMF and official creditors to provide support (negotiating a US41.0 billion rescue package). Nonetheless, after the election, market pressure led to abandonment of the fixed foreign exchange rate regime in January 1999, a policy that had served as nominal anchor since 1994. The real quickly devalued from 1.21 to 2.0

against the US dollar. However, the flexible foreign exchange rate regime, along with inflation targeting and fiscal austerity, would remain in place through the second term President Cardoso (1999–2002) *and* be retained during two terms of President Lula's PT coalition government (2003–10).

In sum, banks in Brazil weathered volatile parameters and downturns during the unprecedented series of crises in developing, emerging and transition countries during the late 1990s and early 2000s that also shaped transition from reformist President Cardoso to PT President Lula. From recovery of the economy during 2004 until the 2008 financial crisis, President Lula's coalition government sought to use government banks to accelerate growth and social inclusion. Once crisis hit again in 2008, federal banks were used to provide lending of last resort. These policies have not undermined economic fundamentals nor eroded the institutional foundations of competitive advantage retained by Brazilian federal banks.

Brazilian Political Elite Perceptions of Federal Banks

The competitive advantages of Brazilian federal banks include strong support for these institutions among political elites. Our survey of 75 Federal Deputies in June 2002 revealed tempered realism about the potential use of government banks for electoral purposes, but strong opposition to privatization of federal banks.[38] While 46.7 per cent of federal deputies interviewed doubted that federal banks would be used to influence elections, 34.7 per cent thought this was possible and 16.0 per cent likely. Politicians recognized the risk of abuse. However, questions about privatization tapped near consensus. A full 89.3 per cent of 75 federal deputies interviewed opposed privatization of either the Banco do Brasil or Caixa Econômica Federal, while 90.7 per cent opposed privatization of the BNDES. Responses about state government banks differed. Nearly half (49 per cent) of federal deputies responded that state government banks still under intervention by the federal government should be privatized. However, opposition to privatization of federal government banks was nearly universal. This is consistent with policy debates about what to do with federal banks reviewed above. Consensus against privatization of federal banks in Brazil is broad but based on shared intuitions of strategy and policy capacity, rather than nationalism, ideology, or economic theory. Opposition to privatization among Federal Deputies is shared. It does not correlate with political ideology or economic views.

Conclusion

Since 1994, Brazilian federal banks have provided alternatives for policymakers and realized competitive advantages over private and foreign banks. Federal banks helped avert the return of high inflation during and after the Real Plan

(1993–4) and induce fiscal and administrative reform of sub-national governments. Federal banks also provided counter cyclical credit to help avert recession and ease adjustment during the unprecedented sequence of financial crises in developing and emerging countries in the 1990s (Mexico 1994–5, Asia 1997, Russia 1998, Argentina 2001, Brazil 1999 and 2002–3). Federal banks have also helped implement new social policies such as family grants through ATM citizenship cards. Data on branch networks, service points, correspondent banking and market shares suggest how institutional foundations provide competitive advantage in federal banking. Data on market share, bad credit, overdue loans, capital risk exposure, levels of reserves and provisions, and measures of efficiency and profitability both clarify the new division of financial labour in Brazil and suggest that federal banks remain viable financial institutions.

Brazilian banking has emerged from monetary chaos and instability in the 1980s and early 90s, survived crises and adjustment from 1994–2004 and helped drive a period of growth from 2004–8 interrupted by crisis during 2008–9. Liberalization or other forces may, in the long term, erode the institutional foundations of competitive advantage exercised by federal banks. Interest rates and bank spreads in Brazil remain among the highest in the world. Although the Bovespa stock market has become among the largest in the world, domestic credit and public finance remain far from mature markets and stable economies. Critics will be proved right if federal banks are mismanaged. However, the record since transition from military rule, opening the industry to foreign competition and the end of inertial inflation and instability supports our central argument. Federal banks remain commanding heights. These institutions have reformed and modernized to help deepen credit and finance, provide policy alternatives and contribute to social inclusion. Brazilian federal banks remain central agents of political economy and public policy. Case study chapters provide a closer look at how these institutions provided policy alternatives and acquired competitive advantages throughout Brazilian history and into the twenty-first century.

3 THE BANCO DO BRASIL

(with Maria Antonieta del Tedesco Lins)

'... [the] Banco do Brasil had, in practice, the power to finance its credit operations via money expansion, turning it into the most powerful public institution in Brazil. Its president had similar prestige as the Finance Minister and normally reported directly to the President.'

M. Nóbrega and G. Loyola,
'The Long and Simultaneous Construction
of Fiscal and Monetary Institutions' (2006), p. 80

The Banco do Brasil was founded before Brazil. Since 1808, government (and national) banks with this name have dominated banking, money management and economic policy. Until creation of the Central Bank in 1965, the Banco do Brasil supervised banks, managed the money supply, promoted exports, controlled imports, provided lending of last resort to banks, brokers and private firms and managed foreign exchange operations and national reserves. Until reforms in the 1980s, the Banco do Brasil remained executor of federal government budgets and retained *free access* to funds at Treasury to settle accounts. The modernization of Brazilian government and the development of specialized agencies for banking, money and finance policy is a story of *extricating* prerogatives from the Banco do Brasil. The gradual transfer of monetary policy to SUMOC (1945), central banking to the Central Bank (1965) and fiscal management to Treasury (1986) and Senate as determined by the 1988 Constitution has produced fundamental change at the bank. Since opening the industry in the 1990s, policymakers and Banco do Brasil executives have adopted market oriented policies and corporate governance reforms inspired by private banking to meet competition. Instead of loosing market share, the Banco do Brasil has remained the largest domestic financial conglomerate in Latin America and, in 2009, the most profitable bank in Brazil.[1]

Organizational scale and political networks have provided the Banco do Brasil competitive advantage over private and foreign banks for two centuries. Periods of liberalism (such as the 1830s and the 1850s) and federalism (1890s) experimented with alternative banking policies and structures. However, the Banco do Brasil remained at the centre of political economy in all other periods of Brazilian history. The first Banco do Brasil (1808–29) embodies nineteenth-century imperial statecraft. The bank financed war and repression of national and liberal forces to consolidate Portuguese monarchy and retain slavery in the Americas. After 1853, the second official Banco do Brasil dominated banking and finance in the latter nineteenth century, providing counter-cyclical credit and lending of last resort. Republicans reluctantly recreated the Banco do Brasil in 1900 and charged the national bank with management of currency boards and, in 1923, central banking. From 1930–45 the Banco do Brasil first mobilized domestic banks amidst revolution and global crisis and depression, then provided directed credit for import substitution industrialization and agricultural expansion to cement the national populist regime of Getulio Vargas. From transition (1945) to the breakdown of democracy (1964), the Banco do Brasil retained predominant market shares and embodied disputes between developmentalists and liberal economists that cross cut divisions within the bank and set Finance Ministers (determined to implement adjustment and reforms) against Banco do Brasil presidents and opponents of orthodoxy in Congress. Instead of liberalization after military coup in 1964, the Banco do Brasil came to allocate immense funds through myriad operations, ranging from bailouts of firms (and itself) to massive amounts of directed credit and periodic rescheduling of debts to industry and agriculture. During military government and prolonged transition, the Banco do Brasil also monetarized bad loans and fed record inflation that transferred over 6 per cent of GDP per year to banks and government accounts during the 1980s and skewed income distribution.[2]

The Banco do Brasil also housed a veto coalition against orthodox reforms through most of the twentieth century. National developmentalists supported by a Banco do Brasil caucus in Congress vetoed transfer of monetary, fiscal, financial and central banking prerogatives from the Banco do Brasil and delayed creation of the Central Bank of Brazil until after the breakdown of democracy in 1964. The Banco do Brasil continued to escape fiscal control under military rule by retaining free access (every Friday!) to Treasury funds until 1986. Reforms since the 1980s have nonetheless radically transformed the Banco do Brasil into a market oriented commercial and investment bank listed on the Bovespa Novo Mercado (New Market) stock exchange (being one of the first Brazilian firms to meet international corporate governance and transparency standards). However, instead of transferring ownership and control of the Banco do Brasil to the private sector through sale of shares on the Bovespa (the hope of PSDB policymakers during the 1990s) the federal government remains majority stockholder. Liberalization, reforms and market oriented policies have thus placed the Banco do Brasil at the centre of social and political networks that cross levels and branches of government, political parties, labour unions, pension funds of major state owned enterprises, mutual funds and organized interests. These networks and institutional foundations have provided powerful competitive advantages over private and foreign banks since liberalization of the industry in the 1990s. The following sections review the policies and performance of the Banco do Brasil since 1808.

The First Banco do Brasil, 1808–29

Having fled the French army to the Americas under British Navy escort, Portuguese King John VI commissioned a national bank on 12 October 1808 to raise funds for the royal treasury, supply credit to government ministries and promote use of legal tender. From its creation in 1809 until refusal of parliament to renew its charter in 1829, Banco do Brasil policies help explain the paradox of Brazilian exceptionalism – that the Portuguese crown prevailed over liberal, regional and national forces in the New World. The first Banco do Brasil embodies imperial financial statecraft and a pact between British bankers and anti-Napoleonic forces of royal government. Despite depletion of gold and a weak tax base in Portuguese South America, King João VI raised funds by selling shares for a new national bank to be granted monopoly over paper currency emissions. This permitted resumption of interest payments to British banks on 1.4 million pounds sterling of debt from war on the Iberian Peninsula. French invasion of Guiana in 1809 required cash to mobilize forces through Pará provincial authorities. The River Plate War (1823–5) and war with Argentina (1826–8) required funds in the south. National and regional uprisings also pressured government finances. From the 1817 revolt in Pernambuco through abdication of Dom Pedro I in 1831 (Emperor of independent Brazil since 1822), domestic revolts repeatedly challenged imperial government in Rio de Janeiro.

The policy advantages of government banking help explain why monarchy prevailed in Brazil. Imperial government and monarchy in the new world would not have survived without the first Banco do Brasil. The Banco do Brasil appears to be the fourth historical example of national banks created to reinforce royal finances. The Swedish Riksbank (1668), Bank of England (1694) and Banque du France (1800) were created by royal grants of monopoly over currency emissions in exchange for preferential sources of public finance.[3] The Banco do Brasil followed these experiences and enforced monetary authority through monopoly over minting and sale of coin and paper money, as well as bank deposits, loans and mortgages, currency exchange letters and government transactions, commissions, interest payments and sales. The crown also granted Banco do Brasil monopoly over exchange of gold, silver, precious metals and trade of promissory notes.

Data on money, credit and public finance confirm the centrality of politics, policies and national banking. Vieira notes correlations between political challenges to the government and currency emissions in the following year.[4] Having emptied both Treasury and the national bank by 1817, the government turned to printing money. Thereafter, Banco do Brasil currency issues outpace reserves. Repressing the 1817 revolution in Pernambuco was financed by printing paper notes in 1818–19. War in the south during 1825–6 was paid for by further issue of notes the following years. Paper notes as a percentage of Banco do Brasil reserves increased from 75 per cent in 1810 (its first full year of operation) to 117 per cent (1811), 287 per cent (1812) and 305 per cent (1813). Thereafter, data reverses the calculation but confirms the trend. Banco do Brasil reserves as a percentage of paper money fell from 48–17 per cent in 1814–27 reaching 8.47 per cent in 1828 before closing the following year.

Unlike the Bank of England, the Banco do Brasil lacked limits on currency emissions. Reserve requirements set in the imperial decree founding the bank were soon ignored. Most observers of early Brazil thereby emphasize the distance of the Banco do Brasil from both ideals of convertible 'hard' currencies and prudent bank policies of holding metal or other reserves. Observing the same phenomena, J. J. Sturz identifies a core competitive advantage of government banking and financial statecraft; *confidence*:

> 'And it is a curious and singular fact in the history of banks that, although the issue
> of notes by the Rio bank exceeded ten times the capital originally deposited in metal,
> not one holder of its notes ever thought of demanding cash for them'. [5]

Client uncertainty and runs on bank deposits can quickly lead to the failure of banks. Sturz implies that the governmental status of the Banco do Brasil helped avert a run on the bank. With gold reserves in its vaults and confidence among depositors, the first Banco do Brasil provided policy options and funds for imperial government.

The legal status of notes issued by the Banco do Brasil replaced use of restamped Spanish silver coin as medium of exchange. This has been criticized as *curso forcado* (forced course) the title of an influential book published in 1848.[6] Nonetheless, from the perspective of *politics*, acceptance of legal currency differs. Government determination of monetary value through a national bank illustrates policy capacity. The confidence of clients in the first Banco do Brasil provided a competitive advantage in the sense of operating at levels of leverage unthinkable for private banks. This, in turn, made it possible for the Banco do Brasil to provide Portuguese monarchy funds for military mobilization and other imperial policies. The ability of the Banco do Brasil to raise funds, print notes accepted as legal tender, provide credit and manage government policy and finances was critical for imperial statecraft. The first national bank remained at the centre of political conflicts through revolution in 1831 and thereafter.

Bank War in Brazil, the 1829 Legislature versus Dom Pedro I

The Banco do Brasil drew fire from liberal and regional opposition groups who refused to renew the national bank charter in 1829. The parallel with US history is compelling. President Andrew Jackson vetoed renewal of the First Bank of the US to weaken Nicholas Biddle and central government. The Brazilian legislature closed the Banco do Brasil in 1829 for similar reasons of opposition to central authority. Disputes over the Banco do Brasil during the 1820s provide new perspectives on conflicts that led to revolution and return of Dom Pedro I to Lisbon in 1831.Thereafter, aversion to a new national bank in Brazil also parallels the predominance of liberalism and federalism in the US. However, one difference is critical. The Banco do Brasil deteriorated during the 1820s in large part because King João VI returned to Portugal in 1821, taking with him reserves held at the national bank and Treasury *and* leaving 8.0 million milréis in debts to the bank (after printing 5.0 million milréis in 1821 to pay debts before leaving the Americas). This would have broken any private bank. Nonetheless, the Banco do Brasil continued to serve Dom Pedro I, the newly declared emperor of an independent Brazil after 1822. In an address to the Constitutional Assembly (shortly before closing it in 1823), Dom Pedro argued that concern about the solvency of the bank was unfounded and that the government intended to restructure its finances. Only 200 thousand milréis in metal reserves remained to cover an estimated over 8.8 million milréis of paper money in circulation. Yet the bank continued to operate six years until liquidation in 1829 (and continued to pay shareholders until 1837!).

Two interpretations of the first Banco do Brasil have prevailed. One emphasizes rents extracted and fraud wrought on the bank by privileged members of court. Another emphasizes the objective weight of government obligations that led to printing paper money. Parliamentary commissions of inquiry are rife with accusations of the former. The data tend to support the latter. Data collected by Sturz, Calogeras, Castro Carreira, and other secondary sources suggest that excessive printing of bank notes caused Banco do Brasil insolvency. However, given that emissions follow political events so closely, bank policy appears driven by political necessity and responses to regional revolts, notwithstanding widespread fraud and abuse. Moreover, comparison of spending at government ministries also suggests that the amount spent by the royal office does not outpace other ministries and agencies. Instead, the war office is responsible for the bulk of increases in government spending during the 1820s.

A different charge was made in parliament by Deputy Odorico Mendes, that of collusion between shareholders and bank directors. For Mendes, printing of Banco do Brasil notes was designed to maintain the income stream of shareholders while sacrificing bank performance to the point of insolvency.[7] The different interests of shareholders and depositors drove cleavages of opposition and support of imperial government during the 1820s. For liberal and regional opposition groups, the Banco do Brasil provided crony credit to crown, court and followers. The national bank funded military forces to defend monarchy and central government by printing bank notes accepted as legal tender. Liberal and regional opposition groups thus perceived the Banco do Brasil as agent of absolute monarchy and central government. Parliament refused to renew the national bank charter in 1829. After 1831, the turn to liberal doctrines of plural commercial banking and the delegation of currency emissions and money management to private banks emerges from this coalition *against* the first Banco do Brasil. Conflicts continued through liquidation of the bank (completed in 1837) because shareholders were protected and paid in full, while depositors were not.

Banco do Brasil policies thereby led to the 1831 revolution and erosion of monetary authority. In the 1820s, inflation of Banco do Brasil notes produced flight toward gold and silver and the resurgence of copper and illicit coins. Use of illicit *xenxem* copper coin, especially in the provinces, indicates a reversion to monetary chaos.[8] In his 1832 report to parliament, Finance Minister Bernardo Vasconcelos describes the causal sequence of revolution as follows:

> '... the disappearance of precious metals, the exhaustion of the bank, the inflation of values, and the loss of trade equilibrium and social relations; interest rates at record levels; foreign exchange at almost zero par; luxury far beyond private fortunes but nonetheless demanded by a court that concealed a lack of merit; injustice; the corruption of manners; immorality of employees; the blind fascination of the crown with certain individuals; an unjust and imprudent war; the destruction of leading men; the emission of an extraordinary amount of money without value; abusive practices; and the excessive generosity of trade agreements that destroyed our businesses, navigation and industry...'[9]

Inflation and disappearance of legal tender during the 1820s, saving shareholders but sacrificing depositors during liquidation of the Banco do Brasil and forced recall and exchange of bank notes at steep discount indicate further ways in which the national bank remained at the centre of political economy during the first Empire.

In sum, Banco do Brasil policies and competitive advantages help explain the fundamental anomaly of early nineteenth century Brazil – that Portuguese monarchy and empire prevailed over liberal and national groups at home and newly independent republican neighbours. The bank inspired and embodied disputes between opposition groups and central government that produced revolution and the abdication of Dom Pedro I in 1831.

Liberal Experiments in Plural Banking and the Banco do Brasil 1853–60

Liquidation of the first Banco do Brasil left the government without a national bank until 1853 when Dom Pedro II asserted control over a private Banco do Brasil built by the enterprising Baron of Mauá. During this 24 year hiatus, policies of decentralization during the 1830s and recentralization during the 1840s gave way to liberal practices of delegating currency emissions to private commercial banks. By 1850, over a dozen private banks issued short-term promissory notes (*vales*) widely used for commercial transactions in place of legal tender. The granting of note issuing authority to private banks and the 1853 reorganization of the Banco do Brasil culminated the turn to liberal policies of money, credit and banking. However, financial crises in 1857, 1859 and 1864 devastated banks, reduced the circulation and acceptance of their notes and led to the centralization of monetary authority and banking.

The Banco do Brasil fell under government control but not ownership in 1853, reflecting the hybrid form of national banks typical of the nineteenth century. In 1853, Treasury Director and future Finance Minister Torres proposed a new national bank to be created through sale of shares to the general public. This was to *avert* direct government control and ensure that public interests be served by liberal principles of private shareholder corporate governance. Legislation in 1853 thereby determined creation of a new Banco do Brasil with 30,000 contos of capital (3.5 million pounds sterling) based on sale of 150,000 shares at 200 milréis. The new Banco do Brasil was to merge Mauá's Banco do Brasil and the Banco Commerical de Rio de Janeiro (BCRJ), reserving 50,000 shares for Banco do Brasil shareholders and 30,000 shares for BCRJ shareholders. Baron Mauá expected to control the new institution. However, Dom Pedro II appointed parliamentary representative João Duarte Lisboa Serra as President of the bank instead.[10]

The new Banco do Brasil moved quickly to acquire regional banks or open branch offices to reassert monetary authority in the provinces. The Banco de Pernambuco was acquired in 1855, the Banco Comercial da Bahia in 1856, the Banco do Para in 1856, and the Banco do Maranhao in 1857. Financial crises in 1857 and 1859 suspended this trend, but acquisitions continued thereafter. In 1862, the Banco do Brasil acquired the Banco Agricola do Rio de Janeiro and prohibited emissions of paper notes by the Banco Rural and Hipotecário, thereby gaining monopoly of currency emissions in Rio de Janeiro. Government liquidation of the Banco do Rio Grande do Sul left only the Banco do Para,

Banco do Maranhão, and the Banco Comercial da Bahia as commercial banks emitting notes (*vales*) widely traded as currencies.

This second national Banco do Brasil remained central to politics, banking and monetary policy until the end of Empire in 1889. Like the first Banco do Brasil, the government commissioned sale of bank shares to increase control over money, credit, and finance while retaining private shareholder ownership to capitalize the bank. The second Banco do Brasil was designed to bring the country closer to a gold standard and monetary and economic stability. Progress was made in the sense that circulation and exchange values for illicit copper and silver coin diminished. However, the milréis never gained full convertibility. Instead, the milréis remained a fiduciary currency; legal tender under Brazilian law, anchored to and managed by a specially designed *fundo disponível* (disposable fund) at the Banco do Brasil.

The second Banco do Brasil confirms the central argument of the monetary principle school – multiple commercial bank emissions tend to inflate currencies and disorganize commercial transactions.[11] Data suggest that the national bank remained the primary source of paper currency (especially during financial and banking crises). From 1853–9, Banco do Brasil increased currency emissions from 8.6–40.6 million milréis (most of the increase in paper notes during the period, 62.2–95.8 million milréis 1854–9). Treasury notes actually *decline* six thousand contos (46.0–40.0 from 1853/4–58/9 fiscal years). The excessive printing and circulation of a variety of notes, paper used as money, and promissory certificates from private banks has been emphasized by virtually every analyst of this period. It is more precise to say that liquidity originated in the Banco do Brasil. Moreover, printing of paper currency by the Banco do Brasil occurs primarily during years of financial crisis, suggesting the new role of this institution as lender of last resort.

In any case, the 1857 and 1859 financial crises produced consensus on the need to end the boom and bust cycles fed by currency emissions from private commercial banks. On 2 April 1859 the government refused eighteen applications to found commercial banks that would have been able to issue paper money. On 30 April 1859 the limit of Banco do Brasil emissions was reduced from three times to twice the *fundo disponível*. Finally, on June 15 the Finance Ministry set a schedule for recall of notes. Further legislation introduced in 1860 and 1866 culminated this shift away from liberal policies of plural commercial bank issues toward the centralization of money and banking.

However, the Banco do Brasil continued to provide lending of last resort during financial crises. The 1864 financial crisis in the US produced a run on the Banco do Brasil and the suspension of currency exchange. The following Caixa case study chapter reports data demonstrating that the recently founded Imperial government savings bank experienced an *influx* of deposits during and after the 1864 banking and financial crisis.

During the panic of 1864 financial crisis, the Banco do Brazil provided lending of last resort at home and management of currency exchange operations in London. A three thousand pounds sterling loan was obtained by the Banco do Brasil from London banks to avert a run on the Brazilian currency. This proved insufficient to regain the confidence of depositors and markets. To stay the flight of deposits, the bank requested permission to temporarily print currency up to four times the *fundo disponível*. The Banco do Brasil thereby survived, but many other banks and firms did not. The collapse of the private bank A.J.A. Souto in September 1864 left depositors with losses of over 41 million milréis. An estimated 118 banks closed by year-end. The Banco do Brasil not only survived, it also provided policy alternatives. Finance Ministry reports suggest that, in 1864, Banco do Brasil management was much more aware of the bank's potential as a lender of last resort and acted swiftly. Between 10 and 20 September 1864 the Banco do Brasil provided an estimated 30 million milréis (3.3 million pounds sterling) in inter-bank loans to domestic and foreign institutions.[12] Competitive advantages reinforced national bank capacity to provide policy alternatives.

The financial crisis of 1864 also coincided with the onset of war with Paraguay, a development that shifted debates away from banking and finance to geopolitics. After having spent the revenue obtained from foreign loans, the government issued an additional 124 million milréis in paper money from Treasury and the Banco do Brasil to pay for war. Total war costs, estimated at 400 million milréis, left the government deeply in debt, while additional currency emissions to meet government obligations further pressured prices and devalued the milréis.

In sum, from reorganization of the Banco do Brasil as a national bank in 1853 through 1889, banking policies shifted back and forth between polar opposites. Finance Ministers first attempted to consolidate currency issues in the third (second official) Banco do Brasil in 1853. In 1857, multiple commercial bank emissions were freed by Finance Minister Bernardo de Souza Franco. By 1860, commercial bank prerogatives were revoked under the *entraves* (constraints) law culminating centralizing reforms begun under Souza Franco's successor at the Finance Ministry, Francisco de Sales Torres Homem, that consolidated currency emissions in the Banco do Brasil. Finally, in 1866, currency emissions were delegated to Treasury, a prerogative it retained until the end of the empire in 1889. Policies thus ranged from liberal policies of almost free banking to attempts by central government to control banking and money in the hope of anchoring the milréis against a gold standard and metal reserves. However, as Vilella notes, 'From 1870 on the monetary and banking question would no longer be as prominent a theme in imperial political economy'.[13] Instead, debates about abolition, immigrant labour, investment and modernization predominated.

The Banco do Brasil as National Bank, 1889–1930

After the military coup ended monarchy on 15 November 1889, republicans perceived the Banco do Brasil as monarchist stronghold and created a new regional bank system. The Banco do Brasil was merged with the Banco Nacional to found the Banco da República in 1893, only to be recreated in 1900 after fraud and mismanagement at the Banco da República brought down President Deodoro da Fonseca and led to closure of the new bank. Thereafter, the Banco do Brasil become, once again, the largest bank in Brazil and primary economic policy instrument for federal government. The Banco do Brasil managed two of *three* currency boards, provided lending of last resort to firms and commercial banks and gained central bank status in 1923. During the Old Republic, the Banco do Brasil provided policy alternatives that ranged from orthodox adjustment policies underwritten by London banks to management of national-liberal subsidy programmes and price protection schemes and management of foreign exchange markets at home and abroad. Once again, policy roles reinforced competitive advantages. From 1906–30, the Banco do Brasil increased market share of domestic credit from 5.6–28.8 per cent.[14]

Redesign of banking under republican government began with emergency decrees in late 1889 and reforms in January 1890 under Finance Minister Rui Barbosa. Barbosa assumed office facing a liquidity shortage and political dilemma. If the market was allowed to correct, recession would disorganize the economy and threaten the federal pact for republican government. If the government were to extend credit and increase paper emissions, this would feed inflation. Political necessity prevailed. Barbosa extended emergency credits to the Banco do Brasil and other private banks, and restored the rural credit programme designed during the last year of imperial government to compensate plantation owners for abolition.[15]

In 1890, two banks were granted authority to print currency against deposits, the Banco do Brasil and Banco Nacional (merged to form the Banco da República in December 1892) while six regional banks were granted authority to print currency anchored on reserves of Treasury Bills (Banco dos Estados Unidos do Brasil, Banco Emissor do Sul, Banco União de São Paulo, Banco Sul-Americano, Banco Emissor da Bahia, Banco Emissor do Norte). This arrangement was a political necessity to accomodate republican forces in states. Issue of government bonds was necessary to reschedule debts inherited from imperial government. Even critics such as Calogeras argue that Barbosa's system of regional banks did not immediately produce a cycle of excessive currency emissions and credit behind inflation and the *encilhamento* financial bubble.[16]

To the contrary, Barbosa agreed that a single monetary authority was superior to plural emissions and sought to increase central government control over banking. In December 1890, merger of the Banco dos Estados Unidos do Brasil and Banco Nacional do Brasil (and recall of 171.000 contos of treasury bills) were designed to counter the volume of paper printed by regional banks. The sum of paper currency emissions from the regional banks under Barbosa through year-end 1890 (he resigned 20 January 1891) suggests that excessive paper currency printing was not the primary cause of the financial crisis that accompanied the organization of republican government.[17]

After Barbosa's resignation, increased paper emissions under Finance Ministers Tristão de Alencar Araripe and Henrique Pereira de Lucena and the mismanagement of regional banks did, in fact, ensue. While merger of the Banco do Brasil and Banco Nacional into the Banco da República in 1892 was designed to centralize authority over banking, money and credit, the merger was accompanied by charges of fraud, mismanagement and imperial conspiracy by the press and opposition groups. President Deodoro's Finance Minister Baron Lucena's loan of over 2 million pounds sterling to four regional banks reinforced republican perceptions of banks as institutional enclaves of imperial elites. On 23 November 1891 an army and navy revolt deposed Marshall Deodoro da Fonseca (the first elected republican President), in good part because of these perceptions of regional banks. For Topik, the cycle of inflation, currency devaluation, and fraud 'end the experiment of encouraging private investment banks through issue of abundant inconvertible currency'.[18]

President Floriano Peixoto therafter pursued state-led policies typical of liberal-nationalism. Emergency credits were extended to save commercial banks from failure in 1892, congress approved 'aid to industry bonds' and merger of the Banco do Brasil and Banco Nacional was completed. Topik describes this merger as 'a seizure of financial power by the state'.[19] Presidential appointment of Banco da República senior staff replayed the removal of Baron Mauá at the Banco do Brasil by Dom Pedro II in 1853. Once again, national banking combined private capitalization with government control. The Banco da República retained a monopoly over currency emissions, concession to manage Treasury surpluses, right to use future Treasury revenue as collateral and other measures that extended government authority over money, credit, and financial markets. The 1893 financial crisis further increased government intervention in banking. Treasury once again assumed monopoly over currency emissions while the government intervened in the Banco da República.

By 1898, a shift to orthodox monetary policies sought to reduce inflation, restore fiscal order and regain the confidence of foreign investors. Finance Minister Joaquim Murtinho (1898–1902) symbolizes this turn to orthodoxy, with his financial Darwinism providing a stark interpretation of monetarist theories.[20] A June 1898 funding loan from London banks included clauses for recall and incineration of milréis for government bonds (in lieu of interest payments from 1898–1901), pledge of Rio de Janeiro customs house receipts toward repayment and supervision of government policies by foreign banks. Recovery legitimized orthodoxy. From 1902–6, Finance Minister Bulhões continued policies of short money and fiscal control to produce surpluses in government accounts for two of his four years in office. Valuation of the milréis from near 7 to 14 pence, a six-fold increase in exports, capital inflows and receding inflation reinforced orthodoxy.

However, domestic banking differed from Kemmerer inspired policies. Instead, the 1900 bank crisis led to cash infusions from the government into the Banco da República, then to intervention and reorganization of the bank into a *third* official Banco do Brasil. Finance Minister Murtinho (normally indisposed to intervene in markets) first attempted to stem the run on deposits at the Banco da República by swapping 186,000 contos of bank debt due Treasury for 50,000 new treasury notes, then provided emergency loans of 900,000 pounds sterling and 10,000 contos. Intervention followed in September 1900. The government then created the third official Banco do Brasil by converting Banco da República liabilities with Treasury into one-third of new bank shares, allocating 1/3 of new shares to existing stockholders, and selling the last third. The trebling of share prices during 1905–6 from 49–155 milréis (reaching 250 milréis in 1908)[21] suggests, once again, the viability of this hybrid form of national bank, an institution that remained under government control but now with mixed ownership of shares.

The Rio de Janeiro financial paper, *Jornal do Comercio*, welcomed the new Banco do Brasil as 'able to exercise the functions of a central bank, having available abundant capital to rediscount the paper of other banks, make advances to other banks, and finally aid them in moments of crisis'.[22] The Banco do Brasil has remained central in domestic banking and political economy since. President Afonso Pena (1906–9) shifted further away from orthodoxy by adopting policies to support world coffee prices, stabilize foreign exchange rates and ensure domestic credit to avert bankruptcies. Influenced by the new currency board and gold standard in Argentina, a Caixa de Conversão (currency board) was created in 1906 with authority to manage money anchored to gold reserves and a fixed exchange rate.[23] In 1906, the Taubaté accord also marked the end of orthodoxy and turn to state intervention under liberal nationalism. Policies sought to stabilize world coffee prices and channel export receipts to domestic producers – both during booms and to socialize costs during downturns.[24]

At first, gold and hard currencies flowed into the currency board from trade and capital account surpluses. Deposits increased from 37 thousand contos in 1906, to over 63 thousand in 1907, reaching 493 thousand in 1908. Far from a blessing, rules in 1906 monetary reforms required channelling these reserves directly into credit through the domestic banking system, increasing credit geometrically. The Caixa de Conversão also increased the capacity of the government to manage financial markets through issue of notes convertible into sterling from its reserves (designed to keep the milréis below official par). However, deficits in foreign trade and the capital account soon revealed problems on the downside. Downturns in foreign accounts proved to rapidly deplete the Currency Board *and* produce geometric contractions of credit. After closing temporarily in 1910, the currency board reopened until a run on hard currencies led to closure again in 1914. These experiences revealed that fixed rules for currency boards reduced monetary policy discretion and produced excessive pro-cyclical credit flows from banks, both on the upside and downside.

A second currency board in 1920 (the Carteira de Emissão e Redesconto, Emission and Rediscount Portfolio) provided policy discretion by granting the Banco do Brasil authority to print currency and exchange commercial paper for treasury notes (through an account managed separately from commercial operations). This account/currency board at the Banco do Brasil was designed to buffer domestic money and credit from fluctuations in trade and capital accounts (a vulnerability confirmed by the 1920 financial crisis abroad).[25] The Banco do Brasil thereafter managed this currency board to clear foreign accounts. However, because presidential orders could emit treasury notes for Banco do Brasil purchase of commercial paper, the Banco do Brasil also became a lender of last resort under direct political control. The Banco do Brasil was placed amidst pressures from coffee producers for credit, prudent management of its commercial portfolio and responsibility for both domestic currency reserves and the money supply.

This set of policies increased government debt and devalued the milréis, leading to abandonment of the Caixa de Conversão and redesign of the Banco do Brasil. Legislation had prohibited trade of government paper and capped emissions at 100.0 million milréis. However, the Banco do Brasil's currency board freed commercial banks to offer an estimated 400.0 million milréis during 1921.[26] The limit on Banco do Brasil currency emissions was tripled to 300.0 million milréis in 1922 and once again increased to 400.0 million milréis in 1923.[27] The milréis consequently plunged from 8.4 pence in 1921 to 5.3 at year-end 1923. The Banco do Brasil also increasingly bought government bonds. In 1921, congress authorized liquidation of 500,000 contos of treasury bills (equal to half the value of notes held by the bank), a development that alleviated government deficits but expanded the monetary base and fed inflation. Monetisation of the fiscal deficit by holding Treasury Bills also threatened to paralyse the commercial operations of the Banco do Brasil.

In 1923, the Bernardes administration proposed transforming the Banco do Brasil into a central bank and created the Instituto do Café to support coffee prices. However, inflation and devaluation reinforced orthodoxy and led to adoption of adjustment policies. In 1923, Banco do Brasil President Cincinato Braga proposed and Congress approved new regulations to limit rediscount operations and clarify its role as lender of last resort. Market perceptions and reform proposals converged on the national bank. The nomination of Braga and presentation of reforms to congress in January 1923 increased pressures on the milréis, falling to 7.5 milréis per pence during first quarter 1922 to bottom at 4.6 pence on 7 November 1923. Meanwhile, opposition in Congress and the financial press denounced use of government notes as Banco do Brasil reserves. The 1922 Congressional Finance Committee report signed by Anibal Freire condemned permissive relations between a discretionary currency board and the Banco do Brasil. While the government defended policy as necessary to sustain credit and growth, Finance Minister Whitaker was forced to resign in December 1922.

The Banco do Brasil also opened offices in London to reduce volatility and manipulation of coffee and foreign exchange markets by British banks. Daily liquidation of import tax revenues in Rio de Janeiro also sought to reduce volatility in foreign exchange markets. These policies increased Banco do Brasil reserves temporarily. In the 1923 Annual Report, Banco do Brasil President Braga records reserves of 90 million milréis (up from 40 million at year-end 1922) and on track to reach the goal of 100 million by July 1924. However, in the 1924 Annual Report, Banco do Brasil President Cincinato Braga laments that short foreign trade surpluses, along with government deficits and debt had reversed gains. Banco do Brasil policies paled before macro phenomena such as declining trade and investment, capital flight and politics. Civil war in Rio Grande do Sul and declaration of a state of emergency in 1924 increased uncertainty, devalued the milréis against foreign currencies and reduced credit and trade flows. In 1924, Braga revised estimates to an expected 5.5 billion pounds sterling shortfall in foreign currency obligations.

After Congressional Finance Committee inquires led to resignation of Braga from the Banco do Brasil presidency in late 1924, the government shifted to tight money policies. In May 1925, President Bernardes argued for recall of currency to value the milréis against foreign currencies. Promises to recall 98 thousand contos through the Banco do Brasil and Caixa de Amortização were exceeded. By April 1925, the Banco do Brasil had recalled 91.900 contos (recalls later reached 139.15 contos) and the milréis rose from the low of 4.6 pence in November 1923 to 7.1 by 1926. This once again reinforced the legitimacy of tight money policy and quantitative theories. However, success also led to maintenance of tight money policies well after recovery had generated trade surpluses and capital inflows, despite demands for liquidity and credit to spur growth.[28]

The Banco do Brasil also played critical roles for revolutionary forces in the late 1920s. For example, Getulio Vargas (as Finance Minister) simply transferred 10 million pounds of sterling and gold reserves from the Banco do Brasil into yet another currency board in 1927 (reserves that were designed to sustain confidence in the 592 billion milréis circulating in the domestic economy). Vargas simply ignored the clause requiring compensation of the Banco do Brasil. He also transferred 11.2 million pounds sterling of government reserves into the currency board where they too were subject to free market prices and exchange. Transfer of 11.2 million pounds sterling from the currency board during the 1930 revolution would leave the Brazilian government without reserves or recourse to finance at home or abroad. An estimated 4.2 million pounds of foreign currency reserves remained at Treasury in 1930. However, this was used by the provisional government to support the exchange rate of the new currency (cruzeiro) abroad while directors of the Banco do Brasil were dismissed. Banco do Brasil directors were seen as oligarchs, just as republicans saw national bank directors as monarchists in 1889.

In sum, from 1889–1930, the Banco do Brasil provided a wide variety of policy alternatives (ranging from orthodox policies of adjustment to statist policies of national liberalism) while realizing competitive advantage and expanding market shares over private and foreign banks.

The Banco do Brasil under Revolution and Adjustment to Global Crisis, 1930–7

After 1930, the Banco do Brasil provided policy alternatives for adjustment to global depression, import substitution industrialization and coalition building. Banco do Brasil policies help explain why crisis and depression abroad were relatively benign in Brazil.[29] The bank helped adjust the economy and redirect production and consumption in accord with new ideas of national populism. During the 1930s, a liberal constitution (1932), communist revolution (1935) and fascist coup (1938) failed to provide frameworks for modern politics in Brazil. Instead, the national populist regime of Getulio Vargas shaped modernization. The policy alternatives and competitive advantages of the Banco do Brasil remained at the centre of developments. During the early 1930s, a new Bank Mobilisation Fund averted banking crisis and assured liquidity and credit. Banco do Brasil management of foreign debt, currency exchange and trade policy helped avert deterioration of foreign accounts. After adjustment, Brazilian GDP grew in real terms at an average of 6.5 per cent per-year from 1934–7. Industrial production grew over 10 per cent per year after 1933, despite notable declines in imports.

Banco do Brasil lending was critical because the 1929 crisis hit Brazil when it was vulnerable. The government was already carrying large stocks of coffee (70 per cent of exports) when forecasts for record harvests in 1929–30 and collapse of demand halved prices.[30] The provisional government hoped that reserves in the Banco do Brasil would be sufficient to cover foreign exchange requirements. However, the bank's currency board/account had been liquidated in 1929. Despite securing a funding loan abroad, the devaluation of the milréis 55.0 per cent against the dollar during 1930–1 and depletion of foreign reserves led to a

moratorium on debt payments. Foreign exchange operations were centralized at
the Banco do Brasil. The national bank was also charged with rebuilding credibil-
ity overseas, as demands from foreign investors multiplied. At home, liquidation
of the Currency Board had dismantled monetary policy, deepened the coffee
crisis and threatened to produce a banking crisis. The provisional government
used the Banco do Brasil Rediscount Facility (*Carteira de Redesconto*) as lender
of last resort to banks and supervisor of the banking system. In expectation of
a return to the gold standard, Finance Minister Whitaker advocated creating a
central bank during the first months of Provisional Government. This proved
impossible. Instead, Whitaker settled accounts between the Banco do Brasil and
Treasury – leaving the bank with large sums of foreign currency to cover withdrawals and meet payments abroad.

In 1932, the still provisional government created a Bank Mobilisation Fund
(*Caixa de Mobilização Bancária*) to restart the economy.[31] This fund set minimum
bank reserves and required commercial banks to deposit further reserves at the
Banco do Brasil to cover institutions in trouble. This restored public confidence,
reduced capital flight, helped avert a banking crisis and reinforced both competitive
advantages of the Banco do Brasil and its reputation as lender of last resort.[32]

The Bank Mobilisation Fund also channelled funds through the Banco do
Brasil to a new *Departamento Nacional do Café* (National Coffee Department,
DNC), created in 1933 at the Finance Ministry. The Banco do Brasil thereby
financed coffee through special credits against future coffee export tax receipts.
The Vargas government would later (1937) decrease price supports and reduce
subsidised credit to coffee. However, because the DNC was unable to repay the
Banco do Brasil, the Treasury itself took out a loan (from the Banco do Brasil
Rediscount Facility) to cover DNC obligations in exchange for canceling pay-
ment of 300 thousand *contos* due Treasury by the Banco do Brasil. The Banco
do Brasil administered a *fourfold* increase of resources for coffee under Oswald
Aranha, Whitaker's replacement at the Finance Ministry.[33]

In 1934, foreign currency earnings from exports were exempted from
exchange controls. In 1935, significant currency outflows ensued once profit
remittances were freed. Negotiations with foreign creditors led to an agreement
for the Banco do Brasil to receive 35 per cent of foreign currency earnings from
exports to repay public contracts. The remaining 65 per cent of foreign exchange
earnings were to be negotiated on an open market, where the private sector
could also purchase quotas. Liberalization of foreign exchange policy and export
increases (led by coffee) improved the balance of trade by 1936.

The Banco do Brasil also financed defeat of the Constitutionalist Revolt
in São Paulo in 1932 and recovery from drought in the Northeast. State and
municipal governments unable to repay foreign investors also appealed to the
bank. The Banco do Brasil was placed once again at the centre of revolutionary
politics, government policies and economic adjustment. As Vieira notes:

The increasingly fragility of the economy and monetary system provided fertile ground for the loss of confidence in the public sector. This favoured political change and revolts which, in turn, because they increased expenses further, made the situation worse.[34]

Amidst myriad pressures for credit and money, the Banco do Brasil provided policy alternatives for the provisional revolutionary government, remained solvent and increased market share. Take, for example, foreign accounts. The Banco do Brasil Foreign Exchange Facility (*Carteira de Câmbio*) retained a monopoly over foreign exchange after prohibition of private transactions in November 1932. Certification of import duties provided control over imports.[35] The Banco do Brasil thereby financed adjustment to the 1929 crisis, managed foreign accounts and obligations and helped shift production and consumption inward.

The Banco do Brasil and National Populism under the Estado Novo, 1937–45

The Banco do Brasil remained at the centre of government policies during the Estado Novo of Getulio Vargas. In 1937, the Vargas administration created a *Carteira de Crédito Agrícola e Industrial* (Agricultural and Industrial Credit Scheme). By the early 1940s, the *Carteira de Crédito Agrícola e Industrial* provided a third of Banco do Brasil credits and 20 per cent of total lending to to industry and agriculture.

In March 1942 the Banco do Brasil was reorganized in accord with the *Lei das Sociedades Anônimas* (Corporate Law). Thereafter, conflicts between monetary policy prerogatives and commercial bank operations became more apparent. In 1942, the Banco do Brasil was reorganized into five portfolios:

Exchange Rate Portfolio (*Carteira de Câmbio*), responsible for exchange rate policy, supervision of banks and the Special Agency for Economic Defense (*Agência Especial de Defesa Econômica*);

Agricultural and Industrial Credit Facility (*Carteira de Crédito Agrícola e Industrial*), that administered directed credits both to producers and via private financial institutions;

General Credit Portfolio (*Carteira de Crédito Geral*), that centralized commercial credit operations;

Export and Import Portfolio (*Carteira de Exportação e Importação*), responsible for foreign transactions, market research and the promotion of Brazilian commercial interests abroad;

Rediscount Facility *(Carteira de Redesconto)*, for rediscounting operations with domestic financial institutions.

The Banco do Brasil remained responsible for collecting federal revenue, authorizing payments and settling foreign exchange operations for government entities. The bank also continued to be the largest single source of finance for the private and public sector while expanding branch offices to provide banking services in the interior of the country. The number of Banco do Brasil branch offices increased from 157 in 1941 to 220 in 1942, reaching 259 by the transition to democracy in 1945. The bank also increased its share of an expanding credit market for agriculture and industry from 19.7–21.6 per cent from 1935–44.[36]

In 1937, the Vargas government decreed a fixed exchange rate, monopoly of foreign exchange and import restrictions. The Banco do Brasil thereafter controlled import policy. The onset of war in 1939 reduced exports to Axis powers and led to difficulties meeting foreign obligations. In April 1939, 30 per cent of foreign exchange from export earnings were allocated to the Banco do Brasil, while the remaining 70 per cent could be traded for cruzeiros at market rates. A separate, lower, official exchange rate was introduced for private financial transactions.[37] Exchange policies encouraged industry to substitute imports.

To counter global instability and export shortfalls in 1942, the Vargas government 'issued' three million contos de réis in war bonds (actually mandatory payroll deductions from public employee salaries and pensions) and one million contos de réis in 180–day Treasury bonds (sold to commercial banks and financial institutions through the Rediscount Portfolio of the Banco do Brasil). The Banco do Brasil also received authorization to increase rediscount operations – a policy that sought to reconcile concerns about inflation at the Finance Ministry while increasing liquidity to maintain growth. However, poor policy coordination and lack of control over the money supply generated, once again, debate about the need to create a central bank. This coincided with the end of Vargas's national populist regime in 1945.

The Banco do Brasil: Developmentalism vs Liberalism, 1945–64

After transition to democracy in 1945, the *Superintendência da Moeda e do Crédito* (Superintendence of Money and Credit, SUMOC) was created to coordinate monetary policy and prepare the ground for a central bank. SUMOC authority was to include issue of money by Treasury, interest rates on inter-bank lending and bank deposits, regulation and supervision of banks, government guaranteed loans and gold and foreign exchange trading. In reality, 'SUMOC remained a toothless tiger'.[38] Few prerogatives were exercised by SUMOC. Instead, the Banco do Brasil retained control over credit, money and banking. The Banco do Brasil also remained exempt from commercial bank reserve requirements and other bank regulations – another competitive advantage. Predominant market share, policy discretion and operational autonomy meant that the Banco do Brasil allocated resources and determined, in practice, the supply of credit and money in Brazil.

The Banco do Brasil also shifted policies toward the private sector and commercial banks after 1945. In real terms, Banco do Brasil loans to the private sector grew over 489 per cent from 1939–52 (private banks increased lending by 110 per cent). Aggressive lending indicates how the Banco do Brasil had became a stronghold of structuralist economic theories and developmentalist policies. However, because Banco do Brasil divisions were also responsible for monetary and fiscal policy, monetarist economists also worked at the bank and advocated more conservative policies. Indeed, when the Central Bank of Brazil was created in 1965, it was staffed almost entirely by personnel from the Banco do Brasil.

Conflicts between developmentalists and liberals occurred *within* the bank. The administration of President Eurico Gaspar Dutra (1946–51) reinforced Brazilian participation in post-war frameworks for international trade and finance. Proposals by the Brazilian delegation to include agriculture at Bretton Woods failed. Thereafter, Brazil faced surpluses from trade in soft currencies and deficits in dollars. In 1946, the government fixed the exchange rate at pre-war parity (CR$18.5/US$1.0) to stimulate imports of capital goods for industrialization. However, by July 1947, exchange controls once again placed the Banco do Brasil at the centre of trade policy. Banks were once again required to sell 30 per cent of foreign currency earnings to the Banco do Brasil at an official rate, remaining free to allocate the remaining 70 per cent. In February 1948, import licensing and other policies encouraged the substitution of imports by industry and consumers.

Unorthodox procedures for monetary, fiscal and financial policy also reinforced Banco do Brasil operations. Currency issues were authorized by officials at the Ministry of Finance, but implemented through the Banco do Brasil Bank Stabilisation Account (*Caixa de Estabilização Bancária*) and Rediscount Facility (*Carteira de Redescontos*). Finance Ministry funds at the Banco do Brasil could involve deposits in the name of SUMOC, or foreign exchange earnings and operations, or through debit or rediscount of government paper through the Bank Stabilisation Account. The latter operation became known as 'camping' paper money (*encampação de papel-moeda*). These operations cancelled debts of Treasury at the Banco do Brasil for an equivalent amount of Banco do Brasil obligations to Treasury in its Rediscount Portfolio. This made federal government budget deficits 'disappear' into the broader money and credit supply. Obligations were removed both from the Banco do Brasil Rediscount Facility and Finance Ministry balance sheets. However, this fed inflation, demonstrated the lack of government control over monetary policy and placed the Banco do Brasil at the centre of disputes over money and subsidized credit.

SUMOC did set commercial bank reserve requirements and auction government bonds on a new open market. However, rediscounting to banks remained at the Banco do Brasil, with cash simply transferred from Treasury when needed. Foreign currency trading also remained under control of the Banco do Brasil Exchange Rate Portfolio. The Banco do Brasil continued to retain control over trade policy with creation a Foreign Trade Portfolio – Carteira de Comércio Exterior (CACEX) in 1953 that both authorized and financed exports and imports.[39]

The Banco do Brasil also increased rediscounting to credit institutions willing to channel resources to agriculture. For structuralist policymakers, agricultural finance both increased agricultural exports to earn the hard currencies necessary to cover industrial imports and ensured domestic food supplies to stabilize prices. The Banco do Brasil thereby channelled credit to agriculture, agroindustry and industry and commerce, the latter in an attempt to overcome bottlenecks in transportation, refrigeration, ports and storage facilities. Policies often conflicted with imperatives of economic management. For example, during 1947–8, the government cut spending and credit to combat inflation, producing a drop in industrial production, rising unemployment and bankruptcies in São Paulo and Rio de Janeiro. The Banco do Brasil acted in an opposite, counter-cyclical direction to appease dissatisfied groups (in part because of its competitive advantage of freedom from reserve requirements). However, the Banco do Brasil was not simply a nationalist stronghold. The bank's Exchange Rate Portfolio also provided multinational enterprises a way to avert caps imposed by SUMOC on profit remittances. Banco do Brasil staff classified profits and dividends as foreign investment for the purposes of SUMOC supervisors – thereby facilitating capital flows out of the country.

The Banco do Brasil also helped liquidate bad loans at private banks. Banco do Brasil credit to cover bad loans at commercial banks increased from 11.0–151.8 million cruzeiros from 1945–50. Opposition groups denounced crony credit policies and their impact on inflation. However, these policies led to nomination of Banco do Brasil President Manoel Guilherme da Silveira to the Finance Ministry in 1949. The bank then continued generous credit policies, especially for agriculture to induce larger harvests.

Tensions between structuralist policies and imperatives of adjustment persisted until military intervention in 1964. Getúlio Vargas returned as elected president in 1951 to face rising inflation and dual deficits in foreign trade and government accounts. Although Vargas' Finance Minister Horácio Lafer attempted to impose austerity, the Banco do Brasil continued to pursue expansion. Two joint Brazil-US commissions concurred with the diagnosis of structuralist economists to the extent that reports recognized the need to alleviate infrastructure bottlenecks. However, Vargas' accusations of under- and over-factoring in remittances of multinational corporations increased tensions and eroded confidence among foreign investors.

As foreign accounts deteriorated and political confrontations escalated, conflicts cross-cut the Banco do Brasil during Vargas's second term (1951–4). Banco do Brasil President Ricardo Jafet opposed austerity, expanded credit operations and sought restrictions on foreign capital. However, Director of the Banco do Brasil Exchange Portfolio, Otávio de Bulhões, defended trade liberalization. An overvalued foreign exchange rate eroded trade surpluses. Nonetheless, liberalization of imports attempted to reduce pressure on domestic prices and supplies. Again, this reflected the diagnosis of structuralist policymakers that inflation was primarily due to the inelasticity of supply. Foreign currency reserves dropped sharply during 1951, exports fell during 1952 and the foreign exchange rate regime collapsed in 1953. International organizations (World Bank and US Export-Import Bank) began to monitor Brazilian economic policy and insist on tighter credit. Meanwhile, legislation increased capital mobility by liberalizing foreign exchange and reinvestment options.[40]

Banco do Brasil policies attempted to avert foreign exchange shortages. First, subsidy was offered to foreign investors through a 10 per cent yearly remittance allowance at an official exchange rate (a policy proposed by the Banco do Brasil). This led to a complex system of multiple exchange rates. Exporters could sell 30 per cent of foreign currency earnings on a free market (once licensed). However, most exports were covered by exchange rates set by the IMF accord, alongside *three* additional floating rates for other products and a fixed exchange rate for public sector imports. Financial transactions were subject to market exchange rates (select foreign loans exempted). The Banco do Brasil also controlled trade finance through its Export & Import Portfolio (*Carteira de Exportação e Importação*). The bank financed coffee and cotton exports, provided rediscount operations for exporters, conducted a variety of foreign exchange operations and continued to emit foreign exchange licenses.

These policies remained in place until Finance Minister Aranha issued SUMOC Instruction 70 (October 1953).[41] This instruction re-established monopoly on foreign currency exchange at the Banco do Brasil, eliminated import controls and designed auctions for foreign exchange and foreign currency promissory notes (*promessa de venda de câmbio* foreign currency promissory notes, PVC).[42] This helped stabilize imports and increase exports and government revenue, albeit not enough to erase deficits.[43]

Meanwhile, political and economic pressures converged against orthodox policies. Inflation increased from 12.0–20.8 per cent during 1952–3. Economic activity slowed, income stagnated and investment declined. This once again placed the Banco do Brasil at the centre of politics and monetary policy.[44] The Banco do Brasil used resources from its Rediscount Portfolio, Bank Mobilisation Account, (and base of consumer deposits) to finance overdue commercial payments and maintain government spending. Credits were provided to banks in financial difficulty to restore confidence and avert a further decline in domestic finance. The Agricultural and Industrial Credit Facility exceeded its budget. Banco do Brasil funds were used to cover checks and avoid a run on commercial banks in Rio de Janeiro and São Paulo in November 1954.

Conflicts between structuralist and orthodox policy options escalated into paralysis and power vacuum, culminating with the suicide of President Vargas in August 1954. Announcement of a 100 per cent increase in the minimum wage on May 1 had deepened differences between national-developmental groups in government and more orthodox economists, foreign investors and international financial institutions.[45] After military intervention was narrowly averted, Vice President Café Filho nominated liberal economist Eugênio Gudin to the Finance Ministry in November 1954. Unable to pursue reforms amidst crisis, Gudin issued a series of SUMOC Instructions to control currency expansion. Caps were set for interest rates on bank deposits. Interest rates for rediscount operations and commercial bank reserve requirements were increased. However, policies designed to reduce the role of the Banco do Brasil in money management were abandoned under political pressure.

Declining demand and prices for coffee exports added to concerns, leading the Banco do Brasil Exchange Portfolio to further overspend its budget and turn to international credit. The Banco do Brasil also refused to cut agricultural finance. Banco do Brasil lending was based on structural theories of inflation. From this perspective, support for agriculture was necessary to adjusting foreign accounts and alleviate inflationary pressures from increased demand and domestic consumption. A credit crunch also hit domestic financial institutions during 1955, leading to appeals for funds from the Banco do Brasil Bank Mobilisation Account. In May 1955, SUMOC Instruction 116 lowered interest rates on loans to banks and discount operations, as well as compulsory reserves for commercial banks. SUMOC Instruction 113 of January 1955 also facilitated the entry of foreign capital and provided alternative sources for long-term investment.[46] These new mechanisms of foreign finance and investment became central to the developmentalist policies of the Kubitschek administration after 1955.

The Banco do Brasil under Kubitschek's Developmentalism, 1956–60

President Kubitschek pursued a variety of audacious development goals exemplified by moving the capital from Rio de Janeiro to Brasília and channelling massive investments into select economic sectors such as auto production and construction. Deficits in government and foreign accounts during 1955 reinforced proposals to tighten monetary policy as Kubitschek assumed office in 1956. The Banco do Brasil pursued the contrary, selling shares in May 1956 to increase reserves and *double* the amount the bank planned to lend. The bank also created new credit lines for small farmers and agro-industry (without guarantee), while pursuing further expansion of branch offices. These policies countered adjustment policies in the Finance Ministry and SUMOC supported by the IMF and international investors. In 1956, Finance Minister Lopes negotiated further agreements with US authorities that included clauses to limit Banco do Brasil rediscount operations, reduce Banco do Brasil interbank credit operations and redirect funds to export financing. These measures produced a credit crunch in 1956–7, but unchecked inflation led Finance Minister Lopes to continue tight money and credit policies.

Adjustment policies failed to reduce inflation or satisfy orthodox reformers while alienating developmentalists and structuralists. By mid-1957 adjustment targets were abandoned. SUMOC officials proposed sale of government bonds during 1957, but banks failed to respond. By 1958, groups seeking to accelerate growth prevailed over groups seeking to maintain fiscal and monetary austerity. The National Stabilisation Plan was abandoned and the government's position in negotiations with the IMF hardened. During 1958, the money supply grew by 30 per cent, primarily through Banco do Brasil finance of Treasury and interbank loans.[47] Lucas Lopes resigned from the Finance Ministry in August 1959, replaced by Banco do Brasil President, Sebastião Pais de Almeida. Developmentalists thereafter predominated in the Kubitschek administration and broke off negotiations with the IMF.

In 1960, the Banco do Brasil resumed currency and swap operations to improve the terms of Brazilian foreign debt and replace funds from the IMF. In 1961, the Quadros administration briefly pursued austerity (nominating Bahia state UDN leader and ex-Banco do Brasil president under Café Filho, Clemente Mariani to the Finance Ministry). But President Quadros's unorthodox populism failed to restore confidence. After his resignation in August 1961 (seven months after taking office), political conflict between the national populist Vice-President Goulart and liberal and internationalist groups escalated. Planning Minister Celso Furtado launched a Three Year Plan in December 1962, with support from the Kennedy administration, to adjust the economy and regain the confidence of foreign investors.[48] However, renegotiation of Brazilian foreign debt stalled, inflation persisted and tight money and interest rate policies deepened the downturn. Although beyond the scope of this study, the breakdown of democracy and military intervention on 31 March 1964 are inextricably linked to the structuralist policies pursued and competitive advantages retained by the Banco do Brasil. This changed dramatically under military rule.

The Unexpected Consequences of Reforms under Military Rule

Economists called to counsel military government believed that inflation had produced financial disintermediation, reduced savings, distorted prices and transferred wealth from the private to public sector and poor to organized interests and upper classes. Monetarist theory differed fundamentally from the traditions of structuralism, national-populism and developmentalism that had informed Banco do Brasil policies for much of the twentieth century. In 1965, the *Plano de Ação Econômico do Governo,* (Government Plan of Economic Action, PAEG) reduced wage adjustments and the money supply. Fiscal reforms, financial reforms, a new accord with the IMF and creation of the Central Bank of Brazil culminated the turn to orthodoxy, while foreign exchange and industrial and agricultural development policies were also centralized under military government.[49] This appeared to confirm the correlation between bureaucratic authoritarianism and the imposition of liberal policies in Latin America in the 1960s and 1970s.[50] While the Banco do Brasil ceded monetary and central banking prerogatives, the bank *expanded* under military government, becoming central agent for large-scale operations to allocate new resources captured by forced savings programmes at home and financial flows from abroad. The Banco do Brasil also continued to operate as agent for the Finance Ministry and Treasury, gaining *new* functions including: Settling check and cash payments (delegated to the Banco do Brasil by the Central Bank); Management of international trade through a Foreign Commerce Account (*Carteira do Comércio Exterior*, Cacex); and administration of official funds and programmes.

By year-end 1965, SUMOC had been replaced by the Central Bank of Brazil and National Monetary Council (*Conselho Monetário Nacional*, CMN) for monetary, financial, budget and public debt management.[51] This marked a turning point for the Banco do Brasil. The bank ceded prerogatives of credit, banking and monetary policy to specialized agencies and the Central Bank of Brazil. The Central Bank assumed the regulation and supervision of banks and financial institutions, the monitoring and control of foreign capital and foreign currency reserves, management of the domestic money supply and agricultural development policies. Policies were to be set by the National Monetary Council under military rule. However, the Banco do Brasil retained both its role as executor of government policy and competitive advantages and market power as largest domestic bank.

Reforms were designed to end distortions produced by Banco do Brasil policies under developmentalism and national-populism. However, after creation of the Central Bank of Brazil and an initial period of adjustment, a new, centralized, state-centred banking system channelled public, private, forced and foreign savings to strategic economic sectors under military rule. Both the financialization of the economy and the concentration of Brazilian banking into a select number of large financial conglomerates with the Banco do Brasil at the apex ensued.[52] Zini estimates that the financial sector grew from 25–44 per cent of Brazilian GDP from 1955–75.[53] Contrary to liberal designs, the market share of government banks increased significantly under military rule. Government intervention also continued through directed credits, subsidized long-term investments and indexation of government bonds against inflation that became both *de facto* currencies and preferred policy mechanism of the Central Bank.[54] By selling indexed bonds the Central Bank could withdraw means of payment from circulation, reduce liquidity and increase interest rates.

Adjustment policies and centralization of banking and credit under President Humberto de Alencar Castelo Branco from 1964–7 renewed confidence among foreign investors, increased financial flows from abroad and produced sustained growth by the late 1960s. A new economic team under Marshall Artur da General Costa e Silva returned to a more structuralist view of inflation as based on demand, implying a return to growth and investment centred policies. The existence of excess capacity after adjustment encouraged this view. The 1967 Strategic Programme of Development (*Programa de Estratégia e Desenvolvimento* PED)[55] exemplified the turn to state-led developmentalism. Government credit policy especially targeted consumer durables and home finance to reinforce domestic demand.

Reforms at the outset of military rule adjusted the economy but soon were replaced by state-led policies that channelled forced savings and foreign investment through the Banco do Brasil and other federal banks. By 1975, the private sector and consumers received more than 95 per cent of Banco do Brasil credit while only 38 per cent of Cr$79.0 billion total deposits at the bank were from individual clients. Furthermore, a *conta movimento* (movement account) simply zeroed Banco do Brasil obligations to Treasury each Friday. Movement account liabilities to Treasury reached Cr$66.2 billion in 1976, over twice the value of personal savings and current account deposits. The Banco do Brasil retained a free hand over credit policy and moved vast sums under military government. The bank ceded formal control over monetary policy to the Central Bank. Reforms after military intervention in 1964 were designed to promote private sector finance, banking and development. Instead, they reinforced the position of the Banco do Brasil at the centre of politics, credit and finance, this time during a period of military rule that allocated massive amounts of forced savings and foreign capital to the private sector and produced record levels of 10 per cent annual GDP growth in the early 1970s. Adjustment to the 1973 and 1979 oil shocks increased the importance of Banco do Brasil lending as military elites bet on skirting adjustment to complete import substitution through state finance of capital goods production.

Adjustment to Foreign Debt and Fiscal Crisis, the Banco do Brasil in the 1980s

Moratorium on foreign debt payments declared by Mexico in August 1982 ended the period of foreign financial inflows. A sudden end of foreign finance, fiscal crisis, accelerating inflation and a sequence of anti-inflation packages (after 1985) that distorted prices and suspended contracts profoundly disorganized the Brazilian economy. The Banco do Brasil remained by far the largest bank in Brazil. However, it was increasingly forced to reconcile its role as agent of directed credit and government policy with market pricing of credit and financial operations. Change at the Banco do Brasil during the 1980s also reflected broader trends in Brazilian banking toward creation of financial conglomerates. During the 1970s, commercial banks began to offer new products and services and create subsidiaries such as investment banks, finance agencies and housing credit societies (*sociedades de credito imobiliário*). Downturns during the 1980s forced banks to ally with industrial or commercial groups such as auto dealerships or consumer retail sales networks. Meanwhile, transition to democracy during the 1980s began to separate monetary and fiscal budgets and clarify accounting procedures, further restricting Banco do Brasil autonomy and prerogatives.

The most important development during the 1980s was the rapid expansion of federal, state and municipal government bonds in bank balance sheets. Federal government paper increased *nineteen* fold in real terms deflated by the Índice Geral de Preços, Disponibilidade Interna (General Price Index, Domestic Supply, IGP-DI), while state and municipal government paper increased *sixteen* fold. Indexation of government bonds became a preferred option for monetary policy during the 1960s. During the 1970s, agents began to use indexed bonds as alternative currency in contracts, rather than the US dollar as most Latin American countries. By the 1980s, the liquidity preference of banks and economic agents increased use of indexed government bonds and produced a dual money economy. In real terms (IGP-DI), short term bank deposits declined five fold from 1980–9, while mid-term deposits doubled but remained far behind the increases in government bond holdings. The foreign debt crisis also reduced the lending capacity of the Banco do Brasil. During the early 1980s, the Brazilian government signed several agreements with the IMF to control money and credit expansion.[56] Banco do Brasil loans declined four fold in real terms from 1978–84. But the collapse of domestic credit was even greater. By 1984, Banco do Brasil liquid assets surpassed the combined value of the *twenty nine* next largest commercial banks.

This dominant position and strong returns at the bank from indexed instruments and high spreads during the instability of the 1980s were invested to modernize the bank. The massive scale and scope of the Banco do Brasil provided competitive advantages that policymakers and senior management used to shift the bank toward market priced lending, adopt corporate governance reforms modelled on private banking and develop new products and services to compete with private and foreign banks. Banco do Brasil reforms would proceed amidst a decade of foreign debt and fiscal crisis, capital flight and disorganization of the economy. After transition to civilian rule in 1985, the country would remain on the brink of hyperinflation until the Real Plan succeeded in restoring price stability in 1993–4.

Paradoxically, strong returns under monetary chaos led the Banco do Brasil to expand branch offices and invest in personnel and technology to modernize. As disorganization of the economy deepened, Banco do Brasil profits soared from record spreads between low interest rates paid on savings and high returns from government bonds indexed against inflation. In 1986, the Banco do Brasil created a retail distributor of real estate bonds and equities (attempting to overcome acute declines in rural lending). In 1987, the bank created new subsidiaries for finance, leasing and credit card administration, while shifting away from subsidised directed rural credits to market criteria in lending decisions. A new savings book, *Poupança Ouro* (Savings Gold), was created to substitute funds from Treasury. A subsidiary investment bank was created in 1989. The Banco do Brasil used its monolithic institutional foundations and strong earnings during instability to competitive advantage in virtually every market and niche of domestic banking and finance.

Reforms during the 1980s attempted to curb the opaque flow of funds across Brazilian federal banks. However, groups in the Banco do Brasil continued to resist orthodox policies and credit controls.[57] Anti-inflation packages provided critical junctures and windows of opportunity for reform. For example, the 1986 price and wage freeze of the Cruzado Plan also included clauses to change relations between the Banco do Brasil, Central Bank and Treasury. In January 1986, the *conta movimento* was closed, ending automatic coverage of Banco do Brasil operations. In 1988, as the new constitution was being written, the government further rationalized flows from Treasury. A new Single Account (*Conta Única*) for Treasury (at the Central Bank) replaced more than *five thousand* government bank accounts, increasing accountability and control. A separate 'monetary budget' was eliminated to require congressional authorization for government expenditures. Treasury also assumed authority over agricultural and export support programmes held since 1965 at the Central Bank.

The Banco do Brasil also grew during the booms produced by heterodox anti-inflation packages. During the Cruzado Plan, the Banco do Brasil almost *doubled* market share from 7.5 per cent of domestic loans in March 1985 to 14.8 per cent by June 1986. The Banco do Brasil retained roughly this share of domestic credits until the Real Plan and price stability forced banks to adjust to new realities. Of Banco do Brasil credits in 1986, 40.0 per cent were financed by internal resources. Agriculture received 37.0 per cent of Banco do Brasil loans, industry 9.0 per cent, commerce and services 27.0 per cent and the public sector and state owned enterprises 27.0 per cent. While cost cutting and administrative reforms were pursued at the bank, the Banco do Brasil retained 2377 branches and 3072 additional mini-branches and other service points across Brazil in 1989, by far the largest domestic banking network.

Banco do Brasil credits fell almost fourfold from just over NCz$40.0 million in 1980 to NCz$11.0 million in 1985 (recovering to NCz$26.0 million in 1989). Banco do Brasil lending to government entities declined from 6.8 per cent of portfolio in 1980 to 1.8 per cent in 1985, but reached 36.5 per cent of total credits at the bank in 1989. Private bank lending to also declined from NCz$61.9 billion (1980) to NCz$ 55.9 billion (1981) but increase thereafter to NCz$71.1 billion during the Cruzado Plan (1986). Private banks also increased lending to government entities from 22.7 per cent (1980) to 44.1 per cent of private bank loans (1985), declining to 34.9 per cent by 1989. The public sector sponged credit from the private sector during much of the 1980s.

Fiscal and foreign debt crisis, record inertial inflation and failed stabilization plans (that froze prices and wages and broke contracts) shaped banking and Banco do Brasil performance during the 1980s. Monetary authorities used the government bond market to reconcile objectives of monetary and credit policy while attempting to rationalize government accounts. Financial intermediation suffered. Credit fell. Long term finance disappeared. Roberto Cysne estimates that inflation transferred between 4 and 7 per cent of GDP from savers to government entities and financial institutions during this period. For the Banco do Brasil, this produced strong earnings, but eroded its ability to provide credit and finance to strategic sectors and consumers. Monetary chaos deepened in the early 1990s. By confiscating an estimated 83 per cent of domestic monetary assets on 16 March 1990, President Fernando Collor induced recession. He also forced the Banco do Brasil to cut personnel, transfer the bank's foreign trade credit portfolio to a new Ministry of Economics and reduced funds for agricultural credit. The Collor presidency was the beginning of the end of state-centred system inherited from military rule. From 1985–94, directed credit at the Banco do Brasil fell from 66.0–8.0 per cent of lending at the bank.

The Banco do Brasil under Price Stability and PSDB Reforms, 1994–2002

After a series of reforms and disputes with groups in the Banco do Brazil, the Cardoso administration attempted to capitalize the Banco do Brasil through a stock offering designed to transfer control of the bank to private shareholders and thereby improve governance. However, instead of producing majority control in the private sector, the reverse ensued. Lack of interest from private investors led Treasury to buy unsold shares and *increase* federal government ownership of Banco do Brasil shares from 29–73 per cent. Like the state-centred bank system that emerged after liberal reforms in the 1960s, unintended consequences once again shaped Brazilian banking. While seeking to downsize and reform corporate governance throughout the 1990s, Treasury also injected a R$8.0 billion to capitalize the bank within BIS Basel Accord guidelines.[58] This section reviews the Banco do Brasil from 1994–2002 as it adapted to price stability, reforms and liberalization of the industry under the Cardoso administration.

Political nominees at the Banco do Brasil first resisted reforms during the Real Plan (1993–4) (Cardoso replaced Ciro Gomes as Finance Minister under President Franco after impeachment of Fernando Collor in January 1993). In 1994, the Programa de Ação Imediato (Programme of Immediate Action, PAI) sought to downsize federal bank branch offices and induce voluntary retirement. Banco do Brasil President Alcir Calliari responded that 'election years were not the best time to close Banco do Brasil branch offices'.[59] The Banco do Brasil also became involved in party politics when PT vice presidential candidate José Paulo Bisol resigned under press charges that he had taken out 16 loans at the bank from 1987–93 to refinance farms without making payments (charge subsequently dropped in a R$1.9 million settlement against the *Zero Hora* newspaper).[60]

After taking office in January 1995, President Cardoso nominated Paulo César Ximenes to the Banco do Brasil presidency. Ximenes sought to close branch offices and reduce reduce staff. A strategic plan published in 1995 called for a shift away from the traditional business lines of social and rural financing toward policies and performance levels of private banking. Conflicts culminated in warning by President Cardoso to an assembly of Banco do Brasil employees that 'I do not have the right to let Brazilians pay for a Banco do Brasil swollen with employees and losses'.[61] Cardoso also criticized continued *double matching* pension payments to the Banco do Brasil pension fund *Previ,* a policy that contributed to the rapid development of the pension fund and its powerful role as shareholder in major Brazilian corporations.[62]

The failed bid to increase private sector ownership and control of the Banco do Brasil led to calls for its privatization. During 1996, Standard & Poor's predicted that the government would have to privatize the bank by 1998. Proponents of privatization included José Jorge, President of Partido da Frente Liberal (Liberal Front Party, PFL) and key member of Cardoso's coalition government. The campaign to privatize the Banco do Brasil gathered strength until Central Bank of Brazil President Gustavo Loyola argued against privatization in August 1996. For Loyola, government control of the Banco do Brasil was necessary to ensure competition in the concentrated Brazilian banking system.

Policies that sustained price stability and the new currency (real) from 1994–99 (high interest rates, an overvalued fixed exchange rate, trade liberalization) affected Banco do Brasil balance sheets. Earnings from high bank spreads under inflation ended. The overvalued real reduced the value of foreign assets held by the Banco do Brasil. However, real income increases under price stability during 1994 and early 1995 fueled rapid growth and demand for credit. By second quarter 1995, Central Bank of Brazil policies sought to check growth by increasing reserve requirements. This aggravated insolvency problems at banks and brought the banking system to the brink of crisis. The Banco do Brasil recorded losses of R$4.2 billion in 1995 and R$7.5 billion in first semester 1996.

The Real Plan also produced a rural debt crisis, with arrears in the sector reaching 40 per cent in 1995. Agricultural policy traditionally involved price supports through the Política de Guarantia de Preços Mínimos (Policy of Minimum Price Guarantees) and subsidised credit from the Banco do Brasil. Fiscal crisis during the 1980s led to the abandonment of these policies. Finance Ministry share of agricultural investment declined from over 75 per cent in the 1970s to *10 per cent* in the early 1990s.[63] This left the Banco do Brasil as primary agent for agriculture and agro industry. In 1986, the Banco do Brasil created a new rural savings account that reserved 65.0 per cent of funds (plus 20 per cent from the bank) for rural credit.[64] Payment of interest differentials on rural credits by the Ministry of Finance continued federal subsidies to agriculture. The Banco do Brasil also channelled 70 per cent of an investment fund (based on Treasury bonds and certificates of deposit) to short-term rural credit operations. The 1988 Constitution also mandated funds for agriculture. Three per cent of income tax revenue and industrial production taxes were directed to less developed states in the North, Northeast and agricultural states of the Centre-West. Despite corporate governance reforms and a shift toward market lending policies, the Banco do Brasil remained agent for massive amounts of subsidized credit for agriculture.

In 1995–2002, the Cardoso administration sought to reduce political control over the Banco do Brasil, downsize staff and branch offices, modernize products and services, increase market lending, investment banking and financial market operations, and transform the bank through corporate governance policies taken from private banking. These reforms left the bank in better condition by 2001. Given the infusion of R$8.0 billion into the Banco do Brasil in 1996, PROEF policies required less cash to bring the bank within Basel II guidelines in 2001. Reforms in 2001 included transformation of the Banco do Brasil into four business groups; wholesale, retail, government and third party fund management. Preparations also began in 2002 for listing the bank on the Bovespa Novo Mercado (New Market), a market with international standards for corporate governance, transparency and financial reporting. Preferential shares were transformed into ordinary shares, minority shareholder rights were increased and new financial reporting standards were adopted. Reforms under President Cardoso thus left a modernized Banco do Brasil for PT coalition government under President Lula (2003–10).

The Banco do Brasil under President Lula and PT Coalition Government, 2003–10

President Lula retained policies of the Cardoso administration such as inflation targeting, tight fiscal and monetary policy and the operational autonomy of the Banco do Brasil. Recovery of investor confidence during 2003 and the return of stronger growth levels during 2004 led to a period of organic growth at the Banco do Brasil. From 2004–8, the Banco do Brasil contributed to the deepening of domestic credit markets and emerged as leading investment bank at the Bovespa stock market. In 2008, when the global crisis hit Brazil and the Bovespa collapsed, the Banco do Brasil provided emergency loans, infusions of capital through stock purchases, and the acquisition of small and mid-sized firms and banks unable to weather the sharp decline in economc activity and shortage of credit. The merger of Itaú and Unibanco in 2008 briefly displaced the Banco do Brasil as the largest financial institution in Latin America. However, acquisition of the São Paulo state savings bank Nossa Caixa, Votorantim Bank and three state government banks placed the Banco do Brasil once again at the top by year-end 2008. Although no longer a direct arm of federal government policy, the Banco do Brasil retains powerful competitive advantages at the centre of the new networks in state, society and markets.

The Banco do Brasil also produced new leadership from party factions and labour unions that became central to PT coalition government under President Lula, especially during his first term (2003–6). PT party faction *articulação* (articulation) leaders include career employees of the Banco do Brasil and presidents of the Brazilian bank workers union such as Luiz Gushiken and Ricardo Berzioni. Both were nominated to ministerial posts by President Silva in January 2003. By August 2003, twenty-one of thirty-three top positions at the Banco do Brasil had been filled by new representatives of the PT, most Banco do Brasil employees and members of the Brazilian bank workers union. Critics decried politicization. However, none of the corporate governance reforms nor market strategies adopted during the Cardoso administration and none of the Bovespa Mercado Novo requirements for transparency and corporate governance have been reversed.

Tensions between the operational independence of the Banco do Brasil and coalition politics continued during the Lula administration. When Banco do Brasil President Cassio Casseb Lima resigned in November 2004 (under charges of irregularities in consulting contracts at the bank), President Lula nominated Rossano Maranhão Pinto, a career employee and Banco do Brasil vice president to head the bank. Appointment of politicians from the Partido do Movimento Democrático Brasileiro (Party of the Brazilian Democratic Movement, PMDB) to cement a coalition government for President Lula's second term were also criticized as politicization of the bank. However, Banco do Brasil officials responded that PMDB leaders brought competitive advantages to the bank based on their networks in the public and private sectors. Networks and relations in President Lula's second term thus differ, given the departure from core offices of the presidency by longtime advisors to Lula that came from the Banco do Brasil and bank workers union. By late 2006 only one of seven vice presidents of the Banco do Brasil was a member of President Lula's Workers' Party (PT).

Further study of recent developments is needed. However, financial results and balance sheets suggest that the Banco do Brasil realized significant competitive advantages during the period of growth (2004–8) and adjustment (2008–9). In 2004–8, the record level of capitalization recorded by Brazilian firms on the Bovespa stock market is closely related to the groups that cross politics, government banks, the bank workers union, the Banco do Brasil employee private pension fund (Previ) and bank consortia often led by the Banco do Brasil investment banking division (and joined by the BNDESpar and Caixa investment banking divisions). Rather than convergence toward private banking and a market-centred financial system, Banco do Brasil policies and market shares during the 2000s suggest that Brazilian federal banks remain at the centre of politics, policy and development strategies and have modernized to successfully compete against private and foreign banks.

Moreover, the massive size of the Banco do Brasil led once again to use of the bank for counter-cyclical lending and leadership in capital markets – without deteriorating bank balance sheets. Since 2003, the Banco do Brasil has remained well within domestic bank regulations and Basel Accord guidelines. During 2002 and 2003, reforms at the Banco do Brasil sought to reduce costs and increase efficiency ratings. Indeed, relations between the Banco do Brasil and President Lula *reversed* past patterns. In the 1950s, national developmentalist groups at the Banco do Brasil resisted more orthodox Ministers of Finance. In 2003 and once again during the 2008 financial crisis, differences between President Lula and the Banco do Brasil were the reverse: Banco do Brasil management refused to cut interest rates and increase loans. In 2003, caution prevailed. In April 2009, Banco do Brasil President Antonio Francisco de Lima Neto was fired after refusing to reduce interest rates on loans.

This reversal of policy disputes indicates transition from the macroeconomics of populism to the microeconomics of government banking in the twenty-first century. Because Banco do Brasil policies and performance remain above BIS and Central Bank of Brazil guidelines, past experiences of passing on bad credit and losses to Treasury to feed inflation and fiscal deficits no longer occur. Instead, the social networks, business relations and political webs of the Banco do Brasil provide policy alternatives for government and competitive advantages over private and foreign banks.

The large losses incurred by the Banco Popular do Brasil and its reincorporation into Banco do Brasil operations in March 2008 also confirm that change is not linear and federal banks are not assured success. Created in 2003, the Banco Popular suffered significant losses and high non-payment levels since inception. After three semesters of operation, losses reached R$ 47.6 million, eroding nearly half of the R$ 116.6 million assets granted by the Lula government upon creation in 2003. By year-end 2005, non-paying loans reached 24 per cent of total loans, leading to reorganization of the bank. Three of six directorships were closed to cut payroll costs by 20 per cent and new risk analysis procedures were introduced. However, further losses of R$ 10,7 million were reported by the Banco Popular do Brasil for first semester 2007 (58 per cent below R$ 25.7 million lost during first semester 2006), while non-paying loans remained at 25 per cent of portfolio. Operations continued through 2007, but accounts and operations were transferred during 2008 to a new Low Income Division at the Banco do Brasil that also manages correspondent banking relations. These mistakes at the Banco Popular do Brasil do not apply to the Banco do Brasil at large.

Data from Banco do Brasil balance sheets in 2002–8 suggests that the bank developed 'organically' in 2002–7 with gradual increases reflecting its competitive advantages at the top of Brazilian banking and finance. Policies changed during 2007 and 2008 as the credit shortage caused by crisis abroad led the Banco do Brasil to provide lending of last resort through interbank investments and loans to small and medium sized banks to avert further declines in domestic liquidity. The Banco do Brasil also acquired a 51 per cent stake in the Votarantim Bank to avert a run on deposits and purchased São Paulo state government savings bank, Nossa Caixa, for R$7.6 billion in 2008. These acquisitions reflected concern about the the merger of Itaú and Unibanco challenging Banco do Brasil's top rank in Brazilian banking.

From 2002 through 2006, balance sheets suggest a period of growth based on loans to the private sector, with deposits and shareholder equity increasing largely apace. After 2006, balance sheets reveal significant capital injections. In 2006–8, Banco do Brasil borrowing from the money market increased from R$49.2 to R$91.4 billion while liabilities with Treasury and BNDES increased from R$14.3 to R$22.4 billion. The asset side of Banco do Brasil balance sheets also changed. Private sector lending increased from R$117.8 to R$181.0 billion from 2006–8 reflecting acquisition of portfolios from Nossa Caixa. Interbank investments increased from R$17.5 to R$95.1 billion, while interbank deposits increased from R$11.6–R$24.2 billion. The counter-cyclical lending strategies of the Banco do Brasil also included increased lending to the public sector, from R$2.4–R$23.0 billion in 2007–8. Government credit policy (release of 40 per cent of compulsory deposits retained at the central bank) led Banco do Brasil deposits at the central bank to decline from R$33.4– R$21.2 billion in 2007–8, freeing multiples of this value for loans and investments.

Table 3.1: Banco do Brasil Balance Sheet Summary, 2002–8, R$ billion.

Assets	2002	2003	2004	2005	2006	2007	2008
Interbank Investments	10.1	5.0	2.7	8.0	17.5	43.4	95.1
Interbank Deposits	7.6	28.3	13.7	20.9	11.6	7.7	24.2
Securities	70.9	69.6	73.4	66.4	73.1	75.2	73.2
Central Bank Deposits*	18.1	18.6	22.1	24.4	28.1	33.4	21.2
Loans to Private Sector	48.9	65.2	75.7	88.5	117.8	146.3	181.0
Loans to Public Sector	5.6	4.3	4.1	3.7	4.3	2.4	23.0
Receivables	29.7	27.3	31.2	35.1	40.4	54.8	80.8
Other Assets	13.7	11.8	30.0	10.8	3.5	4.0	8.8
Total Assets	204.6	230.1	239.0	252.9	296.3	367.2	507.3
Liabilities							
Deposits	97.2	110.0	115.5	137.6	158.8	188.2	271.1
Money Market Borrowing	48.3	40.0	44.5	30.5	49.2	72.2	91.4
Treasury & BNDES	5.9	7.4	10.6	13.3	14.3	17.5	22.4
Shareholder Equity	9.2	12.1	14.1	16.8	20.7	24.2	29.9
Other Liabilities	44.0	60.6	54.3	54.7	53.3	65.1	92.5
Total Liabilities	204.6	230.1	239.0	252.9	296.3	367.2	507.3

* Compulsory deposits for commercial banks according to Central Bank regulations.

Source: Banco do Brasil Annual Reports, Historical Series, 2002–8.

The Banco do Brasil retains dominant market shares. At year-end 2008, the Banco do Brasil retained R$246.3 billion or 20.7 per cent of the asset management market; 28.0 and 24.6 per cent of export finance and import foreign exchange markets; 23.2 per cent of the mutual fund market; and over R$224.8 billion in loans (R$17.6 billion payroll loans (22.4 per cent of market)), a full 59.8 per cent of rural credit system and R$97.0 billion in business loans. Total funding reached over R$362.6 billion. Banco do Brasil customers in 2008 reached 47.9 million, with the bank retaining 39,700 ATM service points and 76.6 million bank cards (23.9 million credit cards and 52.7 million debit cards). Like the Caixa Econômica Federal, the Banco do Brasil also processes government payments, with retirement and social security payments numbering 74.5 million transactions during 2008. Although this implies administrative costs (and receipts) this also brings customers, and prospective customers, into Banco do Brasil branch offices.

During 2008, the Banco do Brasil continued to expand operations, form joint ventures, acquire private and government banks and modernize operations. A secondary offering of stock in January 2008, granting of shares by VISA to the Banco do Brasil, and upgrading of the bank to investment grade BB- by Standard & Poor's in April 2008 suggest that market orientation of the bank continues during the Lula administration, despite pursuit of counter-cyclical credit policies as described above. The Lower Income Segment Department was also charged with regional and sustainable development programmes. During 2008, the Banco do Brasil acquired the state government banks Banco do Piaui, Banco de Santa Catarina (thirty-third largest bank in Brazil with US$3.0 billion assets in 2007), and São Paulo government savings bank, Nossa Caixa (12th largest Bank in Brazil with US$26.7 billion in 2007). The corporate divisions and financial operations of the Banco do Brasil realized competitive advantages and provided policy options during 2008 to counter the credit shortage and help firms and domestic banks to adjust.

Table 3.2: Comparing Banco do Brasil, Itaú and Bradesco, 2002–9.

	Basel Index			ROA			RLA		
	BB	Itaú	Bradesco	BB	Itaú	Bradesco	BB	Itaú	Bradesco
2002	12.2	18.4	17.9	1.2	2.6	2.0	30.2	28.8	28.3
2003	13.7	19.8	19.9	1.1	2.8	1.6	23.1	29.7	22.8
2004	15.2	20.6	18.8	1.3	3.0	2.3	24.0	29.2	30.9
2005	17.1	17.0	17.3	1.2	3.7	2.6	18.7	35.3	28.4
2006	17.3	17.1	18.8	2.8	3.1	2.5	26.7	28.8	26.3
2007	15.6	17.9	15.6	1.4	3.2	2.2	22.2	32.1	24.4
2008	15.2	16.1	16.9	2.5	1.9	1.6	30.4	22.1	21.1
2009*	15.0	16.5	16.6	1.2	1.3	1.4	23.8	18.2	19.5

* Annualized first quarter 2009 results. ROA = Return on Assets. RLA = Return on Liquid Assets.

Source: Banco do Brasil, Itaú and Bradesco Annual Reports, 2002–9.

Comparison of Banco do Brasil returns and capital adequacy with the two major private Brazilian banks, Itaú and Bradesco, suggests that the performance and solidity of the Banco do Brasil remains equal or superior to the two largest private banks in the country. During 2002 and 2003, the capital adequacy of the Banco do Brasil and return on assets remained below levels reported by the two largest Brazilian private banks, suggesting the impact of counter-cyclical lending. However, after 2004, the Basel index of the Banco do Brasil reached 17.1, far above BIS standards of 8.0 and Central Bank of Brazil requirements of 11.0. Furthermore, from 2006 through first quarter 2009, returns on assets, returns on liquid assets, and the Basel index of the Banco do Brasil exceed levels reported by Itaú and Bradesco. Despite providing counter-cyclical credit, the performance and capital adequacy of the Banco do Brasil remains at or above levels reported by the two largest private banks.

In 2006, the Banco do Brasil continued transition to the tighter corporate governance standards of the Bovespa Novo Mercado, selling 52.3 million shares at R$43.5 to generate R$2.3 billion and move toward the Novo Mercado minimum of 25 per cent free floating shares. In 2007, a second R$3.4 billion sale to 119,000 investors underwritten by Previ (Banco do Brasil employee pension fund) and BNDESpar increased the free float of Banco do Brasil shares from 14.5 to 21.7 per cent. In 2009, the Banco do Brasil received approval from the US Securities and Exchange Commission to sell American Depository Receipts on the New York Stock Exchange, while a provisional decree increased the limit on foreign ownership of Banco do Brasil stock from 12.5 to 20.0 per cent in accord with Bovespa Novo Mercado regulations. In 2009, Treasury retained 65.6 per cent of Banco do Brasil shares, Previ 10.1 per cent, BNDESpar 2.5 per cent and 21.7 per cent publically held minority shares (11.1 by foreign entities).

During 2008–9, flight to quality movements in markets and among bank clients once again reinforced the deposit base of the Banco do Brasil while small and medium private banks faced outflows and feared runs on deposits. Crisis abroad led the Central Bank of Brazil to release R$98.8 billion of compulsory reserves and R$42.2 billion in direct funds to ensure liquidity for banks during 2008. The Central bank used another US$71.0 billion of reserves to ease pressures in foreign exchange spot market auctions, repurchase auctions and foreign exchange futures markets. Sales of reserves were designed to protect exporters from devaluation of the real and derivative exposures. Unibanco merged with Itaú in 2009, in part, to counter perceptions that client losses in foreign exchange derivatives could erode returns and endanger the bank. Several small and mid-size banks merged with larger banks to avert liquidity shortages and dispel market uncertainty. Medida Provisória (Provisional Decree 443) freed federal banks to purchase participation in banks and other financial institutions to avert escalation of liquidity shortage into banking crisis. In 2008, acquisition of Nossa Caixa, the Banco do Estado de Santa Catarina (Santa Catarina State Bank, Besc), the Banco do Estado do Piauí (Piauí State Bank, BEP) were completed, while acquisition of the Banco Regional de Brasília (Brazilian Regional Bank, BRB) proceeded.

Banco do Brasil corporate social responsibility and sustainability programmes also reflect transition to international financial reporting and corporate governance standards. Centralization under military rule, capture during prolonged transition, downsizing and reform during the 1990s and market network construction during the 2000s have left the Banco do Brasil as the largest bank in

Brazil and Latin America. Plans for expansion at home include a new focus on home loans and construction, where Banco do Brasil lending increased from R$100.0 million (2008) to R$1.5 billion (2009) and R$3.0 billion targeted for 2010. This implies competition with the federal savings bank Caixa that retains 75 per cent market share. In 2010, the Banco do Brasil also offered new lines of consumer credit (R$30.3 billion in 2009 and R$8.2 billion in March 2010) to build on acquisitions and profits retained from 2009. In 2010, the bank also expanded cellular phone based mobile banking services and begun negotiating purchases of Citizen Bank (US) and Patagonia Bank (Argentina) to support Brazilian business and residents abroad.

The Banco do Brasil thereby increased credit by 33.8 per cent to R$300.8 billion and profits to over R$10.1 billion during 2009 to forecast retaining 20.1 per cent market in 2010 despite the return of private banks to a recovering market. Completion of Nossa Caixa acquisition is to be followed by opening 200 new branch offices (100 in São Paulo) and hire of 10,000 employees (1500 in São Paulo state). The Banco do Brasil also plans invest R$16.0 billion to form a massive electricity conglomerate with BNDES and Previ through merger of Neoenergia and Brasiliana (holding company of Eletropaulo, AES Sul e AES Tietê). To be managed by CPFL (former Companhia Paulista de Força e Luz privatized in 1997), this joint venture involves the Votorantim group, Bradesco, the Camargo Corrêa construction firm, Previ and Bonaire Participações (an associataion of Funcesp, Sistel, Petros e Sabesprev pension funds). This structure indicates how Banco do Brasil remains at the centre of new networks that cross the public and private sectors.

Acquisitions, infusions from the BNDES and Treasury, and counter-cyclical lending increased Banco do Brasil assets from R$521.3 to R$708.5 billion during 2009. This expanded market share and deepened the social, political, and business networks of the largest financial conglomerate in Latin America. The massive scale and competitive advantages of federal banks entered public debate during 2009 when Itaú President Roberto Setubal complained that interest rate reductions of the Banco do Brasil and Caixa constituted unfair competitive pressures on private banks. Responses from Central Bank President Meirelles and Finance Minister Mantega led Setubal to abandon this line of argument and refuse to answer further questions from the financial press. This indicates how bankers, regulators, economists and the financial press in Brazil now agree that federal banks retain substantial competitive advantages over private and foreign banks.[65] They differ about whether these advantages are fair or unfair.

The market value of Banco do Brasil shares on the Bovespa stock market also suggests the performance of this government bank has outpaced the two largest Brazilian private banks. In 2000–3, Banco do Brasil share prices remained below

Figure 3.1: Banco do Brasil Share Price, 2000–4.
Source: Bovespa stock market, available at www.bovespa.com.br.

Figure 3.2: Banco do Brasil Share Price, 2004–9.
Source: Bovespa stock market, available at www.bovespa.com.br.

those of Itaú and Bradesco. However, the share price of Banco do Brasil stock surpasses Bradesco in September 2003. Furthermore, the similar trajectories of Bradesco, Itaú and Banco do Brasil share prices from 2000 through 2004 suggest that the Treasury ownership of the Banco do Brasil did not produce market deviating political intervention.

Comparison of the stock price of the Banco do Brasil with the IBovespa stock index and the share price of Bradesco and Itaú stock from 2004 to March 2009 suggest similar experiences after splits of stock during the period of market capitalization and, subsequently, the substantial decline in price of all three bank shares trading on the Bovespa market after May 2008. Breaks in the data for all three major banks represent splitting shares and provide a further comparison of performance of these institutions on the Bovespa stock market. After raising capital on the stock market, the performance of the Banco do Brasil in terms of market valuation of its stock, has outperformed Bradesco and remained close to Itaú.

In sum, since liberalization of the industry and privatization of state government banks during the 1990s, the Banco do Brasil was transformed from a wholly state owned enterprise into a competitive financial conglomerate under mixed ownership. During the 2000s, the Banco do Brasil reformed to meet corporate governance standards of the Bovespa Novo Mercado. The bank retains top market shares in virtually every aspect of Brazilian banking and finance. In 1996, sale of shares failed to transfer corporate governance and control of the national bank to the private sector. Instead, the federal government increased ownership to 73 percent and, in 2010, retains 65 per cent of shares. Banco do Brasil networks cross banking, financial markets, political parties, social forces and business groups to help the bank realize record profits in 2004–9. The bank also provided counter-cyclical credit to amidst a liquidity shortage and sharp fall in industrial production as the global crisis hit Brazil in second semester 2008. The transparency of Banco do Brasil quarterly reports and advances in Central Bank of Brazil supervision of domestic banking clarify new tensions that have emerged during the PT government of President Lula. These tensions reflect the modernization, competitive advantages and policy capacities of the Banco do Brasil.

Conclusion

Government banks provide policy alternatives and retain competitive advantages. The first Banco do Brasil provided policy options for imperial statecraft. Selling shares of a new national bank in the Americas helped Portuguese King John VI defeat liberal and national movements, consolidate monarchy and maintain slavery in the New World. The second official Banco do Brasil (1853)

was also a privately owned but government controlled national bank that dominated domestic banking, managed money and finance and provided lending of
last resort during financial crises. In 1891, Republicans first delegated banking
to private regional banks then created a Banco da República to incorporate the
Banco do Brasil. However, by 1900 the Banco do Brasil regained its name and
grew thereafter, while also managing two of three currency boards, providing
lending of last resort and gaining central bank status in 1923. After the 1930
revolution, the Banco do Brasil managed foreign obligations and a Bank Mobilisation Fund to adjust to global crisis and depression, then channelled credit
and finance for agriculture and import substitution industrialization during the
national populist regime of Vargas.

After transition to democracy in 1945, money, credit, finance and bank
supervision policies were gradually extracted from the Banco do Brasil. Today,
the Banco do Brasil has lost its monolithic control over policy. Instead, the
Central Bank of Brazil, a variety of executive, judicial and legislative entities,
the media and public, rating agencies and investors now share responsibility for
supervision of banks and government accounts. Democratization has furthered
this specialization and diffusion of prerogatives by increasing transparency and
accountability. Far from weakening the Banco do Brasil, this has left it more
secure to pursue aggressive growth strategies. As the largest domestic financial
institution, it builds on its competitive advantages, market power, brand name
and immense network of agencies, ATMs and service centres. Central bank
reports have described this as organic growth,[66] suggesting that the Banco do
Brasil retains competitive advantages based on longstanding relations that cross
government, business, politics and society. Capitalization on the stock market
and policies to counter the credit shortage and save firms from sharp downturn
during 2008 have not deteriorated the banks portfolio. Markets agree. During
adjustment to price stability in the 1990s, the Banco do Brasil retained 'E' ratings from Moodys. In August 2006, Moodys rated the Banco do Brasil A3 in
its long-term local currency ratings. In April 2009, rating agencies retained the
bank's investment grade rating (despite removal of Banco do Brasil president by
President Lula over refusal to reduce bank spreads and increase flow of credit to
recover the economy).

Since adjustment to price stability, privatization of state government banks
and opening the industry to new foreign competition in the 1990s, the Banco
do Brasil has modernized to retain a predominant role in banking, finance
and political economy. The bank has pursued market-centred commercial and
investment banking operations while retaining the largest domestic branch
network, predominant market shares of deposits, credits, bank assets and leadership throughout specialized financial industries and niches. As largest and most
lucrative bank in Latin America in 2009, the Banco do Brasil remains more than

competitive fifteen years after financial liberalization and entry of leading mul-tinational banks such as Santander, ABN-Amro, HSBC, BNP-Paribas, Credit Suisse, UBS, Goldman Sachs, Dresdner Bank, Deutsche Bank and JP Morgan (alongside foreign banks with over a century in the country such as Citibank). Far from a black hole responsible for financial repression and crowding out pri-vate banks, the Banco do Brasil has served as lender of last resort during the financial crises that wracked emerging markets during the 1990s while banks and the country adapted to liberalization and reforms, emerging during the 2000s to retain a leading role in a new context of transparency, accountability and democracy.

The Banco do Brasil remains under government control and responsible for receiving income tax and revenues for the Finance Ministry, federal govern-ment credit policies, releasing government budget payments, managing export finance and agricultural price support programmes and settling official foreign payments and recepits. As principal executor of federal government banking services, the Banco do Brasil holds deposits of federal entities and pursues finance and credit programmes for foreign trade, agriculture and industry. The Banco do Brasil remains organized along portfolios, such as General Credit, Rural Credit, Foreign Trade, Foreign Exchange, along with Personnel and General Services.

Evidence presented in this case study confirms the competitive advantages and value of policy alternatives provided by federal banks and supports the theory that liberalization, government banks *and* markets maximize welfare. Competitive advantages acquired during two centuries of banking in Brazil enabled policymakers and management to transform the Banco do Brasil into an immense financial conglomerate in the twenty-first century. Since the 1980s, the Banco do Brasil has turned away from the state and deposit base in forced savings to the market, both to capture resources and diversify its finance and credit operations. The bank now provides services such as insurance, pen-sion funds, asset management and other financial products. The achievements of price stability, reforms and democratization during the 1990s have trans-formed the place of the Banco do Brasil in Brazilian political economy. Fiscal, financial, banking and monetary reforms pursued during the 1990s and fur-ther advances in bank supervision, more transparent payment systems and central bank modernization during the 2000s mean that the Banco do Brasil has shed responsibilities more traditionally associated with macroeconomic policy and central banking. The separation of powers and specialization and modernization of Brazilian government implied *extracting* prerogatives from the Banco do Brasil. Given the severity of economic shocks faced by Brazil since the mid-1990s, this proved just in time. Operational autonomy within the new more transparent context of Brazilian banking explain not only the apparent anomaly of competitive advantages and policymaking alternatives in government banking, these advances also explain why the domestic economy and banks were unexpectedly resilient to the global financial crisis during 2007–9. The Banco do Brasil provided policy alternatives and realized competitive advantages to ameliorate adjustment and speed recovery.

4 THE CAIXA ECONOMICA FEDERAL (FEDERAL SAVINGS BANK)

'That all persons in the time of their health and youth, while they are able to work and spare it, should lay up some small inconsiderable part of their earnings as a deposit in save hands, to lie as a store in a bank, to relieve them, if by age or accident they should come to be disabled or incapacitated to provide for themselves; and that if God bless them, that neither they nor theirs come to need it, the surplus may be employed to relieve such as shall.'

Daniel Defoe, *Essays on Projects* (London, 1697), p. 45.

'I know well that the problems that we denounce for some time and continue to denounce, are born more from the lack of implementing laws than the laws themselves. However, we nonetheless must recognize that certain alterations and reforms are indispensible, such as the creation of the Caixa Econômica e Monte Socorro.'

Joaquim José Rodrigues Torres, Viscount of Itaboraí, first director of the Imperial Savings and Pawn Bank, Inaugural Address, November 1861.

'The function of a savings bank, in fact, is not to serve as an institution for investing money. Its business is to enable people to put money aside and even to build up a little capital. But when this capital has been formed, if the depositors wish to invest it – that is to say, to make a profitable use of it – they have merely to withdraw it: the rôle of the savings bank is ended and it rests with other institutions such as we have already studied in dealing with banks and credit establishments, to take charge of it.'

Charles Gide, *Principles of Political Economy*, (1906) p. 510.

Savings banks are an invention of European Enlightenment. Liberal theorists expected that savings banks would become irrelevant once popular classes were incorporated into circuits of money, savings and capital. Thereafter, private banks and stock markets would provide better banking services and more efficient financial intermediation. This has proved wrong. Forces of globalization and increased competition within and across countries make government savings banks a permanent necessity. Government savings banks are still necessary because they provide policy alternatives for economic management and social inclusion. They also retain competitive advantages as banks that ensure their survival. Instead of being replaced by more efficient private commercial and investment banks, government savings banks have reformed and modernized to take competitive advantage of their long traditions, large scale, highly valued brands, greater client confidence and organizational networks that cross political institutions, society and the state. This case study examines the policies and performance of the Brazilian federal government Caixa Econômica Federal (Federal Savings Bank, Caixa) in historical perspective, but especially since transition from military rule (1985), price stability (1994) and capitalization to meet BIS and Central Bank of Brazil regulations (2001).

Savings banks have played an important but largely ignored part in Brazilian political and social economy since a (private) cooperative bank was created in Rio de Janeiro in 1831. The imperial government Caixa Econômica e Monte de Socorro (Savings and Pawn Bank, Caixa) was founded in 1861 to replace failed private and cooperative institutions. The Caixa expanded from Rio de Janeiro to provincial governments after 1874 to provide philanthropic popular savings accounts and reliable pawn services. Deposits were held by Finance Ministry offices until 1888, when Caixas began to hold government bonds as reserves. During the Old Republic (1889–1930), reforms freed Caixas to hold deposits, manage reserves, provide checks and finance home loans and federal government projects. After the 1930 revolution, government savings banks gained further autonomy, becoming central agents of national populist strategies for social inclusion, capital mobilization and industrialization. Caixas expanded operations into urban development and sanitation projects.

After transition to democracy in 1945, the Caixa Central Council was retained while state level Caixas gained further autonomy. Caixas grew above the pace of private banks in most states during the 1940s and 50s, only to suffer under rising inflation and administrative costs (inflation led depositors to withdraw savings earning fixed 5/6 per cent annual returns). After military intervention in 1964, the indexation of savings against inflation led to a recovery of deposits while a new official FGTS payroll surcharge pension fund created in 1966 began to channel forced savings through the Caixa. In 1970, state Caixas lost operational independence and were merged into a single federal government state owned enterprise. Thereafter, the Caixa Econômica Federal became primary agent for military government social policies and channelled funds from new official savings funds to popular and middle class housing schemes and urban sanitation while also financing municipal governments and public sector projects.

After transition from military rule (1985) Caixa management pursued corporate governance reform amidst financial crises abroad, seven anti-inflation packages at home, liberalization of the banking industry and transition toward international capital reserve requirements and more transparent bank reporting and accounting standards. Caixa reforms sought to streamline bureaucracy, reduce non-performing loans and improve products and services to meet new competition. Meanwhile, the Caixa was used by economic policymakers to cushion the cost of adjustment to price stability after 1994 by purchase of bad credits at private and public banks before resale or privatization. The Caixa was also used to provide 'IMF-like' conditional loans to state and municipal governments that imposed payroll reductions, public management reform and privatizations. Capitalization and cleanup of its portfolio in 2001 provided further competitive advantage and profits from large spreads between high interest rates earned from government bonds and low interest rates paid on deposits. Since 2001, the Caixa has returned to traditional businesses of savings, home loans, urban development and sanitation, while diversifying to compete as a commercial and investment bank. The Caixa has led in new markets for microcredit and popular savings while helping to consolidate new federal government social policies such as family grants, income transfers, unemployment insurance payments and pension funds (distributed through a Caixa ATM citizenship card).

Despite these policy alternatives and competitive advantages, the Caixa remains controversial. Critics, such as Miguel Jorge, President Lula's Minister of Commerce and Industry, continue to suggest (in March 2008) that the Caixa should either be merged with the Banco do Brasil or privatized. For liberal theories of bank privatization, government savings banks reproduce underdevelopment. Theories of financial repression suggest that government banks crowd out more efficient allocation of resources that private banks and capital markets should provide.[1] To the contrary, we argue that government banks are institutions that provide policy options and retain competitive advantages. The Caixa thus provides another critical case study. Can government savings banks encourage popular savings without crowding out market forces or being captured by crony credit? A closer look at the Caixa is also necessary because virtually no publications exist on this institution.[2]

Our case study suggests that savings banks may contribute to development by mobilizing domestic savings and expanding access to banking and finance. Experiences of mismanagement and capture by political interests, especially under military rule in the 1970s and prolonged transition to civilian rule during the 1980s, suggest that critics of government banking identify risks. In the nineteenth century, popular savings from the Caixas were also used to pay off war debts of empire and monarchy. The Caixa subsidised mortgages for middle-class public employees under military government. However, since return to democracy and price stability in 1994, transparency, improved bank supervision and modernization of corporate governance have reduced non-performing loans and the ability of organized interests to capture Caixa policies. However, before turning to the Caixa, a comparative perspective demonstrates that this institution is not an outlier. Government (and other types of) savings banks in advanced and developing countries have modernized to compete after liberalization while continuing to provide policy alternatives.

Savings Banks in Comparative Perspective

Europeans have proposed, created, reformed and modernized savings banks since Daniel Defoe wrote in 1697. The original intent of savings banks was to teach popular classes the habit of saving, increase the liquidity of capital and spur economic growth. Savings banks were largely disregarded by economists favouring *laissez faire* policies during the nineteenth century. Nonetheless, philanthropists and (usually local) governments founded savings banks to ameliorate poverty and reverse social exclusion. Almost a century after the *Caisse d'Epargne* was founded in France, Charles Gide argued that savings banks should remain limited, like piggy banks, to collecting small amounts of capital. Neo-liberal theories also expected government savings banks to be replaced by more efficient private commercial and investment banks. The contrary has occurred. Savings banks have modernized and integrated operations in many European countries to expand market shares and sustain social and economic policy alternatives. Government savings banks also remain central institutions in developing and emerging countries. Liberal theories of bank change underestimate the competitive advantages of savings banks and the importance of the policy alternatives these institutions provide.

In Europe, savings banks varied widely, from cooperative and non-profit associations to political and civil organizations and government entities.[3] For example, in Great Britain savings banks took the form of cooperatives and providence associations, especially after the 1832 Poor Law proscribed charity. Savings banks were designed to help workers become financially independent and reduce the fiscal cost of public services.[4] Gosden estimates that membership in UK friendly societies reached over 5.5 million by the 1870s.[5] The founding ideas, organizational form and evolution of European savings banks differed widely. However, local and regional government savings banks were founded in most countries. Some savings banks were privatized during the 1980s and 1990s, most notably in England and Italy (the latter splitting social functions to savings bank foundations). However, like Brazil, most savings banks were not privatized. Instead, these institutions modernized and created national networks to compete with private commercial and investment banks as European Community reforms opened the industry. Since liberalization of banking, most European savings banks have increased market shares and sought to reaffirm social mandates.

The Brazilian Caixa is not an outlier. Our anomaly for liberal theory and explanations also apply to Europe. Since liberalization, savings banks have realized competitive advantages and provided policy alternatives in coordinated market economies. Private banking and capital markets predominate in liberal market economies such as the UK and US. However, since opening Continental European banking during the 1990s, all three 'pillars' of domestic banking have modernized (i.e. private banks, government savings banks and cooperative banks – an expression taken from debates about German banking). The experiences of savings banks in Europe are of special interest because liberalization of banking and monetary unification during the 1990s increased competitive pressures. Bank change across Europe is complex, varied and still underway. However, the successful modernization and integration of government savings banks is marked. The central developments of European savings banks from 1945–2000 can be summarized as follows.[6]

Austria

1991: Wiener Zentralsparkasse amalgamation with Landerbank to become Bank Austria

1992: Central Giro merger with joint stock bank Osterrieichisches Credit-Institut

1997: Giro-Credit amalgamation with Erste Osterrichische Spar-Casse Bank (ex-Vereinssparkasse) to become ERSTE Bank AG listed on stock market. Bank Austria acquires Creditanstalt

Belgium

1942: Association of Belgian Mortgage, Savings and Capitalization

1959: Private Savings Bank Group, 1986 renamed Belgian Savings Bank Group

Denmark

1960s-1970s: 486 local savings bank mergers into two national savings banks (SDS and Sparkekassen Danmark), five regional savings banks and 140 smaller savings banks (merged into 188 savings banks by 1991).

France

1950 Minjoz Act frees savings bank lending

1958 583 savings banks form seven regional associations

1965 Savings for Home Act

1968 Racine Commission report on modernization of savings banks

1973 Checking services provided by savings banks

1979 Nice Conference report informs 1983 Savings Bank Reform Act defining social representation and bank status

1980s-1990s Amalgamation into regional units and closing of regional finance companies

Germany

1947 Union of German savings banks, giro and giro-central associations

1953 Union renamed Deutsche Sparkassen und Giroverband

1992 723 savings banks form 13 regional savings bank and giro-bank associations

Great Britain

1945–1976 Three groups predominate: Trustee Savings Banks (deposits 2,022 million pounds 1965, Post Office Savings Banks (deposits 1,822 million pounds, 1965), Building Societies (total assets 5,532 billion pounds, 1965)

1972–3 Report of the Committee to review National Savings (Page Committee Report)

1976 Legislation to merge savings banks into 17 regional banks with central board

1986 Trustee Savings Bank (TSB) floated as public company on London Stock Exchange

Greece

1956–1990 Postal Savings Bank (PSB) accounts increase from 138,186 – 4,320,531 (over 40 per cent of population), with 12,8 per cent savings deposit market share, 11.4 per cent credit market share and 8.7 per cent total bank assets in 1990.

Ireland

1923–1965 Regulations limiting savings banks to receive deposits at fixed return set by finance ministry

1964 Association of Trustee Savings Banks in Ireland lobby formed

1989 Trustee Savings Bank Act liberalizes savings bank operations to compete with commercial banks

1986–1992 Amalgamation of nine savings banks into Trustee Savings Bank, TSB

1990 Post Office Savings Banks & Trustee Savings Banks deposits = 1,167 million pounds, Building Societies = 3,929 million pounds,

Government savings/financial institutions deposits = 1,407 million pounds)

Italy

1953 Convergence of interest rates paid on treasury certificates at postal banks and savings banks

1960 79 savings banks with 2465 branches (up from 240 in 1940, 506 in 1950)

1963 bank deposit market share of 22.6 per cent, increases to 28.4 per cent in 1990.

1990 Amato Law liberalization of bank system culminating European Community legislation

1990s Privatization of major savings banks

Netherlands

1950s–1960s 'Family' savings banks expand to consumer credit and insurance

1960s Creation of savings bank network to compete with commercial banks

1980s Merger of Post Office Giro, Post Office Savings Bank and Nederlandische Middenstandsbank

Norway

1945–61 Savings bank deposits remain at 50 per cent of market share (commercial banks decline from 48.8 per cent in 1947 to 39.9 per cent in 1970.

1950 Post Office Savings Bank and Post Office Giro created.

1970s–80s Commercial banks regain market share

1987 Savings Bank Act permits capitalization through primary capital certificates (PCCs)

1996 PCCs of 15 savings banks reach NOK 10.4 billion.

1959–96 Consolidation from 600 to 132 savings banks

1996 Savings bank market share at 29 per cent of domestic credit, 45.5 per cent of deposits.

Spain

1947 regulation of social welfare policies of savings banks (24.65 per cent profits 1947–92)

1962 Bank Sector Legislation and creation of ICCA Instituto de Credito de las Cajas de Ahorros supervisory body created, transferred to
central bank in 1971

1939–62 number of savings banks declines 98–84 (29 acquired, 15 created)

1950 branches increase to 1000, reach 2000 in 1956, 3000 in 1962 and
14,414 in 1992

1985 Savings Bank Act to democratize, modernize and reform savings
banks

Sweden

1955 Savings Bank Act sets trustee representation (half local government
appointed half elected by depositors)

1962 Limitation Committee standardizes bank regulations

1969 Savings Bank Act liberalization of savings bank policies and practices

1989–91 Formation of single Savings Bank Group from two savings
bank associations

1992–3 Banking crisis leads to creation of SwedBank (Sparbanken Sver-
ige AB) uniting various bank units under Savings Bank Group.

1995 Savings banks retain 26.6 per cent market share of deposits and
25.4 per cent of private credit

Switzerland

1970–80s Adjustment to dual depressions reduces number of savings
banks.

1971 Association of 248 Swiss Regional Banks formed, but market share
of domestic declines from 25 per cent in 1945 to 12 per cent in 1975
to 5 per cent in 1995.

1994 RBA Holding created to consolidate regional banks.

1990–95 Cantonal banks maintain 35 per cent of savings market.

1995 Regional banks and savings banks (n=127) retain balance sheet of
72.2 million francs, compared to 730.5 million francs at big four private banks and 262.5 million francs of cantonal banks.

Several observations follow. First, savings banks sustain a 'European Advantage' over the US and other countries without these institutions. Unlike the
fiasco of savings and loan bankruptcies in the US in the 1980s and 1990s, local,
regional and national savings bank groups still remain at the centre of domestic banking systems across Europe. Second, far from being destined to failure

under competitive pressures from private and foreign banks, savings banks have instead reformed, modernized, consolidated and adopted new strategies to compete in more open European banking, credit and finance markets. They have also largely avoided the perils of financial market bubbles and crises, especially in comparison to private commercial and investment banks. Third, Canevalli argues that the local organizational networks and lending discretion of savings banks provide competitive advantage and help usher small and medium enterprises through economic downturns. Fourth, the corporate social responsibility policies and charitable contributions of savings banks provide social and cultural investments well above policies of private firms amidst the reduced capacities of Welfare states under fiscal pressure. For example, French savings banks reserve *half* of dividends to fund social responsibility programmes run by bank staff and elected local or regional social and political representatives. Spanish savings banks are also mandated to contribute a share of profits to social, cultural, or community programmes – on average 24.9 per cent of profits during the last decades.

Savings bank change abroad thus confirms our findings from Brazil. Many countries seek to strengthen a select number of large private banks to compete abroad and project national power. However, this should not obscure the modernization and integration of alternative banking and traditional credit institutions at home such as savings banks, cooperative credit societies, credit unions and mortgage associations, many owned or controlled by (usually local) governments. Considered individually, local and regional credit institutions are often very small. However, as a whole they sum to a large part of political economy in most advanced economies. And since opening banking to competition during the 1990s, local and regional government banks and decentralized cooperative banks have *increased* market shares across Europe.[7]

Savings banks thus help explain differences across varieties of capitalism. The varieties of capitalism approach raises profound questions about creating and sustaining comparative and competitive advantage, the ability of governments to control business cycles and the importance of different policy traditions. The theory of institutional foundations of comparative advantage helps explain why the domestic impact of globalisation has differed. Instead of convergence toward private commercial and investment banking and capital markets through privatizations, banking and finance in most advanced economies are based on politics and business strategies that involve collaboration as much as market competition. Hall and Soskice, Sharpf and Ostrom stress how the limited exchange of information, the monitoring of behaviour and sanctions against those who would defect from cooperation pervade policymaking across Continental Europe.[8] Continental European banking involves powerful business associations and trade unions, networks that link banks, firms, social forces and government agencies and legal and regulatory systems all designed to promote collaboration as much as competition. Savings banks and cooperative banks remain at the centre of social and political networks that shape corporate governance, reinforce competitive advantage and inform strategies of private enterprises in Europe. Alternative banking across Europe reflects long histories that have accumulated large amounts of capital in deeply embedded local markets and institutions. Far from being condemned by more liquid financial markets or large private banks with greater economies of scale and better aggregate measures of efficiency, the integration of regional and local savings banks and cooperative banks have produced competitive advantage, better performance, increased market shares and renovated institutions for social and economic policy coordination.

Government savings banks also remain important in developing and emerging countries. If savings banks are an invention of European enlightenment; then they are also a legacy of European colonisation. Savings banks were critical for state formation after independence throughout Asia, Africa and the Middle East.[9] They remain so in the twenty-first century. Given the modernization of banking through the adoption of information technology, electronic and mobile banking, the recognition of microcredit and finance in development and the importance of access to finance and banking services to alleviate poverty and promote social inclusion, it follows that government savings banks may provide policy alternatives and retain competitive advantages. Government savings banks (often postal savings banks) provide policy alternatives even – and perhaps most importantly – in weak and failed states for public management, social inclusion and reconstruction after war and natural disasters. Further considerations are beyond the scope of this study. However, a glance at savings banks in advanced and developing countries suggests that the Caixa is not an exception. A historical approach to the Caixa clarifies how savings banks provide policy options and retain competitive advantages.

Government Savings Banks under Monarchy and Empire, 1861–89

In 1831, a private cooperative savings bank was founded in Rio de Janeiro. By June 1837, deposits summed to 2,546 million milréis while another 220 million milréis had been accumulated by the Bahia Savings Bank (founded 1835). After liquidation of the Banco do Brasil in 1829, Sturz estimates that 1/5 of Brazilian domestic government debt was held in the Rio de Janeiro Savings Bank. Over a dozen private savings banks were created during the early nineteenth century in Brazil.[10] However, the failure of most led to the founding of an imperial government savings and pawn bank in 1861. The Caixa Econômica e Monte de Socorro was commissioned as part of banking and finance reforms in 1860 that ended currency emissions by commercial banks and concentrated monetary policy at Treasury.

The 1860 decree also set rules and regulations for Caixas. Deposits were limited to four milréis per week and capped at fifty milréis per savings account. Interest on savings was fixed at 6 per cent per year, paid twice yearly.[11] Further regulations in 1861 provided government guarantee of deposits (a competitive advantage that became apparent once 118 private banks failed in the 1864 banking crisis), subordinated Caixas to the Finance Ministry and described their mission as:

> '...responsibility for receiving deposits of popular savings and capital reserves across the Brazilian territory to increase their liquidity, encourage saving habits and facilitate the development and circulation of wealth.'[12]

In 1874, Finance Minister, President of Treasury Courts and Conservative Party leader Viscount Rio Branco reviewed the performance of savings banks favourably, emphasizing their contribution toward the social improvement of labourers.[13] The philanthropic structure of the imperial government savings bank is suggested by the voluntary service of directors and refusal to suspend caps on weekly and total deposits (despite pressures to permit commercial and large private deposits).[14]

The organizational structure of Caixas remained centralized and relatively simple. Governance was conducted by a Conselho Inspetor e Fiscal (Fiscal and Inspection Council) composed of a President, Vice-President and eight counsellors chosen by government. The Council hired employees, set salaries, elaborated budgets and managed contracts and funds. Savings bank agencies retained four employees (treasurer, librarian, doorman and gopher) and servants as required. Pawn services were also offered.

Caixas thus remained simple deposit taking agencies for Treasury until 1888. Until transition to republican government in 1889, the evolution of deposits and withdrawals reflects this structure. Table 4.2 reports the value of deposits, withdrawals and balance of funds placed in Treasury (ignoring their fate for the moment) from 1862–89. Of special note is the geometric expansion of deposits precisely during and after the 1864 banking crisis. As noted in the preceding chapter, the failure of the Souto bank in 1864 brought down 118 banks and losses to bank depositors over 110 million milréis. The 1864 bank crisis is considered the most serious financial crisis in nineteenth-century Brazil. It also provides compelling evidence of the competitive advantage of government banking. A substantial influx of deposits during and after the 1864 crisis 'kick started' Caixa operations four years after opening the bank. The only years thereafter when withdrawals outpaced deposits were 1873–4 (when international financial crisis and depression once again shook Brazilian banking), 1878, then again in 1883–4 and 1886–9. However, outflows never erased the balance of funds generated for

Treasury from Caixa savings deposits. At year end 1889, after collapse of Imperial government on 15 November, deposits (99,000:601$000) remained 2,488 million milréis (2,488:557$000) above the sum of withdrawals (98,158:940$000).

Table 4.1: Caixa Deposits, Withdrawals and Balance at Treasury, 1861–89, $000.

	Deposits	Withdrawals	Balance
1861	11597	221	11376
1862	49117	12124	36993
1863	53015	13998	39027
1864	195333	41388	153944
1865	809481	275924	533557
1866	1374456	786787	587668
1867	1843115	1124040	719075
1868	2159469	1674374	488094
1869	2322090	1925117	386973
1870	2637469	2119118	518210
1871	3606959	2196161	1410798
1872	3822693	3167813	634821
1873	3478447	3304451	173995
1874	3577437	3702302	−875135
1875	3566880	4064543	−598763
1876	3550479	2509000	1041479
1877	4480605	4244108	236497
1878	4309916	4472617	−162701
1879	4547242	4230764	30478
1880	3526773	4933023	1406230
1881	3932637	3787647	144990
1882	4394209	3990067	404142
1883	4344889	4527633	−182764
1884	4307528	4919069	−611541
1885	4992271	4323067	669204
1886	4717637	5367300	−650663
1887	7505003	7826546	−321543
1888	7552840	8662808	−1109968
1889	7331014	9956930	−2625916
Total	99000601	98158940	2488557

Source: Finance Ministry Reports, 1870, 1880, 1889. Available on Centre for Research Libraries, Brazilian Government Document Digitization Project.

The Caixa chanelled funds from individual savings to the imperial government Treasury while increasing autonomy and providing policy alternatives. At first, Caixas ran on funds from 10 per cent charges on pawn operations. In 1865, the Caixa extended an interbank loan to the Banco Brasileiro e Portuguez, effectively acting as lender of last resort in the wake of banking crisis. During 1866,

30,000 milréis were retained by Caixas in reserve against future banking crises. By 1869, a State Council Finance Section Special Commission called for expansion of Caixas to the provinces and major 'court' cities (cities surrounding the Rio de Janeiro capital). In 1874, the Caixa was authorized to purchase government bonds, allowing the government to apply Caixa surpluses to the general budget. This reform was introduced precisely when debts from war with Paraguay were coming due and markets priced further credit dearly.[15] In 1880, the failure of a private savings bank, Coruja & Cia, produced a run on deposits at the Rio de Janeiro Caixa, a phenomena repeated in 1882 when the new Macahé branch office ran short of cash. In 1888, further reforms of banking, finance and the Caixas were introduced. In 1889, the Caixas retained 60,047 savings accounts amidst a population estimated at 14.3 million.

Table 4.2: Caixa Deposits compared to Banco do Brasil and Bank System, 1862–89, million milréis.

Year	Caixa	(Mkt Share)	BB	(Mkt Share)	Other Banks	(Mkt Share)	Total
1862	0.5	0.2 %	15.9	38.1 %	25.3	60.6 %	41.7
1864	2.4	1.0 %	7.6	16.7 %	35.5	78.0 %	45.5
1870	3.4	6.8 %	6.0	12.0 %	37.8	75.9 %	49.8
1875	4.2	4.4 %	31.6	33.7 %	58.1	61.8 %	93.9
1880	13.2	10.1 %	64.4	49.2 %	59.7	45.6 %	130.8
1885	14.0	8.4 %	64.7	38.6 %	95.8	57.1 %	167.7
1889	11.4	5.6 %	52.5	25.9 %	147.3	72.8 %	202.2

Source: Goldsmith, p. 41 and Finance Ministry Reports.

The growth of savings banks also reflects the top-down, centre-periphery politics of Brazilian monarchy. Imperial decree 5594 (April 1874) called for provincial governments to create savings banks. In 1867, Finance Minister Visconde do Rio Branco had authorized Provincial Presidents to retain 1 per cent of lottery receipts to offset administrative costs of savings bank agencies, while reserving 1 per cent of deposits for Treasury. Legislation in 1874 encouraged pawn services at agencies. In 1886, Ministry directives called for creation of Caixa branch offices at provincial government facilities and post offices, while legislation in 1887 determined creation of Caixas at Finance Ministry offices (Mesas de Rendas Coletas) in provinces or, lacking such offices, postal agencies. Table 4.3 reports the balance of provincial Caixa operations from 1875 through 1881. In addition to the 2,488:557$000 accumulated by the 'court' Caixa (Rio de Janeiro), the balance of 6,545:294$000 from provincial Caixas provided further funds for imperial government.

Table 4.3: Balance of Provincial Caixa Operations, 1874–81, $000.

Province	Created	Receipts				Costs		Balance
		Deposits	Interest*	Income	Total	Withdrawals	Pawns	
S. Pedro	May 875	2499883	210624	1570	2712956	1656723	1570	1053760
S. Paulo	Sept1875	1517474	70610	1020	1589112	1058273	1026	529811
Minas	Oct 1875	134293	15235	26	449555	74237		75267
Matto Grosso	Oct 1875	626361	60868	266	687496	412630	8131	266734
Espírito Santo	Dec 1875	407483	38401	486	446372	256544	486	189341
Santa Catarina	Jan 1876	359449	36083	283	395815	222990	2369	170455
Paraná	July 1876	396583	36438	301	433322	215759		217562
Goyaz	July 1876	444584	39698	232	484516	270854	232	213428
Para	July 1876	2461508	178360	728	2640598	1375558	728	1264310
Amazonas	May 1877	281278	15882	68	297229	184209		113020
Pernambuco	June 1877	1058087	66148	1736	1125972	565300	1953	547694
Maranhão	July 1877	1012742	58964	805	1072512	614779	805	459927
Bahia	Feb 1878	1945648	153175	681	2099505	951993	681	1126394
Alagoas	July 1878	164237	10727	231	175195	88041	231	85683
Ceará	Feb 1879	499494	25995	159	525648	293580	159	231908
Total		13809104	1017208	8592	15135803	8241470	18371	6545294

*Interest from Treasury and Pawn Operations

Source: State Council and Finance Ministry (Conselho do Estado e Ministério da Fazenda), *Parecer da Commissão sobre as Caixas Econômicas e Montes de Soccorro*. (Rio de Janeiro, 1882), Appendix D.

Debates in Finance Ministry reports and State Council commission studies reveal increasing concern with savings bank policies. During the 1864 banking crisis, Caixa staff were overwhelmed by 300–400 daily requests to open accounts, characterized as fraudulent third party deposits to circumvent caps on deposits and secure government guarantee on savings.[16] By 1869, Finance Ministry reports also express concern about an 'upmarket' shift in deposits. While 3,285 deposits were made below 5$000 (194:500$000 total) over five times as many deposits (20,172) were made at the limit of 50$000 (3,249:750$000 total). This elicited four concerns from the Finance Ministry, Caixa management and the Finance Section of the Imperial State Council; The need to expand staff to meet demand, fear of fraud, concern about mission drift and, most importantly, the institutional stability of the Caixas.

After 1871, Finance Ministry reports and two special commissions on the Caixa argued that accepting large deposits had shifted Caixas away from their philanthropic mission and threatened stability by subjecting its balance sheet to liquidity risk. The upmarket shift had subjected Caixas to panic withdrawals and runs on banks that had produced dozens of private bank failures in 1864. The

1871 Finance Ministry Report argues that large deposits threatened to transform the Caixa from a philanthropic savings bank into a deposit bank:

> '... the great majority of Caixa clients in this city are people with 50$000 a week available. These small capitalists have converted the establishment into a deposit bank, where they come to deposit their money under guarantee at better interest rates than anywhere else.' Finance Ministry Report, 1871, pp. 51–2

This tension between, on the one hand, expanding the bank by accepting upmarket deposits and, on the other hand, retaining the social mission and financial solidity of Caixas indicates the emergence of a specific policy debate focused on savings banks, philanthropy, social economy and development in Brazil.

A State Council report also stressed the underdevelopment of the Caixa in comparative perspective. The number of savings accounts in Rio de Janeiro (1/50.4 residents) pales in comparison to comparable data from savings banks in Great Britain (1/20 residents), France (1/28) and Brussels (1/6). Nonetheless, social data on savings account holders suggest that a significant number of depositors were from popular classes. After 1881, Finance Ministry Reports intermittently include data on the social profile of new clients. The 1881 Finance Ministry Report registers 11,176 new savings accounts, of which 3,586 were opened by workers, 1,499 by domestic servants, 155 by stevedores and 43 by agricultural workers. A further 1,623 savings accounts were opened for minors and 1,047 by women, after Caixa granted women control over savings accounts, unless receiving written prohibition by husbands (a policy upheld by courts after being challenged by the Pernambuco Caixa).

The number of accounts and social profile of Caixa clients indicates the level of social exclusion under imperial government, monarchy, slavery and underdevelopment in nineteenth-century Brazil. Caixas also provided policy alternatives for imperial government that led to the transfer, loss or devaluation of popular savings. Caixas emulated the philanthropic and charitable mission of European savings banks. In Brazil, Caixas bought government bonds and chanelled popular savings into commercial investments by crown, court and members of the imperial financial and economic elite. Savings deposits from Caixas helped fund discretionary government spending, most notoriously to refinance debts accumulated from war with Paraguay (1864–70).[17] Wasteful spending on war with Paraguay, inflation, fiscal crisis and the militarisation of imperial politics are seen as the primary causes of the breakdown of monarchy, military coup and transition to republican rule in 1889. The evidence from Caixa balance sheets suggests that popular savings accumulated during the latter nineteenth century were largely lost during this sequence. This pattern would continue during inflation, financial crises and monetary disorganization in the Old Republic after 1889.

Caixas Econômicas in the Old Republic, 1889–1930

After provisional republican government inquiry into personnel and salaries at Caixas failed to reveal abuses, the structure and operations of imperial savings banks were retained. Honorary service at top management continued. Staff and salary policies remained unchanged. In 1892, a Decree separated Caixas from the finance ministry, creating 'independent' and 'annexed' Caixas depending on their ability to generate surpluses and run independently. Cursory comments about savings banks during the Old Republic (1889–1930) in primary and secondary accounts suggest that these institutions withered under orthodox liberalism. Some provincial (now state) Caixas failed to become financially independent and were 'returned to a corner of some public agency'.[18] This is misleading.

Data suggest that Caixas grew substantially during the Old Republic, once again revealing competitive advantages and providing policy alternatives. Caixas recovered from problems at the end of the empire and expanded, even during the financial crisis that marked the first years of the Old Republic. From the first full year of republican rule and financial crisis (*'encilhamento'* during 1890) through 1899, deposits at Caixas (175,488:043$000) outpaced withdrawals (154,688:231$000) producing a balance for reserve funds and patrimony of 23,810:112$000. This is further evidence of the competitive advantage of government banks. The 1890 *encilhamento* stock market crash led to widespread bankruptcy of brokers, financial agents and banks. Not the Caixa. During 1890, deposits of 9,310:750$000 outpaced withdrawals of 7,200:019$000, producing influx of 2,110:231$000 – this during what is widely considered to be, after 1864, the worst financial crisis in Brazil until 1929.

The 1892 committee of inquiry report into Caixas Econômicas records a total 90,630 savings accounts. By 1898, the Finance Ministry records 123,816 savings accounts. By 1899, Caixa reserves and patrimony funds (latter created in 1895) reached 1,223:555$000, representing a decade of consistent reserve accumulation (except for 1896). However, a financial panic during second semester 1900 produced a run on banks, *including* Caixas. Withdrawals from Caixas during 1900 reached 33,295:725$000 producing a net loss of 13,437:770$000. Once again, management criticized the use of Caixas as commercial banks as responsible for losses, especially after a Ministry of Finance directive increased the cap on weekly deposits from four to ten milréis (10:000$).

'... we predicted problems when, in 1898, the cap on deposits was raised from 4:000$ to 10:000$, because experience demonstrates that the development of these institutions should be measured more by the number of deposits than the value of deposits. Savings banks are essentially previdentiary and should not receive capital that does not represent the savings of workers.'

1902 Finance Ministry Report, p. 683

For the Caixa Fiscal and Inspection Council President, the run of withdrawals on the institution during the 1900 banking crisis revealed that reforms had 'perverted the functions of the Caixa, reducing it to a bank'.[19]

Top down change also continued: Decree number 11.820 of January 5, 1915 signed by President Venceslau Brás and Finance Minister João Pandiá Calogeras, called for *each* state government to create a savings bank (but continued to annex to Finance Ministry offices deposits of Caixas unable to sustain operations). And contrary to Caixa Council recommendations, this decree also expanded bank services at Caixas by easing caps on weekly deposits and loans (after a surge of inflation), providing checking services to clients (apparently commercial; only checks above 50 milréis for clients with over 50 conto balances) and freeing savings banks to provide other services.

The institutional development and social profile of Caixas during the Old Republic counter stereotypes of orthodox liberalism and stagnation. Operating results and balance sheets suggest that Caixas increased their financial autonomy and provided services to bankless Brazilians at a significant level. Finance Ministry annual reports include annual overviews of Caixa performance and indicate organizational change. Reforms in 1888 (the last year of monarchy) ended the policy of depositing funds at Treasury and created reserve funds at Caixas based primarily on government bond purchases. After 1888, Caixas channelled half liquid receipts from savings deposits and interest from bonds to purchase further bonds, a process that accumulated reserves over 9.9 thousand contos or million milréis by 1924.

Instead of depositing funds at Treasury (1861–73) or purchasing government bonds (1874–88), Caixas after 1888 accumulated government bonds as reserves and 'patrimony'. In turn, reserves and patrimony were delegated to state Caixas able to generate sufficient funds from savings, pawn operations and interest earned on government bonds.

The Autonomy of Caixas in Brazilian States

The evolution of the São Paulo state Caixa suggests that several state savings banks (not state government banks but independent savings banks) developed at a significant pace to become competitive banks with significant market shares during the Old Republic. Table 4.4 reports the number and total value of deposits received by the São Paulo Caixa, interest paid to clients and (after 1888) retained by the bank, as well as the number and total value of withdrawals made by clients. From creation of the São Paulo Caixa in 1875 to 1920, the increase from 37,000 milréis to 64 million milréis suggests that this institution gained significant market share of the estimated 2.33 billion milréis of total bank deposits in 1920. The trajectory of deposits and withdrawals also indicates how savings banks grew by the accumulation of small deposits while weathering periods of financial crisis.

Table 4.4: São Paulo State Caixa Econômica, 1875–1920.

Year	Deposits Number	Deposits $000	Interest Clients $000	Interest Caixa $000	Withdrawals Number	Withdrawals $000
1875	1005	37293	297		77	5415
1876	3459	120696	3054		759	69342
1877	3786	141270	5412		890	101692
1888	5027	190356	7097		1102	126903
1889	7471	301392	13126		1684	185950
1880	816	331588	17687		2347	278490
1881	9779	394879	23033		2361	290478
1882	13196	520522	30193		2940	392264
1883	13891	552613	35538		3687	474046
1884	15385	614896	39039		4244	572966
1885	19248	793254	51178		4188	542917
1886	2024	934003	63473		5093	745285
1887	9793	1254326	62458		6359	1530443
1888	8802	1180491	62216	6029	5319	1094793
1889	10806	1499287	70921	7092	7323	1532241
1890	1277	2553898	80300	12617	6748	1584580
1891	1717	5056330	189985	37997	8202	2889729
1892	1495	4478723	257939	51587	9164	4002967
1893	13405	3877730	278345	55669	10452	4481420
1894	11644	3662065	338467	49693	9045	3857000
1895	17072	5364896	297823	59564	9625	4135335
1896	17017	5299322	342811	68562	11424	6014528
1897	14207	4472608	311571	63314	10628	4977122
1898	12786	4474752	292676	43995	10881	5052229
1899	14943	5741916	349028	34897	11185	4393253
1900	14998	5793991	388648	37864	13041	6548920
1901	17176	7015462	408601	40869	12327	5318470
1902	20164	7879337	527606	52760	13915	6067209
1903	23543	11072382	611146	64114	15991	78909689
1904	24401	10174455	810243	81321	17865	9635269
1905	21009	7403393	720845	72981	19163	11433346
1906	2602	9591847	728283	72828	17235	7523604
1907	35162	13516090	932438	92243	20961	9990813
1908	39795	14412756	10990412	109016	27536	13345695
1909	46033	15941718	1200743	120074	32374	14551217
1910	55199	20263278	1364656	136465	35383	17396514
1911	65521	27962334	1657291	165729	40408	21061627
1912	77753	36870951	2181660	218166	51405	29886249
1913	70171	30397576	2269381	226938	64229	39367279
1914	49743	19152363	1811708	181170	62274	27961881
1915	62893	23544952	1769629	176849	56775	19843571
1916	83383	33623508	2488590	277198	61262	24301493
1917	78643	33644028	2500307	272549	71495	36869770
1918	82196	38631775	2798937	271831	66878	30640779
1919	99642	53253184	3307211	323121	81442	48362613
1920	115526	64052663	3739264	363162	87882	56486748

Source: Repartição de Estatística e Archivo do Estado. *Annuario Estatístico de São Paulo*, 1920. p. 308.

Immigrants, workers, women and special groups such as orphans and widows became São Paulo Caixa clients. Of 16,009 new clients opening savings accounts during 1920, 6,833 were women, 5,266 were illiterate, 3,000 were labourers or artists, 414 rural workers, 112 railroad workers, 1700 employees in commerce, 888 were orphans, 408 were domestic servants and 7,057 were immigrants (7,229 declared no profession).[20] The São Paulo Caixa was used by popular classes. Of 115,000 deposits during 1920, over 31,000 were under 50 contos.[21] These deposits summed to 953 million contos. Compared to the consistent influx of large deposits recorded during the empire and early old republic, the data from the 1920s suggests that popular classes increasing used savings banks.

In sum, Caixas during the Old Republic gained institutional autonomy in states by retaining deposits in reserve instead of simply placing funds at the Finance Ministry. In 1915, Caixas were freed to provide checking services, home loans and public sector finance and expanded operations. Data on the social profile of the São Paulo Caixa suggest that bankless groups such as women, immigrants, labourers and orphans summed to a substantial part of clients. The philanthropic character of these institutions continued. Whether fixed interest rates under increasing inflation chanelled savings to or from popular classes remains an open question.

Caixas Econômicas and National Populism, 1930–45

'Savings Banks have experienced a new and beneficial expansion. Some now provide solid foundations for our still imperfect credit system. And, as important as their role in the formation of national capital is the educational role they have exercised on diverse social groups, by stimulating savings and a methodical accumulation of reserves that contribute directly to the constitution of family assets.'

President Getulio Vargas, 29 August 1939

After the 1930 revolution, government savings banks were perceived as agents for financial education, social inclusion, savings mobilization, import substitution industrialization and faster growth. Their governance, organization and regulation as philanthropic savings and pawn institutions limited to paying fixed interest on savings accounts were seen as constraining the growth of Caixas Econômicas and national development. Brazilian savings banks suffered two waves of panic withdrawals during 1931 and 1932 alongside private and commercial banks. However, after the normalization of the banking system by 1934, Caixas President Solano Carneiro da Cunha sought to expand services and streamline management. A Superior Council (five members nominated by Vargas) and Administrative Councils in states (three members nominated by Vargas) were created. Instead of transferring deposits to Treasury Offices (Delegacias da Fazenda), decree 24,427 of June 1934 generalized the practice that autonomous[22] state savings banks would retain funds as reserves against loans and financial operations. Savings banks thereby became more like banks. Home loans and finance to state and municipal governments for infrastructure development increased. Caixas acquired new competitive advantages, becoming both exempt from taxes on commercial bank transactions and official retainer of funds held in escrow pending judicial decisions. Caixas also retained legal monopoly over pawn services.

During the 1930s, savings banks gained autonomy and complexity. They developed guidelines for 'independent' and 'associated' agencies (the latter foreshadowing correspondent banking), set new regulations for hiring staff by exams, capital reserve requirements and loan approval procedures while conducting promotional campaigns to encourage citizens to open savings accounts.[23] From 1934 to 1940, savings banks increased share of domestic credit markets from 6.0 per cent to 10.5 per cent, with loans increasing from Cr$444.912.000 to Cr$1.372.698.000. De Placido e Silva reports twenty-fold (nominal) increases in the value of savings deposits at Caixas after the 1930 revolution.[24] Balance sheets suggest that Caixas focused on low-income home loans. In 1936, of the 1,623 housing loans reported by the Rio de Janeiro Caixa, 1,050 were at the minimum value of 50 contos, while 306 loans were made between 50 and 100 contos and 112 loans between 100 and 200 contos.[25] Caixas under Vargas' national populism are thus consistent with the commanding heights tradition. Directed credit from Caixas and other government banks were used to accelerate modernization. In Brazil, Caixa specialization in housing and urban development during the 1930s and 40s contributed to social inclusion, the inward turn of economic activity and the substitution of imports. Deposits at government savings banks peaked during the 1930s at almost 60 per cent of the total value of paper money reported by the IBGE. Caixa market share of bank deposits increased from under 20 to over 30 per cent during the 1930s (declining slightly during the early 1940s). Like much of the administrative machinery and political legacies of Vargas, the Caixa inherited substantial competitive advantages after transition from national populism to democracy in 1945.

The Caixas and Disequilibria under Developmentalism, 1945–64

Examination of savings banks after 1945 is critical given the negative perception of government banking and clientelism, corporatism and populism that are seen to predominate during the period of competitive electoral politics that ended in military coup on 31 March 1964. The first characteristic of government savings banks from 1945–64 of note is their size. Deposits at Caixas during the 1950s remained at roughly one third of paper money circulating in the Brazilian economy. After declining in the early 1940s, Caixa market share of bank deposits increased after transition from the Estado Novo to democratic government in 1945. Caixas do not correlate with particular political regimes. Both the increase of deposits after transition from national populism in 1945 and the decline of Caixa market share of bank deposits during the 1950s suggest that other factors (such as inflation) are at work. Given that inflation increased from 2.6 per cent in 1947, to between 12 and 25 per cent in the mid-1950s and an estimated 91.9 per cent during 1964, the flight of clients from savings accounts with fixed annual returns of 6 per cent is understandable.

Exemption from taxes on commercial bank transactions, official escrow funds as a liability base, and the large network of Caixa branch offices provided competitive advantages over private banks. Caixa branch offices appear to have brought financial services to areas poorly served by private banking.[26] Data from the 1959 Caixas Annual Report suggests that a total of 483 branch offices were operating in Brazil, with 226 standard agencies, 149 postal agencies, 100 affiliated agencies and 8 correspondent agencies across twenty Brazilian states. Data from the 1969 Annual Report suggests a greater geographical reach. Of the 514 Caixa offices, 163 were located in capital cities, while 351 were located in the interior of states. Regulations of Caixa 'Postal Agencies' were set in November 1948 (Decree 25.733). Inspired by the US Postal Bank and echoing initiatives in nineteenth-century Brazil, this also foreshadowed a government concession in 2001 to provide banking services in postal offices (won by Bradesco).

This network of branch offices appears to have pressured the balance sheets of Caixas. Administrative costs increased above inflation during the late 1950s, especially personnel costs. From 1955 to 1959, administrative costs increased from R$739.662.000 to over Cr$2.3 billion, while personnel costs increased from Cr$613.783.000 to Cr$1.9 billion.[27] The latter increase of 284 per cent outpaces inflation (228.3 per cent). Inflation also eroded the deposit base of Caixas. The dual impact of flight from deposits (earning fixed 6 per cent annual interest rates) and rising administrative costs first eroded returns, then required cash infusions from the federal government. In 1955–9, returns decreased from 0.8 per cent of deposits to 0.1 per cent of deposits. Upon separation from *Delegacias Fiscais* (Fiscal Stations) in 1946, *Contas Patrimoniais* (reserves) set aside by savings banks totaled Cr$274 million. Reserves increased to Cr$1.17 billion in 1957 before being consumed by deficits. By 1959, Caixas required cash infusions in thirteen of twenty-one states. Deficits totaled Cr$480 million in 1959 (eight Caixas supplied a Cr$1.39 billion surplus, São Paulo state alone reporting profits of Cr$116 million for 1959).

Further research into the politics and policies of the Caixa in 1945–64 under the macroeconomics of populism and the disequilibria of developmentalism will be needed. The stereotype of Caixa policy during this period is one of middle class capture. Instead of serving for social inclusion, Caixa home loans to public sector employees appear to confirm the traditional image of rent seeking and dependent middle class veto of further social inclusion that arrested political development in Brazil during this period. However, the large scale, organizational complexity and autonomy of Caixas in the diverse settings of Brazilian states from 1945 to 64 suggest that these institutions cannot be disregarded simply as middle class capture. Reading of the bi-monthly *Revista das Caixas Econômicas*, published by the Caixa Superior Council from 1949 until closed by military government after 1964, suggests the emergence of a sophisticated epistemic community concerned with popular savings, banking theory, risk analysis and bank operations. Issues of the *Revista das Caixas Econômicas* report independent evaluation of the structure, policies and performance of dozens of savings banks abroad written by Caixa staff based on field research, review of developments in monetary theory and policy, municipal finance development, and independent monitoring of legislation, regulation and legal cases in judiciary relevant to banking and savings bank policies and ranking of state Caixa performance. Caixas also held annual planning conventions with representation from independent state Caixas. These events were open forums for strategic planning that defined annual corporate priorities published in the *Revista* and circulated internally by the Central Council. This decentralization, complexity and autonomy would be reversed under military rule. So too would the open corporate planning debates and social economy focus of the *Revista das Caixas Econômicas*. The downmarket policy experiences and strategies of the Caixa under democracy before 1964 were lost under military rule.

Centralization of Caixas under Military Rule, 1964–85

Caixas were reorganized as part of financial reforms under military government. Creation of the Central Bank of Brazil (1965), the Sistema Financeira de Habitaçao (Home Finance System, 1966), the Banco Nacional de Habitação (National Housing Bank, BNH, 1966), the Fundo de Garantia por Tempo de Serviço (Official Pension Fund, FGTS) and introduction of monetary correction to protect savings against inflation fundamentally altered Brazilian political economy. Reforms were designed by economists such as Roberto Campos and Otávio Gouveia Bulhões to extricate monetary, fiscal and credit policy and bank regulation and supervision from the monolithic Banco do Brasil. Reforms also freed firms from permanent employment contracts (required by 1941 legislation) by creation of an official pension fund through 8 per cent payroll surcharges (FGTS). The military government also reduced the institutional autonomy of state Caixas. By 1970, independent state Caixas were merged into a centralized state owned enterprise charged with management of military government official savings, directed home credit programmes, social policies and urban development finance.

Caixa financial reporting of select aggregate results on the national level also reflects the centralization of these institutions under military rule. Instead of pre-1964 practices of detailed financial reporting, open debate of economic trends and savings bank policies and publication of debates from annual Caixa management congresses, the military government 1) suspended the Caixa Central Council 2) stopped publication of the *Revista das Caixas Economicas* and 3) suspended annual policy and planning congresses. President Costa e Silva then charged a commission composed of three executives close to the military with review of Caixas and development of plans for reorganization. Meanwhile, economic recovery and increasing deposits from both official savings programmes and the general public produced strong surpluses at Caixas; NCr$89.0 million in 1968 and NCr$167.2 million in 1969.[28] This leveraged expansion, with loans almost doubling from NCr$754.7 – NCr$1,397.2 million on a deposit base that grew from NCr$884.6 – NCr$1,002.3 million.

In 1970, Caixas were consolidated into a single state owned enterprise, the Caixa Econômica Federal (Federal Savings Bank, Caixa) responsible to the Finance Ministry. The Superior Council was eliminated and the bank was redefined as agent of federal government credit policy. Decree 759 constituted the Caixa S.A. through transfer of liquid assets in state Caixas and 2.5 per cent of lottery receipts, endowments that summed to NCr$353.0 million in March 1970. The Caixa became responsible for the implementation of the official savings programme (Programa de Integração Social, Programme for Social Integration, PIS) and social policy fund (Fundo de Assistência Social, Social Assistance Fund, FAS) under the Social Development Council. The bank retained legal monopoly over lotteries, managed directed credit programmes for housing, sanitation and infrastructure projects through state and municipal governments and distributed educational loans.

Control over forced savings, social policies and finance for state and municipal governments transformed the Caixa into a prized political resource. For example, São Paulo governor Paulo Maluf launched his political career as President of the São Paulo Caixa after being nominated by President Costa e Silva in 1967. The number of political nominations and administrative posts at the Caixa increased under military rule. Instead of imposing market discipline, politicization and use of Caixa jobs to build party-electoral machines occurred under military rule (elections were held for municipal, state and federal legislatures and most mayorships during military rule). After transition to democracy, one of the major challenges of reforms at the Caixa was to reduce the up to *2,000 political appointments* in each of the twenty-seven superintendent state offices of the bank. Reforms after military intervention in 1964 were reputed to be liberal.

However, the centralization, politicization and bloating of administrative staff at the Caixa confirms the unintended state-centric consequences of military rule in Brazil on banking.

This also characterizes Caixa liabilities. Under military rule, the Caixa shifted away from consumer deposits to rely increasingly on official forced savings as the primary source of funds. From 1971–6, deposits from the official pension fund FGTS increased from 24.9–45.9 per cent of Caixa liabilities.[29] Meanwhile, savings deposits declined from 20.1–11.0 per cent and interbank deposits declined from 13.3–4.9 per cent of toal liabilities. Caixa assets also suggest a shift in policy toward the private sector. While home loans remained approximately one third of Caixa assets, from 1971–6, lending to the private sector increased from 58.5–66.3 per cent of Caixa assets.

The Caixa confirms evidence from Banco do Brasil and BNDES case study chapters. Instead of liberalization after the 1964 coup, the administrative centralisation and shift toward forced savings programmes suggests state centred policies. Furthermore, traditional policies of the Caixas (the philanthropic intent of popular savings in the nineteenth century and policies for popular housing since the 1930 revolution) were diminished under military government. One of the most accepted characterizations of military rule in Brazil is its orientation toward dependent middle classes. Social policies once designed for popular inclusion were captured by or reoriented towards middle class groups and organized interests under military rule. This shift toward the middle classes also occurred at the Caixa. The inaugural address of Humberto Barreto as President of the Caixa Econômica Federal on 11 May 1977 claimed that the problem of popular housing in Brazil had largely been resolved and that Caixa home loans would henceforth, under his management, be directed towards middle income families to address their housing shortage.

The Caixa in Transition from Military Rule

After 1985, Caixa management pursued corporate modernization while the bank acquired new roles and portfolios amidst inertial inflation, seven anti-inflation policy packages and prolonged transition from military rule that let traditional elites use government banks to sustain party-electoral machines. From 1985–94, the Caixa remained at the centre of disputes between traditional elites and new leaders of democratic transition. Inertial inflation upped the political ante by leaving the Caixa as *de facto* lender of last resort. Before the Real Plan ended inertial inflation (1993–4), record spreads between interest rates paid on deposits and earnings from indexed government paper produced strong profits at the Caixa, profits that often escaped standard bank accounting and reporting standards. From 1994 until capitalization of the bank to meet BIS and Central Bank capital reserve requirements in 2001, the Caixa provided critical policy alternatives to sustain price stability and implement fiscal reforms amidst international financial crises. Political disputes and macroeconomic emergencies often delayed plans to rationalize and modernize the bank. Nonetheless, the Caixa emerged in the 1990s after from military rule with dominant market shares in home loans and urban development while continuing to manage federal government social policy.

Caixa market shares in lending to the public and private sectors from 1968–2003 are reported in Figure 4.1 to introduce this trajectory during and after military government. The two latter peaks of Caixa lending to the public sector indicate expansion of Caixa lending to nearly 50 per cent of total lending to government entities (during the worst period of inertial inflation of 1989 and after renegotiation and caps on lending to sub-national government entities in 1997). The preceding peak of Caixa lending to the public sector, in 1978, culminates a period of more organic growth after reforms at the outset of military government led to recovery of Caixa lending to the public and private sectors from under 10 per cent to 20 and 30 per cent of total lending respectively. A single peak in the market share of Caixa loans to the private sector from 1968–2003 also suggests that Caixas became lenders of last resort under inertial inflation and monetary chaos. From 1968 to 1975, Caixa share of domestic loans to the private sector doubles from 8 to 19 per cent, then to a full 50 per cent in 1989 when inflation reached over 1700 per cent. Caixa market share drops thereafter during the 1990s to 6 per cent of total private sector lending in 2001.

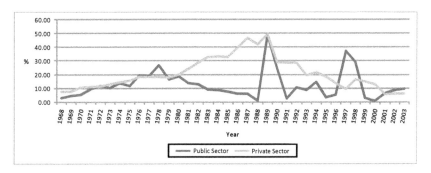

Figure 4.1: Caixa Market Share of Credit to Public and Private Sector, 1968–2003.
Source: IBGE, Estatísticas do SéculoVinte, 2003, available at www.ibge.gov.br and Central Bank of Brazil, available at www.bcb.gov.br.

Peaks of Caixa lending to the public sector during 1989, 1994 and 1997 reflect the use of the government banks as lender of last resort under high inflation, instability and the imperatives of adjustment during economic packages. Caixa market share reaches half of loans to the public sector during the penultimate surge of high inflation in 1989. After peaks during the Real Plan in 1994 and renegotiation of sub-national government debts during 1997, Caixa market share of loans to the public sector declines, remaining under 10 per cent by 2001.

In sum, indexation of savings accounts against inflation in 1965 and the centralisation of Caixas in 1970 produced a period of growth at the Caixa under military rule. Forced savings were channelled by the Caixa into urban development and housing, while political appointments and social policies built political careers under the peculiar two party system under military government (1965–79). During the 1980s, inertial inflation, the disorganization of the economy, and failed economic packages left the Caixa as lender of last resort responsible for half of lending to the public and private sector by 1989. To offset losses in 1992, the central bank infused R$1.2 billion into the Caixa. After 1990 and especially after price stability in 1994, Caixa market shares to the private and public sector declined to approximately 10 per cent.

After adjustment and reforms during the 1990s, the Caixa has retained or expanded market shares since capitalization in 2001. A closer look at Caixa policies by economic sector reveals how the federal government savings bank realized competitive advantages after transition to democracy.

The Caixa in Home Loans and Construction

After 1985, the Caixa transformed policy experience into competitive advantage in home finance and construction. In 1986, the Caixa acquired the National Housing Bank (Banco Nacional de Habitação, BNH) including its home loan portfolio, management contracts for FGTS funds, and personnel and programmes. The Caixa became responsible for management of the Fundo de Apoio a Produção de Habitação para a População de Baixa Renda (Home Construction Fund for Low Income Populations, FAHBRE) and the Fundo de Assistência Habitacional (Home Assistance Fund, FUNDAH). The Caixa thereby became responsible for writing and reviewing national plans for housing and sanitation. In 1986, the Caixa also replaced the BNH as coordinator of the Plano Nacional de Habitação Popular (National Popular Housing Plan, PANHAP) and the Plano Nacional de Saneamento Básico (National Sanitation Plan, PLANASA). Acquisition of BNH management divisions and policy coordination capacity transformed the Caixa into coordinator and agent for government policy, programmes and directed credit for home finance and construction.

During the 1960s, dual directed credit and free mortgage markets were regulated by the Sistema Financeiro de Habitação (Housing Finance System, SFH). SFH reforms chanelled FGTS and voluntary savings through the Sistema Brasileiro de Poupança e Empréstimo (Brazilian System of Savings and Loans, SBPE). The SBOE required that 65–75 per cent of bank savings deposits be invested in home loans, 80 per cent of funds as directed SFH credit and 20 per cent at market rates called Carteiras Hipotecárias (Mortgage Portfolios). In 1986, the Caixa acquired the Fundo de Compensação de Variações Salariais (Salary Variation Compensation Fund, FCVS) created at the BNH in 1967 to guarantee home loans, capitalize SFH home insurance and liquidate obligations from SFH credit insurance. The SFH system increased the number of homes financed from 8,000 to 627,000 in 1965–80. However, subsidies remained registered in FCVS accounts, reaching R$72.0 billion at year end 2008 a value that remains in escrow on the liability side of Caixa balance sheets (albeit as federal government treasury obligation administered by the Caixa).

The Sistema Financeiro Imobiliário (Home Finance System SFI) created in 1997 attempted to free market forces and securitize mortgages, a system that remained dormant (producing between 28,000 and 37,000 homes per year) until further reforms in 2003 succeeded in capitalizing the system. In 1997, legislation regulated creation of Mortgage Credit Security Companies, Mortgage Receivable Certificates, and removed legal impediments for use of real estate as collateral on loans and securities. Further reforms during the 1990s include creation and regulation of Fundos de Investimentos Imobiliários (Real Estate Invesment Funds, FII) that require 75 per cent investment in real estate developments. These policies encouraged primary and secondary markets for mortgages and mortgage backed securities. The Caixa used its policy experience and political and social foundations of competitive advantage to lead in these new markets and retain dominant shares as these markets took off during the 2000s. Since reforms in 2003, home finance increased from the 28,000 to 37,000 levels recorded in the 1990s to 195,900 in 2007. The Caixa led this transition from a directed credit system designed under military rule to a dual system of downmarket directed credit and market priced home finance capitalized through investment funds and mortgage backed securities traded on the BMF-Bovespa stock market.

After military rule, Caixa management first had to clean up and write off the portfolio of home leans inherited from the BNH. Presidents Itamar Franco (1993–4) and Fernando Henrique Cardoso (1995–2002) offered several opportunities for clients to liquidate late or non-paying home loans at substantial discount. In 1995, the Caixa resumed use of FGTS funds for downmarket home finance after a five year suspension. The Programa Carta de Crédito FGTS (FGTS Letter of Credit) limited contracts to acquisition of first homes by those earning less than 12 minimum salaries. To reduce costs for potential lower income clients, the Caixa signed agreements with producer associations in home construction (Associação Nacional dos Comerciantes de Materiais de Construção, National Home Construction Merchant Association, ANAMACO), notaries (Associação dos Notários e Registradores, Notary and Registry Association, ANOREG) and regional home realty associations, Conselhos Regionais de Corretores de Imóveis (Regional Realtor Councils, CRECI). By 1998, the

FGTS letter of credit programme reached R$5.9 billion in contracts for over 408,000 homes.

In 1996, a provisional decree also facilitated renegotiation of mortgages, providing up to 95 per cent discounts on balances due for liquidation of late or non-paying loans. The Caixa thereby liquidated over 32,000 mortgages, generated R$335.0 million and reduced the level of non-paying loans in its portfolio. The Caixa later liquidated a further 207,000 non-performing home loans, generating R$1.9 billion in receipts. The Cardoso administration subsequently launched *four* new programmes for directed home credit and popular housing subsidies. The Programa Pró-Moradia (Pro-Home Programme); the Programa Carta Crédito-CEF (Caixa letter of credit); Programa de Apoio à Produção de Habitação (Programme for Assistance to Home Construction) and; Crédito Lastreado em Antecipação de Recebíveis (Receipt Anticipation Credits). The Caixa was contracted to implement the Programa Pró-Moradia, involving demarcation, regularisation and purchase of urban plots, the design, construction and/or reform of homes and the recuperation of deteriorated popular housing projects. By 1998, home construction reached R$65.0 billion, with R$56.5 billion originating in funds from the Caixa, R$8.5 billion from FGTS funds and budget allocations of R$712.1 million.

In sum, the Caixa provided policy alternatives and realized competitive advantages in home finance and construction industries.

Caixa Public Finance

After transition from military rule, the Caixa also provided policy alternatives and reasserted competitive advantage in public finance. Savings banks in Brazil have purchased government paper since the 1830s. Caixas also transferred deposits to Treasury for most of the nineteenth century. In 1915, Caixas gained autonomy to retain deposits and turn a profit from banking and financial services. This included public finance. After the 1930 Revolution, Caixas became primary agents for sub-national government finance, especially in sanitation and urban development. This continued during the 1970s when the Caixa began to channel official savings to development projects under military rule. Since transition to democracy in 1985, the Caixa was contracted to implement the following projects:

1) Inter-American Development Bank National Programme for State Fiscal Management (R$2.7 billion)
2) Programa Pro-Saneamento (Pro-Sanitation Programme), 1996 (368 contracts with R$731.2 million FGTS funds)
3) Federal government budgeted programmes

a) Programa Habitar Brasil (Habitate Brazil Programme), integrated sewage and water contracts, home construction and community development (728 contracts, R$209.1 million)

b) Programa Ação Social em Saneamento (Social Action Programme in Sanitation, PASS), 1996. Focus on water, sewage and waste removal services in worst urban neighborhoods (949 contracts, R$227.6 million).

c) Pro-Infra, Programa de Infraestrutura (Infrastructure Programme) 1996. Transportation and infrastructure for tourism and industry, with priority for poor neighborhoods (256 contracts, R$132.8 million).

These contracts helped deepen Caixa networks in the public and private sector, policy experience, and competitive advantages in public finance. In 1997, Caixa operations with municipalities were consolidated in a single programme entitled 'Caixa – o Banco do Município' (Caixa, bank of Municipalities). Since then, the Caixa has convened annual seminars on municipal development, organized 18 regional offices for staff training and created a proprietary data set on municipal finance to retain competitive advantage.

Experience in municipal finance also led to use of the Caixa from 1995–7 as an 'IMF-like' lender to state and municipal governments unable to pay employees and settle accounts. Under inertial inflation before 1994, state and municipal governments simply delayed payments to adjust accounts. After the Real Plan, sub-national governments were forced to confront fiscal realities. To induce adjustment, the Caixa was used to extend financial support to state and municipal governments on the condition that personnel costs be cut, state government banks be privatized and public administration modernized. This role of the Caixa as a domestic IMF anticipated a series of fiscal reforms adopted during the late 1990s that culminated in the Fiscal Responsibility Law passed by Congress in 2000.[30] Reforms ended emergency measures and conditional lending to subnational governments at the Caixa that had generated tension between the bank and policymakers.[31]

Caixa conditional lending to state and municipal governments began in October 1995 to resume late payment of public employees in Alagoas, Minas Gerais and Piaui states. Despite opposition of Caixa president Sergio Cutolo, Finance Minister Malan extended further loans to a total of seventeen state governments, reaching R$458.9 million by 1996.[32] Conditions included a cap of personnel costs at 60 per cent of liquid receipts, ceilings for public employee salaries, requirements to draft privatization programmes and increase taxes, modernize state finance secretaries through computerization, targets for zero fiscal deficits and prohibition of loans against future budget receipts or federal government transfers. The political logic of conditionality was not simply partisan. Terms were toughest with PSDB governors Alencar of Rio de Janeiro and Azcredo in Minas Gerais, while Governor Souto of Bahia (PFL) and Governor Arraes of Pernambuco (PSB) received loans *without* conditionality clauses requiring privatizations. And conditionality was imposed. Finance Minister Malan suspended loans to two states for not meeting reform targets in contracts. Seven states reported reducing a total of 28,977 state government jobs.

These operations deepened policy experience and capacity at the Caixa. For example, during 1996, the Caixa processed 5,109 new applications from 1,231 mayors for new credits toward urban development projects involving sanitation, infrastructure and housing. While Fiscal Responsibility Legislation would prohibit municipal finance until 2006, these experiences placed the Caixa in an advantageous position when the Central Bank ceded authority over municipal finance to Treasury and President Lula increased the flow of funds to states and municipalities (first in the Growth Acceleration Programme of 2006 then during 2007–8 as counter-cyclical policies). As the municipal finance market returned during the late 2000s, the Caixa used its institutional foundations, policy experience, and political and social networks to competitive advantage.

The Caixa and Policies for Adjustment and Stabilization

The Caixa also acquired private and public bank portfolios with bad loans for resale or privatization. As noted, a banking crisis after the end of inertial inflation required acquisition of several large private banks by the federal government. Central Bank president Persio Arida and Finance Minister Malan prepared private banks for resale by purchase or transfer of bad loans to the Caixa. The Caixa was used to remove bad credits from balance sheets *and* infuse cash into banks under intervention by the federal government before resale or privatization. The Caixa received R$1.68 billion under the PROER programme to acquire 39,722 mortgages from the private bank Econômico before sale of the institution. The Caixa also received R$786.0 million under PROER to acquire the mortgage portfolio of Meridional bank, cancelling debts of the bank with the Caixa for cash differences that removed bad loans from the Meridional and permitted sale of the bank in 1997.

The Caixa also increased interbank loans to ensure the liquidity of private banks during the first years of price stability. The value of Caixa interbank lending increased from R$550.0 million in 1994 to over R$7.7 billion in 1996. This attracted criticism from Caixa officials and the press. The mandate of the federal government savings bank was to finance housing, sanitation and urban development, not serve as lender of last resort to private banks. Nonetheless, imperatives of adjustment led Ministry of Finance officials to use the Caixa for purposes beyond its core business. This occurred once again during the credit shortages caused by financial crisis in 2008, when the Caixa loaned Petrobras R$2.0 billion in a letter of credit to avert a cash shortage and late payment that would have further devalued Petrobras shares during times of uncertainty on the Bovespa stock market.

Caixa Corporate Governance Modernization

After transition to democracy, new Caixa management attempted to reform internal bank procedures and modernize corporate governance. Centralisation of Caixas under military rule, capture of Caixa policies by middle class groups such as public employees and political control over the bank by traditional elites during the prolonged period of transition produced conflicts. Corporate governance reforms during the Cardoso (1995–2002) and Lula administrations (2003–10) sought to reduce the control of traditional elites and party machines over centralized decision making. During 1994, internal reforms entitled Programa de Racionalização e Competitividade (Programme of Rationalization and Competitivity) were commissioned by Caixa management. A bewildering variety of complex Caixa operations left by a succession of diverse policymaking roles had left Caixa bureaucracies dispersed, incoherent and largely unresponsive. The goals of the Programme of Rationalization and Competitiveness were to:

1) Centralise formulation, implementation, evaluation and control of corporate strategy.
2) Decentralise operational procedures to increase agility.
3) Integrate three core business segments; commercial, developmental and service provision.
4) Rationalize quality and efficiency, especially in terms of service provision and development.
5) Rationalize organization by eliminating levels of hierarchy to increase competitivity.
6) Prioritize business activities.
7) Strengthen management functions and decisionmaking bodies.
8) Reduce operating costs.

Overlapping administrative sectors and an excessive number of political appointments made the Caixa inefficient, unprofitable and immune to change. Operating expenses consumed cash needed to invest in technology. Corporate headquarters and branch offices had increased from 20 to 40 per cent of administrative costs. Service receipts remained at 17 per cent of Caixa receipts, far below the average of 35 per cent at Brazilian banks. Late and non-paying loans at the Caixa had reached *48 per cent* in 1994 (*85 per cent* in several regions).

Caixa management attempted to reorganize the bank into three subsystems; central governance, logistics and business. Central governance was to formulate bank strategies (through six central coordinators) and supervise (through twenty-four new regional coordinators and fifty-five new process managers) the implementation and evaluation of policies at points of sale. Logistics, composed of 158 new logistics centres, was charged with operationalizing products and services and assessing and reforming bank operations. The business subsystem was designed to develop management tactics for meeting bank goals and commercialization of products and services through eighty-four new business offices. Reforms attempted to renovate management by relocating and retraining personnel rather than downsizing or voluntary retirement programmes.

Political conflicts converged on the Caixa as the Real Plan stabilized prices and launched Finance Minister Cardoso in the 1994 presidential campaign. During 1993–4, Caixa Presidents Danilo de Castro and José F. Almeida (appointed by President Itamar Franco) often opposed Minister Cardoso's policies. Reforms also encountered persistent opposition from political elites, especially from political machines in less developed states and members of the PFL party. For Cardoso, rationalization of the Caixa (reduction of personnel costs and discretionary lending) was seen as imperative for economic adjustment. For the PFL and political elites, reforms threatened to reduce control over jobs and projects in popular housing, urban development and sanitation with large contracts and political returns. Conflict erupted in 1994 over a provisional decree reducing the number (1,500!) of political appointments per state to managerial positions at the Caixa. PFL leader Vice President Maciel suspended reforms upon assuming presidential duties (vice presidents assume the presidency while presidents are abroad). Despite reforms, the Caixa remained central to coalition government under Presidents Cardoso (1995–2002) and Lula (2003–10). The Caixa Presidency is valued as a political nomination equal to the most important federal government ministries. Caixa vice presidencies, especially of those of housing, sanitation and urban development, also remained prized for their large budget lines for projects with high appeal among politicians, construction firms and voters.

In sum, the Caixa was used in the 1990s to help sub-national governments adjust to price stability and to acquire bad loans at failed private banks to facilitate their resale. However, improvisation during adjustment and banking crisis were temporary. It reflected recentralisation typical of post-transition governments in Latin America that struggled to impose fiscal control and reform public sectors. By the late 1990s, policymakers turned to broader reforms and policies.

Caixa Capitalization and Reorientation, 2001–8

The Finance Ministry capitalized the Caixa in June 2001 to meet Central Bank requirements that financial institutions retain a minimum Basel Index of 11 per cent. Capitalization increased the Basel Index of the Caixa from 4.9 per cent in June to 14.8 per cent in December 2001. Policies included:

1) swap of R$86.7 billion of assets and liabilities for higher interest bearing treasury bonds;
2) transfer of R$26.7 billion in housing loans and R$13.0 billion of debts held by the Caixa from federal government renegotiation of state government debts (its role as 'domestic IMF');
3) injection of R$9.3 billion for capitalization;
4) payment of R$8.0 billion in exchange for Caixa liabilities to the federal government unemployment insurance funds (FGTS) and;
5) payment of R$5.7 billion for additional assets transferred to the Emgea assset management entity.

The recovery of bad and non-performing loans and sale of assets at the Emgea asset management entity since 2001 sum to over R$13.0 billion suggests that the total cost of capitalization remains below R$25.0 billion.

Was it worth it? This section reviews the policies and performance of the Caixa since capitalization in 2001. Four reforms of corporate governance were adopted in 2001 to ensure the continuity of the Caixa as agent of government policy while ensuring against losses. First, a new management model was introduced to avert crony credit and ensure banking prudence. Second, greater transparency was adopted for distribution of government mandated services, grants and social programmes. Third, a series of measures exchanged assets and restructured bank capital. Finally, non-performing assets and housing loans inherited from the BNH were sold to Emgea, a specially created asset management entity of the federal government. Since 2001, Caixa executives have sought to expand core business areas, reinforce the bank's role in social policy and promote both new programmes of popular credit downmarket and compete in investment banking. High interest rates after 2001 provided a window of opportunity and further time to modernize. High spreads between low interest paid on Caixa savings deposits and high interest bearing government bonds reinforced returns.

In terms of home loan and construction industries, the Caixa continues to implement directed credit programmes for popular housing while expanding into new regulated markets for home loans, construction and mortgage securities. The Caixa continued to serve as agent for new social policies such as family grants and income transfers. While the Caixa suspended most public finance from 2001–6, President Lula placed the bank at the centre of the Programa de Aceleração do Crescimento (Growth Acceleration Programme, PAC) that has chanelled funds to municipal governments. Corporate governance reforms also were pushed into the background until Caixa President Jorge Mattoso resigned in 2005 (after releasing a client's confidential account data under pressure from Finance Minister Palocci). Since 2005, Caixa President Maria Fernanda Ramos Coelho has increased transparency, accountability and social responsibility programmes at the bank. Since 2003, the Caixa has been called on by President Lula to increase the pace of growth, provide counter cyclical credit during downturns and to reduce consumer and corporate interest rates and bank spreads.

Table 4.5: Summary of Caixa Structure and Performance, 1995–2008.

	Assets	Profits	Deposits	Employees	Branches	Basel	FA/Equity
1995	82.6	67.2	50.3	99,866	2,316		
1996	90.7	235.1	51.5	99,343	2,105		
1997	99.9	87.5	54.1	96,300	1,803		
1998	94.8	169.3	49.9	94,859	1,819		
1999	68.4	157.1	34.4	94,194	1,919		
2000	64.4	136.2	32.2	104,253	1,921		
2001	43.6	–126.5	29.8	98,971	2,013	13.5	63.8
2002	36.3	146.2	21.6	106,548	2,147	14.6	53.7
2003	52.1	261.7	28.1	100,498	2,046	19.2	41.3
2004	55.6	299.9	34.5	100,164	2,135	20.2	36.1
2005	80.6	485.2	45.6	106,729	2,321	27.8	20.1
2006	98.1	487.4	56.7	104,934	2,428	25.2	19.7
2007	140.9	448.5	80.0	106,770	2,052	28.8	12.8
2008	126.6	573.5	70.8	103,895	2,069	20.6	11.9

Note: Assets & Deposits = US$billion. Profits = US$million. Basel = BIS Basel Accord index of capital reserve adequacy. FA/Equity = Fixed Assets / Equity, a summary indicator of bank modernization.

Source: Central Bank of Brazil, Top fifty Banks in Brazil, available at www.bcb.gov.br.

Review of balance sheets and policies since 2001 suggest that the Caixa retains its core business in urban development, home loans, real estate, fund management for government programmes and services and lottery administration. However, investment banking, management of third party funds and the creation of of new products and services have both increased profits and popular access to banking and social services. The bank has turned record profits since 2001. The Caixa became the fourth largest Brazilian investment bank by 2003 and gained dealer status from the Central Bank for trading in primary and secondary markets for government securities. The Caixa has expanded its role in bond markets. At year-end 2003, the Caixa held R$76.7 billion in Brazilian government bonds (over 10 per cent of total government debt), assets earning over R$13.5 billion that year. Since recovery of the Brazilian economy in 2004, the Caixa continued to improve its balance sheet and converge toward international bank reporting and performance standards (full transition to International Financial Reporting Standards set for 2010).

Data on assets, deposit base and the number of employees and branches suggest that the Caixa emerged from reforms and downsizing during the 1990s to expand organically since capitalization in 2001. Caixa assets declined from over US$99.9 to US$36.3 billion from 1997–2002 after reorganization and capitalization (reflecting a three fold devaluation of real against the dollar). Deposits also declined from US$54.1 to US$21.6 billion from 1997–2002. During the second Cardoso administration (1999–2002) the number of Caixa employees declined from 104,253–98,971 and branch offices from 2,316–1,803. However, under the Lula administration, Caixa staff increased to 104,934 employees and branch offices to 2,428 by 2006.

Since capitalization in June 2001, the ratio of fixed assets over equity and Basel Indexes indicate substantial change and transition toward international banking standards. The Basel Index of the Caixa (a measure of the adequacy of reserves against possible losses), increased from 4.9 in March 2001 before capitalization to reach 27.8 and remain twice above the Central Bank minimum of 11.0 at 25.2 in 2006. The ratio of fixed assets as a proportion of equity also declines markedly from 63.8 at year end 2001 to 11.9 in 2007.

Transition toward international accounting standards breaks the time series of Caixa Annual Reports. However, reporting standards used by the Caixa since 2005 provide greater clarity about policies and performance. Table 4.6 reports returns on stockholder equity, assets, Basel solvency index, immobilization index, provisions as a percentage of credit, bank efficiency index and coverage of personnel costs. Caixa performance indicators confirm findings reported in Chapter 2 that Brazilian federal banks produce strong profits and returns while setting aside more provisions and reserves against risk than private or foreign banks. From 2005–8, Caixa returns on stockholder equity remained above 20 per cent per year, reaching 30.6 per cent in 2008 despite the impact of the global financial crisis. Caixa returns on liquid assets remained between 0.9 per cent and 1.3 per cent, just below levels recorded by private and foreign banks. The Basel Index of the Caixa remained well above the 11 per cent level required by the Central Bank, declining from 27.9–20.6 from 2005–8.

The immobilization index of the Caixa increased slightly from 20.1 to 21.0 per cent from 2005–8, suggesting transition toward international banking standards. However, the value of provisions as a percentage of credit operations remains much higher than international practices, albeit declining from 10.1–8.6 per cent from 2005–8. Finally, the deterioration of aggregate measures of efficiency from 64.5–71.4 form 2005–8 suggests a serious distancing from international standards that tend to approach 50.0. If this trend continues, the Caixa may be unable to compete with more efficient private and foreign banks over time.

Table 4.6: Caixa Performance Indicators, 2005–8.

Indicator	2005	2006	2007	2008
Return on Stockholder Equity	26.1	26.0	22.6	30.6
Return on Liquid Assets	1.1	1.1	0.9	1.3
Basel Solvency Index	27.9	25.3	28.9	20.6
Immobilization Index	20.1	19.7	12.9	12.0
Provisions % Credit Operations	10.1	9.8	9.1	8.6
Efficiency Index	64.5	64.2	75.5	71.8
Coverage of Personnel Costs	92.5	89.6	94.3	86.8

Source: Caixa Econômica Federal, Relatórios de Administração, 2005–8.

However, one of the central arguments of this book is that bank efficiency measures should not be considered in isolation. The Caixa retains a larger organizational structure than private or foreign banks because of policy making roles and social and political networks. However, these differences provide competitive advantage in banking. Moreover, higher Caixa personnel costs reflect a corporate policy to favour full-time contracts with organized labour over outsourcing – a policy that reinforces social and political networks but increases personnel costs.

The liability side of Caixa balance sheets from 2005–8 suggest that the bank has distanced itself from reliance on official savings programmes and funds from Treasury in favour of current accounts and savings deposits. Bank deposits (current accounts) increased from R$6.9 to R$13.2 billion in 2005–8, while savings deposits increased from R$53.2 to R$92.5 billion. The increase of mid-term savings deposits originated from sale of savings certificates instead of escrow held by the Caixa, the latter subject to judicial review and removed from balance sheets in 2008. The value of government funds and programmes increased from R$7.9 to R$11.0 billion in 2005–8, but remains less than 10 per cent of total deposits. The total value of deposits increased from 106.9 billion in 2005 (15.6 per cent market share) to over R$165.5 billion in 2008 (a significantly lower 12.9 per cent share of a market that increased from R$682.6 billion to over R$1.27 trillion from 2005–8.

In 2005–8, Caixa lending continued to focus on home finance, increasing from R$20.2 to R$45.0 billion. However, increased lending to consumers (R$8.9 to R$13.7 billion) and business (R$5.7 to R$15.1 billion) suggest diversification of the Caixa across credit markets. In 2005–8, the total value of Caixa lending more than doubled, from R$37.2 to R$80.0 billion. Breakdown of data on Caixa home loans suggests that the bank continues to provide directed credits for acquisition of low income housing while expanding market priced mortgages. The Caixa retains monopoly over use of FGTS funds for home finance, increasing such transfers from R$4.4 to R$10.0 billion in 2005–8.[33] However, market priced mortgage lending also increased five fold from R$1.9 to R$10.6 billion in 2005–8. Meanwhile, directed credit programmes tapping FGTS funds declined to R$1.4 billion by 2008. If compared to the value of home loans extended by the Caixa during the 1990s (R$2.8 billion in 1994 reaching R$6.7 billion in 1997, over half FGTS funds), this suggests a substantial shift toward market priced mortgages at the Caixa during the 2000s.

And unlike the high levels of bad and late credit reported during the adjustment to the end of high inflation in 1994–6 and financial crises (1994–5, 1997, 1998, 1999, 2001, 2003), the level of late loans at the Caixa fell substantially during the years of economic growth and credit expansion in 2004–8. The percentage of late over total loans at the Caixa fell from 6.8 to 4.0 per cent from 2006–8 for commercial loans generally, from 6.2 to 5.9 per cent for consumer loans, and 7.5 to 2.2 per cent for loans to business.[34] In contrast to problems abroad, the value of late home loans as a percentage of total home loans at the Caixa fell from 3.1 to 1.7 from 2005–8.

Caixa credit risk matrices in 2001–8 provide further evidence of improvement in performance and the greater transparency provided by improved Brazilian bank reporting standards (See Table 4.7). In 2001, Central Bank regulations abandoned previous bank reporting of two categories of good and bad credit (good loans <90 days overdue, bad loans >90 days overdue) in favour of international standards of AA-H credit classification and requirement that banks increase or decrease provisions according to the value of loans in these categories. Provision requirements vary from 0 per cent against AA loans to 100 per cent against loans classified as H (over 180 days late).

The value of late loans held by the Caixa over 180 days decreased from 10.4 to 5.1 per cent of total from 2001–8. Furthermore, all categories of late payment (except for loans between 15 and 30 days late) decreased significantly in 2001–8. In comparison, loans classified as AA (paid and guaranteed) and A (paid on time) increased from 5.9 to 9.4 per cent and 24.3 to 33.3 per cent of total loans. The only category of late loans that increased over the period were those 15–30 days overdue (from 12.7 to 27.1 per cent), reflecting the impact of adjustment to international crisis in 2008 (bulk of increase occurs after 2006).

Table 4.7: Caixa AA-H Credit Classification, 2001–8.

	Days Late	Provision	2001	2002	2003	2004	2005	2006	2007	2008
AA	<15	0 per cent	5.9	5.6	6.6	6.3	5.4	5.0	6.3	9.4
A	<15	0.5 per cent	24.3	26.4	31.3	28.8	39.3	43.5	40.1	33.3
B	15–30	1 per cent	12.7	12.6	13.7	13.9	14.3	15.8	20.6	27.1
C	31–60	3 per cent	20.3	16.6	14.5	16.9	16.7	19.2	19.4	19.2
D	61–90	10 per cent	17.8	26.1	20.7	21.7	13.3	6.0	4.5	3.3
E	91–120	30 per cent	1.8	1.9	2.0	2.0	2.2	1.3	0.9	0.7
F	121–50	50 per cent	4.9	1.5	1.5	1.4	1.0	0.7	0.7	0.7
G	151–80	70 per cent	1.5	0.8	0.9	1.0	0.8	1.0	1.0	0.9
H	>180	100 per cent	10.4	8.7	8.5	7.7	6.8	7.2	6.1	5.1
R$ bn			20.94	23.53	26.14	30.16	38.55	47.36	57.39	81.8

Source: Caixa Annual Reports, 2002–8.

A central argument of this study is that Brazilian federal banks have realized competitive advantages over private and foreign banks since liberalization of the industry in the 1990s and transition to new technologies. The Caixa has also increased volume and market shares in card payment markets – one at the center of transition from the old culture of cash and check payments to new use of electronic payments. The number of Caixa debit cards increased from 22.4–48.2 million from 2002–8. Caixa market share of debit cards increased from 19.6 per cent in 2002 to 23.0 per cent in 2005, remaining at 21.9 per cent in 2005.[35]

Two examples illustrate competitive advantages of the Caixa in the card payment industry. Like other banks in Brazil, the Caixa shares an agreement with Visa (now Cielo) for payment processing. However, unlike other banks in Brazil, the Caixa was contracted by the federal government to distribute ATM citizenship cards to recepients of family grants and other transfer programmes and social policies. The Caixa stamped its brandname on the federal government ATM citizenship card and continues to do so, despite charges of unfair competition from private domestic banks. A Caixa request to transform its 110 million ATM citizenship cards into bank cards, currently pending at the Central Bank, would dramatically increase the number of bank card holders in Brazil (estimated 182.4 million at year end 2007).

The Competitive Advantages of Social Policy Agency

The reorientation of the Caixa since 2001 also involved the development of new programmes to encourage downmarket banking and microfinance. In 2002, the bank launched a new account for popular savings and banking-services, Caixa Aqui, that requires neither minimum deposit, nor proof of income, nor proof of residence. If Caixa Aqui clients retain a positive balance for three months, they become eligible for loans up to R$200.00 at interest rates of 2 per cent per month (no questions asked). By February 2004, 1.27 million new accounts had been opened. By year end 2004 accounts surpassed 2.2 million. By 2008, the number of Caixa Aqui accounts opened had reached over 6.8 million (over 2/3 of the total number of 9.87 million popular bank accounts opened according to the Central Bank of Brazil).[36] The Caixa has realized competitive advantages far and above private and foreign banks in reaching downmarket to bring bankless Brazilians into the formal economy.

The Caixa also remains agent for payment of federal government grants, especially since a variety of social policies and transactions were consolidated in Citizenship Cards in July 2003. For example the Caixa processed over 172 million transactions involving R$2.1 million during 2003 for programmes such as Young Agent, student allowances, propane gas assistance, food allowances, family and income allowances, crop guarantees and programmes to eradicate child labour (down from 225.9 million transactions valued at R$3.1 million during 2002). A consequence of Caixa contracts for federal government social policy is that the bank remains owner of the largest data base on social policy in Brazil. Again, this implies a different profile of costs and competitive advantages than private and foreign banks. For example, during 2003 and first semester 2004, the Caixa registered 3.6 million new households and added a separate registry of 4.3 million households (from the school grants programme), increasing the number of households registered to over 13 million by June 2004. This has implications for public policy. While President Silva created two new ministries and a variety of programmes to expand social policies, the Caixa remains at the centre of new social policies because it owns and manages social policy data bases and retains a brand name and national network of branch offices that make it possible to reach those in need.

In sum, since capitalization in 2001, the Caixa has provided social policy options, directed credit and managed a variety of policies during adjustment, recovery and pursuit of faster growth and popular inclusion. Data used to control for abuse of public banking such as bad credit, administrative costs and profit/loss reporting suggests that the Caixa remains within international banking standards and central bank regulations. Higher administrative costs and lower efficiency ratings remain a concern. However, levels of bad credit reported by the Caixa since capitalization in 2001 suggest convergence toward levels reported by private and foreign banks operating in Brazil. And Caixa profits often *outpaced* private and foreign banks while the federal government savings bank has led in terms of popular bank accounts, transition to card payments, provision of social services through bank cards, correspondent banking and other downmarket strategies to reach bankless Brazilians.

Conclusion

Since 1861, Caixas have expanded and contracted under a variety of political regimes and economic circumstances. Founded as part of conservative party reforms under monarchy in 1861 as a philanthropic savings and pawn bank, Caixas were opened in provinces after 1875. From 1861–88, Caixas simply deposited funds at the Finance Ministry. From 1889–1930, republican government retained voluntary service and the philanthropic mission of Caixas, while increasing their autonomy and introducing bank services such as checking, home loans and lending to the public sector. From 1930–45, Caixas became central to national populist strategies of popular inclusion and state-led development under Getulio Vargas. After transition to democracy in 1945, Caixas first expanded but inflation in the 1950s eroded deposits. Increasing administrative costs combined to reduce earnings and erode reserves. After military intervention in 1964, the indexation of savings (1965), consolidation of state government Caixas into a single state owned enterprise (1970) and use of forced savings led to expansion of the Caixa as instrument of military government social and credit policy. During the 1980s, inertial inflation and political vacuum during prolonged transition from military rule left the Caixa as lender of last resort open to political abuse. Price stability in 1994 forced the Caixa to adjust to the end of easy profits from high bank spreads, while policymakers used the bank to acquire bad debt from private and public banks and induce reform of sub-national governments. Reforms reduced Caixa size and market shares during the 1990s. However, since capitalization in 2001, the Caixa continued to implement federal government social policy while expanding traditional business such as home loans and urban development, pursuing new strategies of investment banking and the expansion of popular credit and savings accounts.

This case study begets a question. Does capital flow to or from popular classes through government savings banks? Since the seventeenth century, advocates suggest that savings banks may help those worst off. Scholars in the new political economy and the Marxist tradition suggest that government savings banks tend to extract value from popular classes. The evidence presented in this chapter suggests that the fortunes of popular classes (and other social groups) did change dramatically across Brazilian history. Large gains and losses under volatile conditions of dependent development mark the Brazilian experience. But the causal process is not uniform. Reforms favouring popular inclusion at times added value and promoted improvement. Savings were often eroded by inflation. And sometimes savings accumulated simply because economic growth creates virtuous cycles. This case study traced vast sums that have flowed to and from Brazilian citizens through Caixas Econômicas. Perhaps the central conclusion is that transparency and accountability are critical. Experiences such as adventures in war under monarchy and machine politics under military rule confirm the worst fears of critics of government banking. Savings banks have served to extract rent, provide crony credit and impose losses on those who can least afford it. However, a proviso matters. These phenomena occurred largely under monarchy and military rule.

Since transition from military rule (1985), price stability (1994) and capitalization of the Caixa within international and Brazilian central bank standards (2001), this institution has outperformed commercial competitors. The Caixa remains, according to aggregate measures of cost per loan, less efficient than many private and foreign banks because of its broader network of branch offices and aversion to outsourcing labour. The Caixa also still pales against European savings banks that are deeply embedded in local and regional institutions and markets. A legacy of military rule remains. The Caixa is still a centralised agent for Brazilian *federal* government social policy, an institution that seeks to decentralize, delegate initiatives and reach out to social movements and other forces of democratization. The Caixa seeks not to command heights but to command depth. This case study suggests that savings banks can provide new channels for social inclusion and financial development, while using scale, scope, brand name and vast networks in Brazilian politics, society, business and government to realize competitive advantages in banking and finance. However, paradigms and practices of social banking from abroad suggest that decentralization and democratization have just begun.

The policies and performance of the Caixa since price stability, liberalization of the banking system and entry of new foreign competitors confirm our theory of government bank change. The Brazilian financial system is not converging toward private banking through privatizations. The policy alternatives provided by the Caixa are valued by political elites, social forces, and business groups. The social networks and political webs that embed Caixa policies and performance provide competitive advantages over private and foreign banks. This supports theories of relational banking and institutional foundations of competitive advantage. Brazil still lacks the deeply leveraged banks and embedded markets of advanced economies. And high interest rates and barriers to competition in the very concentrated banking system may still shelter the Caixa in ways not sustainable over time. However, the record to date is clear. The Caixa has provided policy alternatives for development, social inclusion and democratization while realizing competitive advantages over private and foreign banks. As banking is revolutionized by new information and communication technologies, the competitive advantages of savings banks help sustain their social mandates.

Appendix: Legislation on Savings Banks

Decree 575, 10 January 1849
  Sets requirements for private business corporations.
Law 1083, 22 August 1860.
  Bank Regulations and Savings and Pawn Bank operating principles.
Decree 2.723, 12 January 1861.
  Creates Caixa Econômica e um Monte de Socorro in Rio de Janeiro
Decree 2.847, 16 November 1861.
  Further regulation of Caixa
Decree 3.699, 19 Septemner 1866.
  Increases pawn limits to Five years.
Decree 5.594, 18 April 1874.
  Creates and Regulates Provincial Caixas Econômicas e Montes de Socorro.
Decree 3.313, 16 October 1886.
  Regulates lottery, orphan loans and savings deposits.
Decree 9.738, 2 April 1887.
  Annexed Caixas without pawn services to Provincial Treasury offices.
Decree 1168 December 1892.
  Regulates Caixa organization in states.
Law 559, 31 December 1898.
  Introduces interstate deposits across Caixas.
Decree 2.591, 7 August 1912.
  Introduces and regulates payment and acceptance of checks.
Decree 11.820, 15 December 1915.
Regulates division of independent and annexed (to State Treasury offices)
  Caixas, based   on receipts sufficient to pay costs and accumu-
  late reserve and patrimony funds. Introduces loans backed by federal
  government bonds, letters and notes below ten contos. Women freed
  to open and solely operate accounts unless expressly prohibited by
  husband.
Decree 17.146, 16 December 1925.
  Introduces payroll lending for federal employees.
Decree 19.834, 8 April 1931.

Eliminates Caixa autonomy, placing them under Finance Ministry.

Decree 19.870, 15 April 1931.

Requires deposit of escrow (depósitos judiciais) at Caixas.

Decree 19.987, 15 April 1931.

Requires deposit of all contractual guarantees at Caixas.

Decree 20.225, 18 July 1931.

Limits payroll lending to Pension Funds of state and federal government employees, Caixa employees, Military clubs and non-profit entities.

Decree 20.383, 9 September 1931.

Increases to 20:000$000 limit on value of federal government depoists at Caixa earning interest.

Decree 24.427, 4 June 1934.

Reorganizes Caixas, creating Superior Council, entrance examinations and monopoly of pawn operations.

Law 370, 4 January 1937.

Regulates bank deposits.

Decree-Law 854, 12 November 1938.

Regulates lottery concessions (modified by Decree-Law 2.980, 24 January 1941 and Decree-Law 6.259, 10 February 1944).

Decree-Law 8.257, 30 November 1945.

Grants independence to Caixas in states of Amazonas, Pará, Maranhão, Ceará, Espírito Santo, Santa Catarina and Mato Grosso.

Decree-Law 8.455, 26 December 1945.

Decentralizes organization of Caixas in states.

Decree 25.733, 29 October 1948.

Authorizes postal savings offices.

Decree 50.954, 14 July 1961.

Transfers Lottery to Caixa Superior Council.

Law 4.380, 21 August 1964.

Introduces monetary correction of home loans, creates Banco Nacional da Habitação (National Housing Bank, BNH), Sociedades de Crédito Imobiliário (home credit societies), Letras Imobiliárias (mortage securities), Serviço Federal de Habitação e Urbanismo (Federal Housing and Urban Service). Directs 70 per cent of lottery receipts to home contruction below sixty times minimum salary.

Decree 55.279, 22 December 1964.

Adapts Caixas Econômicas Federais to the Sistema Financeiro da Habitação (Home Finance System).

Decree-Law 204, 27 February 1967.

Ends lottery concessions and destines lottery receipts to social and medical projects.

Decree 63.417, 11 October 1968.
  Installs comission to present proposal for reform of Caixas.
Decree-Law 759, 12 August 1969 (and Decree-Law 66.303, 6 March 1970).
Create state owned enterprise, Caixa Econômica Federal via commission of Giampaolo Marcello Falco, Sebastião José França dos Anjos e Cláudio Alberto Leão de Medeiros.
Decree 66.027, 31 December 1969.
  Destines 2.5 per cent of lottery sales at Caixas to fund Caixa Econômica Federal.
  Complementary Law 6, 30 June 1970.
  Concedes tax exemption to Caixa Econômica Federal.
Decree 81.171, 3 January 1978.
  Approves new Caixa statutes.
Decree 97.547, 1 March 1989
  Statutes of Caixa Econômica Federal.
Decree 2055, 31 October 1996.
  Alters Caixa Statutes Article 8 on use of FGTS funds.
Decree 2254, 16 June 1997.
  Approves Caixa legal statutes.
Decree 2644, 29 June 1998.
  Alters composition of directorship and regulates staff careers.
Decree 2943, 20 January 1999.
  Approves Caixa legal statutes.
Decree 3851, 27 June 2001
Approves Caixa legal statutes and determines asset transfers to Emgea and infusion of capital.
Decree 3882, 8 August 2001.
  Alters legal status of Caixa.
Decree 4371, 11 Septemer 2002.
  Approves Caixa legal statutes.
Decree 4376 13 September 2002.
  Approves Caixa legal statutes.
Decree 5056, 29 April 2004
  Approves Caixa legal statutes.
Decree 6132, 22 June 2007
  Approves Caixa legal statutes.

5 THE BANCO NACIONAL DE DESENVOLVIMENTO ECONÔMICO E SOCIAL (NATIONAL BANK FOR ECONOMIC AND SOCIAL DEVELOPMENT, BNDES)

For almost three decades since its creation in 1952, the National Bank for Economic Development (BNDE) set new standards for institutionalization that had a broad impact on the economic bureaucracy and policy-making in general. The bank set the standard for administrative professionalism and its *técnicos* gained a reputation as among the most competent in Brazil. Managers codified bank procedures and defended them and the bank in intrastate politics. The BNDE also developed a distinctive mentality of nationalist developmentalism that informed its policies and policy battles.

Ben R. Schneider,
Politics within the State: Elite Bureaucrats &
Industrial Policy in Authoritarian Brazil
(Pittsburgh, PA: University of Pittsburgh Press, 1991), p. 35.

The BNDES is a paradigmatic development bank. The trajectory of the BNDES involves a sequence of policies and business practices that have shaped Brazilian development. During the 1950s, the BNDE supplied directed credit for transportation, electric energy, infrastructure and steel production. During the 1960s, the bank diversified under financial reforms. During the 1970s, the BNDE helped complete state-led import substitution industrialization by channelling foreign finance and forced savings into capital goods, project lending and regional development programmes. During the 1980s, the bank shifted away from public investment because of fiscal crisis and foreign debt. During the 1990s, the BNDES became agent for privatization of state owned enterprises. The bank remained virtually the only domestic source of long-term finance during a decade of financial crises in emerging markets (1994–2003). Since 2000, the BNDES has shifted toward 'second generation' reforms designed to finance the private sector, free market forces and deepen capital markets while attempting to increase lending to small enterprises. From 2004–8, capital inflows and a booming domestic stock market reinforced the capacity of the BNDES to underwrite long-term investments and transform large Brazilian firms into multinational corporations. The bank once again provided critical counter-cyclical lending during the 2008 financial crisis. This case study captures much of development trajectory of Brazil and provides an additional perspective on Brazilian federal banking. The reality that the second largest domestic creditor and primary source for long term finance remains a government owned development bank.

The BNDES has also been at the centre of debates about development policy. Since founding in 1952 as part of US–Brazil Commission recommendations, debates within the bank have involved political parties, other ministries and agencies responsible for economic policies, public opinion and academic debates. Secondary studies and BNDES documents, publications, balance sheets and staff memoirs provide a clearer record of this very large financial institution.[1] The epigram from Schneider sums previous research. Willis and Martins also stressed the fundamental importance of the BNDE in Brazilian government planning and economic policy before 1964.[2] However, like many institutions, the BNDES *lost* institutional autonomy and operational independence under military rule (1964–85). The bank turned to more liberal policies and privatizations in the 1990s. This policy shift was profound. A paradigmatic development bank in state-centred Brazil became primary agent of privatizations during the 1990s. Since 2000, BNDES policies have been described as neo-developmentalist, a doctrine that first attempted to shift market-centred policies toward small, medium and micro businesses, but under the Lula government has increasingly sought to transform select Brazilian firms into multinational enterprises while also shaping domestic growth. Before turning to the case study, brief review of development banking abroad sets the context and comparative perspective.

Development Banking

Development banking describes a variety of institutions that financed industrialization during late development across Continental Europe, Asia, Latin America and other developing nations.[3] These were commanding heights in the traditional sense. Government development banks were founded to provide finance and credit on terms beyond that which private banks or markets were willing to provide.[4] Given that private banks were unable to measure and unwilling to bear long-term risks associated with infrastructure investments,[5] Continental European governments founded industrial development banks in the early nineteenth century.[6] The French government Credit Mobilier soon became both model abroad and shareholder in other European development banks as its ability to finance railroads and accelerate industrialization became widely acknowledged.[7] The Credit Mobilier also became a model for banks in Asia, such as the Industrial Bank of Japan and Industrial Bank of India.[8] Development banks were also founded after World War I for European governments to provide cash, subsidised loans and guarantee of bank bonds for industrial reconstruction.[9] After World War II, the Kreditanstalt fur Weidaraufbau (Reconstruction Credit Agency, KfW) and Japan Development Bank were created to channel Allied government funds for reconstruction. German and Japanese development banks thereafter adopted new policies and strategies as development challenges evolved. Newly independent countries in Africa and Asia also created development banks after World War II to channel World Bank loans and foreign aid.[10]

Gerschenkron, Myrdal, Lewis and other economists argued that development banks were essential to accelerate industrialization in late development. Development banks were central to the commanding heights approach. Johnson's study of the Japanese Ministry of Technology and Industry (MITI) remains a classic account of finance, late development and government intervention.[11] Hirschman argued that economic development in Latin America required inducement mechanisms and policy coordination to channel foreign assistance as well as public and private investments.[12] State development banks and agencies were also cited as critical agents for accelerated growth in developing countries of Asia.[13]

However, times have changed. The different character of manufacturing, information technology, financial markets and banking in the twenty-first century suggest that more complex tradeoffs between markets and government intervention now obtain.[14] Woo-Cumings summarizes three problems with development banks.[15] First, because development banks tend to deeply leverage large industrial groups with bank credit, state-owned and private enterprises avoid going public through issues of equities. Second, the massive scale of political and economic interests associated with development banks often increase moral hazard and require costly bailouts. Development banks can protect outmoded industry, impede economic innovation and sustain bad equilibrium. Large scale development projects are also notorious for their impact on the environment. Finally, Woo-Cumings argues that development banks tend to unfairly transfer the cost of risk through either inflationary finance that monetarises industrial losses, or through government infusions of equity that hides losses in government accounts. For Woo-Cumings, the Asian financial crisis during 1997–8 reinforced views that development banking places domestic political economies at greater risk.[16]

Development banks fell from favour after 1980 as policies of liberalization and privatization were adopted to free market forces. Development banks also inspire essentially contested, diametrically opposed theories and concepts about government intervention, banks and financial markets. For critics, development banks reproduce financial repression, favour rent seeking and unfairly subsidize industry. Their centralized technocratic decisions tend to remain beyond public scrutiny and may have profound environmental impacts. However, for economists and policymakers in developing countries, these banks were created precisely because of market failures. Development banks were created because private banks were unwilling to provide long term finance for industrialization and infrastructure. Development banking also presents difficulties for international trade negotiations, given the need to reconcile comparative advantage, relative prices and subsidies. Opposing theories frame this case study. However, it is important to note that a positive sum, bi-lateral policy consensus was behind the creation of the BNDE. The BNDE emerged from US–Brazilian diplomatic collaboration, received funds and training from multilateral institutions and has involved other foreign agencies and investors since. The following sections examine BNDE(S) policies and performance since founding in 1952.

From US–Brazilian Joint Commissions to UN-ECLA – BNDE Plans, 1949–53

After World War II, Brazilian diplomats sought to secure foreign finance and investment during negotiations at Bretton Woods and the signing of Inter-American treaties. However, given greater needs in Europe and Asia and challenges from the USSR and China, broader policies along the lines of the Marshall Plan or Asian development finance remained on hold. Instead, Brazil hosted a series of bi-lateral commissions that advocated private and domestic resources. In 1947, a US–Brazilian Technical Commission was charged with writing development plans for Brazil. In 1949, the Abbink Mission published a review of the Brazilian economy and called for joint ventures among public, private and foreign investors to overcome bottlenecks in transportation and energy. A US–Brazilian Joint Commission designed plans for collaboration and, in September 1951, the US and Brazil signed agreement to share foreign and domestic funding. The World Bank and US Eximbank approved $500.0 million in credits for projects defined by a second US–Brazil Joint Commission, while a Brazilian Economic Re-Equipment Fund (Programa de Reaparelhamento Econômico) based on a 15 per cent premium on income tax provided further resources.[17] The Vargas government also published the Plano Salte (Jump-Ahead Plan) for 1952–3, a plan designed to accelerate industrial growth through Banco do Brasil credits underwritten by Treasury. The BNDE was created in June 1952 to manage these development projects.

From 1952 through 1955, the bulk of BNDE finance was directed to transportation and electric energy. Funds from the Inter-American Development Bank, 4 per cent of Federal Savings Bank (Caixa) deposits and 3 per cent of federal government social security funds provided further working capital for the BNDE. Roberto Campos recalls five criteria for early BNDE project approval (reduction of bottlenecks, generation of foreign exchange, utilization of local inputs, utilization of private finance, and forward and backward linkages). However, targets and funding levels forecast in the Joint US–Brazil Technical Commission were not met, especially in foreign finance. And once conflicts between the Vargas administration and foreign business escalated over charges of under-factoring profit remittances, the World Bank suspended relations with Brazil.[18] During 1954 and 1955, the BNDE exceeded reserves to cover project financing until the government extended a 15 per cent forced savings programme for five years and created four funds and an electric energy tax to finance infrastructure projects.

The meeting of the United Nations Economic Commission on Latin America (ECLA) in Rio de Janeiro during 1953 and creation of a BNDE-ECLA working group became a turning point for the bank and Brazilian economic policy.[19] The BNDE-ECLA working group shifted emphasis to internal savings.[20] Celso Furtado's 'Perspectivas da Economia Brasileira' (Perspectives for the Brazilian Economy) summarized this new ECLA-BNDE view and became core reading in BNDE management training after 1956.

The BNDE remained a very small organization. The bank was first managed by an administrative council staffed by members of the US–Brazil Joint Commission and consultants. By 1953, staff reached 150 (six lawyers, ten economists, twelve engineers, 31 technical assistants and 91 administrative staff). In 1952, funds for one major project were disbursed.[21] In 1953, five contracts were funded.[22] Through the second half of the 1950s, the BNDE funded between twenty and thirty projects per year.[23] As Leff notes, 'once the railways had been provided with new equipment in the early and mid-1950s, the great bulk of the Development Bank's resources went into four public sector projects – two in steel and two in electricity'.[24] Early BNDE lending thus targeted transportation, infrastructure and electric power generation and distribution.

The suicide of Getulio Vargas in August 1954 increased political tensions and conflicts over development policies. Provisional government and elections the next year led to adoption of new policies at the BNDE. However, the second cycle of BNDE investments and policies were shaped by the development targets of President Kubitschek for 1956–60.

Kubitscheck's *Plano de Metas* and BNDE Developmentalism, 1956–60

The Kubitschek administration centralized planning in a National Development Council and increased the pace of investments to spur economic growth.[25] BNDE Presidents served as Executive Secretary for the National Development Council, while the bank also staffed executive groups created for each industrial sector. Electric energy provision was delegated to independent autarchies through funds provided by federal government, administered by BNDE and coordinated by state governments and state owned enterprises.[26] BNDE representatives also participated in the SUMOC monetary authority and the Customs Commision, charged with coordinating development programmes with economic trends.[27] Government banks financed 14.5 per cent of investments toward Kubitschek's targets from 1956–60, while federal government budgets accounted for 39.7 per cent, state government budgets 10.4 per cent and investments from private and mixed-enterprises 35.4 per cent.[28]

During the late 1950s, the BNDE also shifted from direct finance to shareholding and other forms of participation with state, mixed and private enterprises while serving as guarantor for finance in foreign currencies backed by Treasury. Direct credits decline from 100–51 per cent of BNDES operations from 1955–9.[29] This transition coincides with the expansion of BNDE finance beyond sectors favoured during the first cycle of investments (railroads and electric energy). The bank shifted to finance of basic industries. The origins of BNDE resources also changed. Early reliance on specially designed taxes, savings bank deposits and social security funds were replaced by sectoral funds voted by Congress or channelled from foreign aid or international financial institutions. Total BNDE resources increased from 2 billion cruzeiros in 1955 to over 25 billion cruzeiros by 1959.

The BNDE was also charged with supervising government investments in state owned enterprises. BNDE planners helped avert repetition of mistakes and funding delays experienced during the first lending cycle (1952–5). The Brazilian congress renewed the BNDE charter in 1956 for 10 years, stipulating a minimum of 25 per cent of BNDE finance and credit for underdeveloped regions. In 1956, the BNDE also introduced monetary correction that indexed contracts against inflation, increased personnel and opened regional offices. The bank also hired a new generation of staff that became central to the identity, independence and policies of the BNDES over the next twenty years.[30] BNDE underwriting of credits in foreign currency also increased from US$8.0–US$263.79 million from 1954–60.[31] And while projects in electricity and transportation predominated during the mid-1950s, by 1960 80 per cent of transactions involving foreign currency at the BNDE were channelled to basic industry. This shift of Brazilian economic policy and BNDE lending away from basic infrastructure toward import substitution industrialization is a paradigmatic experience of commanding heights. The BNDE allocated directed credit for rapid industrialization.

By the end of the 1950s, three cycles of BNDE investments had been completed. Investments in steel, electric energy and railways had matured and led to the creation of state owned enterprises for each sector. Eletrobras, a state owned energy monopoly, ensured subsidised electric energy for industrial development.

Rede Ferroviária Federal S.A., the national rail company, provided transportation despite massive foreign direct investment in auto production and public construction of highways during the 1950s.[32] The role of the BNDE in two failed attempts to stabilize the Brazilian economy under democracy during the early 1960s involves broader conflicts between populist government, political coalitions, national developmentalists and groups favouring more orthodox policies to sustain foreign investment. The breakdown of democracy and military intervention on 31 March 1964 is beyond the scope of this study. However, from the perspective of the BNDE, military rule inaugurated a period of more orthodox policies of economic adjustment and market-centred financial reforms.

The BNDE under Military Government and Financial Reforms, 1964–7

Reforms during the first years of military rule[33] included creation of new funds and subsidiary divisions at the BNDE to channel forced savings, government resources, foreign investment and private finance to strategic industrial sectors. Policies were based on liberal economic ideas and military doctrines of national security and development.[34] During the 1960s, the BNDE sought to mobilize private capital through issue of government bonds and provide new incentives for firms to offer equity and investors to purchase shares. The BNDE served as intermediary to channel new sources from world liquidity and foreign banks seeking opportunities beyond advanced economies. BNDES regional offices were also created for regional development programmes.

In 1964, a science and technology development fund was created at the BNDE.[35] After transfer to the Planning Ministry and up-scaling to agency status, this fund supervised transfer, development and diffusion of technology throughout the 1970s.[36] Another BNDE fund for project development was created with USAID and Inter-American Development Bank support. The BNDE also helped create and finance networks of Brazilian industrial firms to gain scale and reduce cost of imported machinery and equipment. The BNDE Industrial Finance Agency and Fundo de Desenvolvimento Técnico e Científico (Technical and Scientific Development Fund, Funtec)[37] channelled resources originating in loans and aid from bi-lateral and multilateral agencies, foreign and domestic financial markets and Banco do Brasil credits. These funds linked networks of buyers and sellers of heavy industrial equipment to modernize Brazilian industry through domestic product quotas and finance at below market rates with longer terms. BNDE networks and financing programmes helped deepen industrialization through the 1970s.[38]

In 1965, two financial agencies were also created at the BNDE. The Programa de Financiamento às Pequenas e Médias Empresas (Finance Programme for Small & Medium Enterprises, Fipeme) channelled resources to small and medium enterprises. The Fundo Agroindustrial de Reconversão (Fund for Agroindustrial Conversion, Funar) was created to administer funds allocated in the federal government budgets inder the Lei do Estatuto da Terra (Law of Land Statutes) and provide incentives, subsidies and grants for agro-industrial development projects. In 1966, the Fundo de Desenvolvimento da Produtividade (Productivity Development Fund, Fundepro) was created to channel finance to regional and state government banks.[39] Three BNDE credit lines were created for underdeveloped regions.[40] A further subsidiary was created in 1967 (later spun off) for small and medium enterprises; the Centro Brasileiro de Assistência Gerencial à Pequena e Média Empresa (Brazilian Centre for Management Assistance for Small and Medium Enterprises, Cebrae).[41]

These BNDE innovations were part of policies designed under military government to mobilize private capital and deepen the Brazilian financial system.[42] However, like the unexpected consequences of reforms discussed in preceeding case studies, BNDE policies also reinforced state-led finance and state owned enterprises under military rule. Instead of building the private sector and pursuing liberalization policies, policymakers under military government increased the scale and scope of government banking. The BNDE was transformed into a state owned enterprise in 1971. New subsidiaries and programmes increased staff at the BNDE from 600–1,500 from 1971–5. BNDE policy under military rule also reinforced statism. During the 1970s, the BNDE channelled resources to basic industries at negative real interest rates and used subsidies to purchase shares in private companies.[43] Monetary correction was used to direct credit and realize subsidies. BNDE loans were often adjusted at 1/5 of indexes used to protect contracts against inflation. This implied 4/5 reductions in the cost of debt as inflation reached record levels.

Reforms also placed the BNDE at the centre of networks of regional and state government development banks. The Fundo de Modernização e Reorganização Industrial (Regional Industrial Modernization and Reorganization Fund, FMRI) was created in 1970 to channel 25 per cent of BNDE finance to underdeveloped states and regions as required by the first National Development Plan. The BNDE also completed viability studies for economic sectors and geographical regions[44] while attempting to maximize technology transfers.[45]

Forced savings programmes created under military rule also increased BNDE capital for industrial development during the 1970s.[46] From 1966–70, the Imposto de Operações Financeiras (Financial Operations Tax, IOF) served as capital base for BNDE lending. In 1974, the BNDE became responsible for administration of two official savings programmes, the Programa de Integração Social (Programme for Social Integration, PIS) and Programa de Formação do Patrimônio do Servidor Público (Programme for Formation of Public Servant Patrimony, Pasep). These funds from payroll taxes were designed as worker retirement and savings funds and remain central for the bank in the twenty-first century. These two funds summed to almost two thirds of BNDES liabilities in 2004.

Contrary to the market centred intent of reforms under military rule in the 1960s, the BNDE and other federal banks became exclusive agents of long-term credit and finance during the 1970s. Collapse of domestic stock markets in 1972 also dashed hopes of accelerating growth through equity issues. Instead, state owned enterprises increased their share of stock market transactions from 31.9–61.3 per cent from 1967–73.[47] The capitalization of private companies on stock markets fell from 0.43 per cent of GDP (1970–3), to 0.11 per cent (1974–9) reaching 0.18 per cent of GDP (1980–3). In comparison, federal government finance increased from 3.2–23.2 per cent of total domestic investment from 1967–79. BNDE long-term investment increased from Cr$437.0 million – Cr$175.4 billion from 1967–79. The Banco Nacional de Habitação (National Housing Bank, BNH) created in 1968 increased lending from Cr$ 1.4 billion in 1968 to Cr$ 359.1 billion in 1979. Federal banks thereby allocated massive resources from public savings and foreign investment to state owned enterprises and home construction under military government.

The oil price shock in 1973 is widely considered as a turning point in the international economy. This coincided with pre-election politics (in limited electoral-college under military rule) and election of General Geisel to the Presidency in 1974, followed by an audacious attempt to deepen import substitution industrialization rather than slow the economy. This provides further evidence against correlation between military rule and liberalization in Brazil. From 1973–9, government investments increased from 17.0–30.0 per cent of total value of long-term investments.

The BNDE and State-Led Import Substitution Industrialization: PND II, 1974–9

The BNDE remained central for Geisel's attempt to spurn orthodox adjustment in favour of state-led strategies to complete import substitution industrialization. The II Plano Nacional de Desenvolvimento (Second National Development Plan, PND II) embodied this counter-cyclical strategy based on directed credit and state-led finance.[48] Unlike reforms in the 1960s, the PND II omitted initiatives and policies for private finance and banking. Plans were instead based on the assumption that profitable investments would attract the private sector. The BNDE would lead by providing project finance.[49] Economic policy and planning was also centralized by creating a Conselho de Desenvolvimento Econômico (Economic Development Council, CDE) composed of five economic ministries directly responsible to the presidency. Federal banks were placed under authority of the Council to coordinate design and implementation of policy.

By 1975, interest rate hikes designed to reduce the money supply created a credit crunch for the vast array of PND II industrial development projects. This placed the BNDE and its ability to lend at below market interest rates at the centre of political and economic pressures. The government used BNDE credits as counter-cyclical policy and lender of last resort. This downturn after a period of strong growth during the late 1960s and early 1970s also revealed a new dynamic emphasized in preceding chapters. Government paper indexed against inflation became a major source of income not only for banks and financial institutions, but also for commercial and industrial firms. This liquidity preference toward liquid short term instruments indexed against inflation has been described as the 'financialization' of the Brazilian economy, a phenomena that would accelerate until price stability returned under the Real Plan (1993–4). The breakdown of monetary order, erosion of confidence in the stock market after collapse in 1971 and the high cost and short term of credit transformed the BNDES into the only source for long term lending in Brazil.

BNDE policies deepened networks and relations across state, domestic private and multinational firms in Brazil during the 1970s by channelling vast amounts of foreign finance into the economy and participation in the creation of new associations and co-funding arrangements, especially in energy, basic industries and capital goods production.[50] New BNDE subsidiaries were created. The Programa de Operações Conjuntas (Programme of Joint Operations, POC) substituted the Fipeme in 1974 and delegated risk analysis and credit approval to partner banks and financial institutions. The BNDE thereby maintained a centralized structure without branch offices while substantially increasing the flow of credit to and through other federal and private commercial banks. Observers of the late 1970s emphasize the importance of BNDE policies for concerted intervention and rapid growth from 1974–80.[51] BNDE polices complemented protectionist trade policies, government procurements of capital goods and technology development policies to complete import substitution industrialization under military rule.

Three BNDE subsidiaries were created during the 1970s to capitalize firms through equity issues: Insumos Básicos S.A. (Basic Inputs, Fibase); Mecânica Brasileira S.A. (Brazilian Machinery, Embramec) and; Investimentos Brasileiros S.A. (Brazilian Investments, Ibrasa).[52] BNDES subsidiaries were fused in 1982 to create BNDES Participações S.A. (BNDES Participations, BNDESPAR). In 1976, the BNDE also created the Programa de Estímulo ao Desenvolvimento do Mercado de Capitais (Programme for Stimulation of Capital Market Development, Procap) that guaranteed share purchases. The BNDE also encouraged alternative energy development.[53] BNDE(S) investments in domestic stock markets failed to take off in the 1980s and '90s, but have proven central in the unprecedented capitalization of the Bovespa stock market since 2000.

In 1979, the BNDE was transferred from the Ministry of Planning to the Ministry of Industry and Commerce (where it would remain until 1982). Schneider sees this as the culmination of a process under military rule designed to limit BNDE autonomy, also exemplified by the appointment of political allies of the president opposed to the national-developmental views of bank officials.[54] Transfer of the BNDE to the Ministry of Industry and Commerce also allowed the bank to *escape* monetary and fiscal controls set by the Ministry of Planning and National Monetary Council while approximating BNDE programmes and other policies for technology and industry.[55]

The context for Brazilian development and BNDES policies changed profoundly after the Mexican government declared moratorium on payment of foreign debt in August 1982. This stopped foreign financial flows into Brazil until liberalization policies and price stability began to recover the confidence of foreign investors twelve years later. The second oil shock of 1979 and the Latin American debt crisis during the 1980s forced a shift in policies away from state-led strategies. The BNDES escaped austerity during 1979, but lending reductions imposed by the National Monetary Council during 1980 reduced BNDE programmes. In retrospect, import substitution policies during the 1970s left Brazil with a more complex and diverse industrial park. However, the dual foreign debt and fiscal crises during the 1980s and new realities of information technology and private sector driven innovation challenged policymakers to develop new policies under tough circumstances of foreign debt and fiscal deficits. One internal change at the bank was the elaboration of economic forecasting within the BNDE. The excessive optimism of development plans in the 1970s and overshooting of financial markets in 1979 demonstrated the need for better internal forecasting, risk and credit analysis.[56]

The preceding case study chapters on the Banco do Brasil and Caixa found reforms under military rule in the 1960s to have produced state-led directed credit and policy centralization. This also holds true for the stock market. Instead of private banking and dispersed individual shareholders, the BNDES became primary agent in equity markets during the 1970s and early 1980s. BNDE equity holdings increased in real terms from CR$ 32.1 billion in 1978 to over Cr$62.0 billion in 1985 before privatization sales began. While the bank incurred a Cr$90.4 billion loss on equities during 1986, losses from equity operations normally remained low. Lower than the costs of socializing risks emphasized by critics of government banking such as Woo-Cumings. Further study of BNDE policies and equity market transactions is needed. However, the replacement of private by public finance suggests that reforms introduced in the 1960s failed to free market forces and or mobilize private capital through equity markets. Liberalization policies would be reinforced by foreign debt, inertial inflation and fiscal imbalances during the 1980s.

Foreign Debt and Fiscal Deficits: The Adjustment of the BNDES, 1982–90

The Latin American debt crisis shifted BNDES policies away from state led development strategies toward the privatization of Brazilian state owned enterprises.[57] The policies described above such as subsidiary purchase of shares in private firms, the subsidization and guarantee of equity sales and purchases and other incentives for capital market development transformed the BNDES into the primary institution responsible for the dismantling of government ownership and floating state owned enterprises on equity markets in the late 1980s and through the 1990s. This involved massive subsidies to the private sector and a massive transfer of assets from public to private ownership.[58] This was done in part from ideological design and part because of the reality that resources no longer flowed from abroad. Privatizations were also designed to shed large state owned enterprises often overstaffed and stripped of assets through murky transactions under military rule. From 1986–90, a series of Central Bank resolutions and National Monetary Council directives capped and finally banned government bank lending to state owned enterprises. After transition from military rule in 1985, foreign debt, fiscal crisis, record inflation and a series of anti-inflation packages that distorted prices and broke contracts summed to monetary chaos.

In real terms, BNDE finance declined 51 per cent from 1980–9. By 1990, BNDES credits and finance had fallen to almost one-quarter 1975 levels. As Bonelli and Pinheiro note:

> The macroeconomic and fiscal crises over the last 13 years seriously reduced the volume of resources available to the BNDES and, consequently, the volume of BNDES loans. From 1975 through 1985, BNDES finance reached a fifth of domestic capital formation, increasing the relatively high levels of investment during this period. At present, the bank finances, directly and indirectly, approximately eight per cent of brut investment in Brazil.[59]

Times were bad for the BNDES. However, they were worse for private banks and capital markets. Despite the marked declines in BNDES lending, the bank remained the only domestic source for long term funding during the 1980s. The BNDES became arbitrator of bankruptcies, selecting who in domestic industry and commerce would survive. This reality during the 1980s was shared by the Caixa and Banco do Brasil. Federal banks became *de facto* lenders of last resort. Because the BNDES could subsidize equity purchases, launch and liquidate firms, privatize state enterprises and buy or sell shares, the bank made and unmade many private firms. The BNDES thereby served as policy lever as government priorities shifted from large-scale basic industries to information technologies and exports.

BNDES's predominant position in stock markets transformed the bank into principal agent of privatizations. Twenty state owned enterprises were sold from 1981–4 generating US$190.0 million for government. Of the 268 state owned enterprises identified by government census in 1979, 76 were private firms assumed by the government, many by the BNDES, because of defaulting on finance and credit. Sale of these firms during the 1980s provided the BNDES with experience and precedents that transformed the bank into the primary agent of privatizations during the 1990s. In late 1985, the BNDES sold new shares to capitalize the state oil company Petrobrás. In 1987, the BNDES accelerated sale of state owned enterprises.[60]

Amidst foreign debt, fiscal crisis and transition to democracy, the BNDES also improved internal planning, analysis and forecasting. By 1990, the BNDES maintained among the best departments for credit rating, project analysis, economic forecasting, regional economics and commercial and financial law in Brazil.[61] Staff also produced discussion papers that shaped policy debates. A study produced by BNDES and Petrobras staff in the 1980s entitled 'competitive integration' was later described by newspaper columnist Luis Nassif as 'The Programme that Changed Brazil'. Competitive integration called for capitalization of large Brazilian enterprises to compete abroad as multinational corporations.

Privatization of the Developmental State, BNDES Policies in the 1990s

Pressures of foreign debt and fiscal crisis reached critical juncture in 1990 when President Collor confiscated an estimated 83 per cent of domestic financial assets and accelerated policies of liberalization and privatization.[62] The monetary shock of the Collor Plan forced federal banks to reorient policies and rely on internal resources. The BNDES shifted policy to the private sector. A ban on government bank lending to state owned enterprises reinforced this shift. From 1990 through 2002, the BNDES privatized 119 state owned enterprises and generated an estimated US$70.3 billion for government accounts. Despite opposition from governors, political parties and social movements, privatization of state owned steel, electric energy, petrochemical and telecommunications monopolies were completed during the 1990s.[63] However, instead of privatizations shrinking BNDES market share, the reorientation of the BNDES toward the private sector increased the share of BNDES in Brazilian political economy and banking. From 1975–85, BNDES finance remained approximately 20 per cent of gross domestic capital formation. By 1990, BNDES share of gross capital formation had declined to 3.25 per cent. However, by 1999 the BNDES had increased share to 6 per cent.

The BNDES organized privatization auctions and financed newly privatized firms to expand basic services and infrastructure. The fiscal, financial and credit retrenchments of the 1980s were over. From 1993 to 1998, BNDES credits multiply fourfold, from R$6.73 billion (US$3.22 billion) to R$27.79 billion (US$16.34 billion). Privatizations profoundly altered Brazilian political economy and the place of federal banks. For the BNDES, policies shifted from the public to the private sector while promoting exports to reduce the vulnerability of the Brazilian economy.

In 1991, the BNDES created an export promotion programme, later renamed BNDES-Exim (BNDES Export-Import Bank), to channel export finance to medium size enterprises.[64] By 1999, BNDES-Exim credits reached a quarter of BNDES lending. The BNDES also attempted to shift away from large projects toward small and medium enterprises, commerce and the service sector. This increased the number of BNDES credit operations. By 2000, the number of loans had tripled from levels in the early 1990s, reaching 144,000 in 2004. A Fundo de Garantia Para a Promoção da Competitividade (Guarantee Fund for Competitivity Promotion, FGPC) created in 1988 shared risks with commercial banks in operations for small and medium businesses.

From 1990–2000, BNDES policies also sought to deepen domestic equity markets, free market forces and support fiscal reforms. By 1993, the BNDES had privatized eight state owned steel enterprises and initiated the liquidation of the government holding entity Siderbrás.[65] The bank organized twenty two privatization auctions during 1994. During 1995, the BNDES began privatization of public services such as electric energy, highways, railways and ports.[66] The bank also induced reforms in state government through the Programa do Governo Federal de Apoio à Reestruturação e ao Ajuste Fiscal dos Estados (Federal Government Programme for Assistance in Reform and Fiscal Adjustment in States). In 1995, concessions to distribute electric energy in several Brazilian states were auctioned. During 1996, state owned petrochemical enterprises were privatized, further electric energy and transportation privatization auctions were held and the Rede Ferroviária Federal SA (RFFSA) was sold, bringing the total number of privatizations to forty seven.

The largest privatization was Telebrás, the state owned telecommunications monopoly that was split into auctions held in 1998 totalling over 22.0 billion reals, the last major privatization under a fixed foreign exchange rate. Again, privatizations did not imply downsizing at the BNDES. From 1993 to 1998, BNDES finance increased four fold from R$6.73 billion to R$27.79 billion (deflated to December 2001). Finally, share sales of Petrobras[67] and privatization of Banespa (São Paulo state government bank) during 2000 generated R$14.4 billion reals for the federal government. In one of the first measures designed to encourage broader individual participation in the stock market, the Petrobras auction permitted use of social security savings (Fundo de Garantia por Tempo de Serviço, FGTS) for purchase of shares.

In 1998, the BNDES also commissioned consultancies to draft a national development plan in accord with new budget policies to set three-year plans and annual budgets. Plans centred on adopting both second generation reforms designed to free market forces and large financial operations designed to project Brazilian business abroad.[68] The BNDES has continued to focus on these two strategies. During the 1990s, BNDES export-import operations included large-scale exports of equipment for hydroelectric dams in China, acquisition of Embraer aircraft by commercial airlines in the US, export of buses to Cuba and finance to meet clauses for domestic content in construction of oil exploration platforms.[69] Meanwhile, the BNDES continues to provide regional development finance according to constitutional mandate. From 1997–2001, BNDES lending for regional integration programmes for the North, Programa Amazônia Integrada, (Amazonia Integration Programme), western Rio Grande do Sul state (Programa Reconversul) and centre-west region (Programa Centro-Oeste) summed to R$23.1 billion.[70] The BNDES also delegated administration of fixed income funds to private financial institutions such as Fundos Regionais de Empresas Emergentes (Regional Emerging Entreprise Funds) and Fundos de Empresas Emergentes de Base Tecnológica (Emerging Tech Firm Fund).

The BNDES has shifted lending to the private sector, but a significant portion of development bank resources still originate in official savings programmes. The 1988 Constitution altered the PIS-Pasep savings programmes and introduced a new Fundo de Amparo ao Trabalhador (Worker's Assistance Fund, FAT) discounted from paychecks.[71] The BNDES is guaranteed 40 per cent of this forced saving fund, with the mandate that bank investments generate income and employment.

The end of major privatizations by 2000 was followed by a period of transition at the BNDES and adoption of neo-developmentalist policies under PT President Lula. Plans during the final years of the Cardoso government (2000–2) sought to shift the bank further in the direction of investment banking and the private sector. In 2002, the strategic plan published by the bank entitled 'Vision 2005' reflected the market-centred conceptions of BNDES president Francisco Gros and sought to deepen domestic capital markets. However, change was placed on hold until the new government and bank president took office in 2003.

The BNDES under President Lula: Neo-Developmentalism, 2003–10

BNDES policies under President Lula and PT coalition government first reassessed development policies but largely maintained the dual strategy of second generation reforms, direct and indirect lending policies, and increased financial market operations and incentives to globalize select Brazilian corporations. From 2003–10, four economists were selected by President Lula to serve as BNDES President. The first was Carlos Lessa, professor of economics and former rector of the Rio de Janeiro federal university. Lessa attempted to shift BNDES policies away from the private sector and introduce new lending policies designed to encourage networks of domestic producers. Lessa failed to generate internal support in the bank and after repeated confrontations with Minister of Commerce and Industry, Luiz Fernando Furlan (officially his superior) was dismissed by President Lula on 18 November 2004.

The second BNDES President under President Lula was Guido Mantega, long-time economic advisor to Lula, coordinator of the PT economic programme for presidential contests since 1989 and first Planning Minister under President Lula. Mantega served as BNDES president from November 2004 until March 2006 when he was chosen to replace Finance Minister Palocci. BNDES Vice President Damion Fiocca thereafter remained as BNDES President until PMBD economist Luciano Coutinho was named in May 2007. Coutinho is professor of economics at the University of Campinas and representative of the left-nationalist wing of the PMDB party, a critical member of President Lula's coalition government during his second term (2007–10). Despite discontinuity under four presidents since 2003, the BNDES has developed new policies designed to encourage the formation of large Brazilian corporations able to compete as multinational enterprises on the world stage and new lending policies to support networks of productions in critical sectors.

Since 2007, BNDES President Coutinho has pursued a full service approach, attempting to help start-up small and medium firms, provide funds to expand successful firms, and participate in venture capital funds to help enterprises transit toward corporate governance standards and initial or secondary offerings of stock on the Bovespa exchange. In 2008, as financial crisis led to a shortage of credit, collapse of share prices, and sharp decline in industrial production by fourth quarter 2008, the BNDES also provided lending of last resort to major Brazilian corporations while retaining long term goals for massive investments in deep sea petroleum production.

Table 5.1: BNDES Interbank and Non-Bank Loans, 1995–2008, US$ Billion.

	Interbank Loans			Non-Bank Loans		
	BNDES	per centMkt	Total	BNDES	per centMkt	Total
1995	15.6	(32.4)	48.1	8.0	(3.8)	207.1
1996	18.1	(35.4)	51.1	10.9	(4.9)	219.8
1997	19.7	(27.8)	70.7	14.5	(6.8)	210.3
1998	21.6	(35.5)	60.8	23.0	(11.3)	202.0
1999	20.4	(41.0)	49.7	15.0	(3.5)	142.8
2000	24.3	(43.9)	55.3	15.2	(9.6)	157.7
2001	25.9	(50.4)	51.5	14.5	(10.4)	139.1
2002	23.3	(44.3)	52.5	13.7	(13.0)	105.1
2003	26.1	(41.9)	62.2	20.0	(14.1)	141.5
2004	30.6	(40.8)	74.9	21.8	(12.2)	178.6
2005	34.3	(37.3)	91.8	27.7	(11.3)	243.1
2006	38.8	(35.0)	110.6	32.9	(10.2)	323.1
2007	52.4	(33.5)	156.3	43.2	(8.8)	488.5
2008	53.0	(49.3)	107.3	45.6	(9.6)	474.3

Source: Central Bank of Brazil, Top Fifty Banks, 1995–2008.

BNDES lending since 1995 suggests the realization of competitive advantages typical of a large, centralized development bank. Contrary to the extensive branch office networks retained by the Banco do Brasil and Caixa, the BNDES retains fewer than 1900 employees (compared to 105,000 at Caixa) in the Rio de Janeiro and four regional offices. Since 1995, the BNDES increased its market share of non-bank loans from R$8.0 billion (3.8 per cent) to R$20.0 billion (14.1 per cent) during the economic downturn, risk aversion and credit shortage in 2003. Under President Lula, BNDES market share of loans to non-financial entities increased from 8.8–9.6 per cent of total from 2003–8. Once again, the BNDES has increased its market share of lending to non-financial sector since liberalization of the industry and privatization of state government banks.

BNDES inter-bank lending also increased substantially. Since the Real Plan ended inertial inflation in 1994, the BNDES has expanded its market share of interbank lending from 15.6 billion (32.4 per cent) in 1995 to 53.0 billion (49.3 per cent) in 2008 during credit shortage and stock market collapse. During previous years of financial crisis and economic reversals, the BNDES also increased interbank lending significantly. For example, during the 1999 and 2001 crises, BNDES interbank lending increased to 41.0 per cent and 50.4 per cent of total. This marked presence in interbank loan market reflects the role of the BNDES in providing indirect lending to targeted sectors through private, foreign and other government banks in Brazil.

Table 5.2: BNDES Loan Approvals by Programme, 1995–2007, R$ Billion.

	1999	2000	2001	2002	2003	2004	2005	2006	2007	2008
Direct Lending										
Finem	5.1	5.5	6.8	13.3	7.9	11.4	13.2	14.5	22.0	28.5
Capital Markets	1.6	1.9	0.9	0.8	0.9	0.6	2.0	3.4	3.5	10.4
Export-Import	2.3	3.4	3.9	7.7	6.3	5.6	6.7	4.0	1.3	3.2
Sub-Total	9.1	10.9	11.8	21.9	15.3	17.7	22.0	22.1	26.9	42.4
Per cent	(50.5)	(47.4)	(46.8)	(58.5)	(45.6)	(44.7)	(46.9)	(43.0)	(41.5)	(46.4)
Indirect Lending										
Finem	3.1	4.0	3.7	1.6	1.2	1.6	1.8	2.7	5.1	6.0
Finame	1.6	2.5	3.3	4.0	5.3	6.6	9.3	10.7	17.0	22.1
Finame Agro	0.7	1.3	1.8	3.0	2.8	4.5	2.1	1.4	2.0	2.7
Finame Leasing	0.0	0.00	0.2	0.2	0.3	0.2	0.4	0.6	1.4	1.6
Export-Import	1.4	2.3	2.0	4.0	5.6	5.4	7.3	9.7	6.7	9.5
BNDES auto	1.8	1.7	2.2	2.4	2.7	3.4	3.6	3.5	5.0	5.5
Sub-Total	8.9	12.0	13.4	15.4	18.2	22.0	24.9	29.2	37.9	48.4
Per cent	(49.5)	(52.6)	(53.2)	(41.5)	(54.4)	(55.3)	(53.1)	(57.0)	(58.5)	(53.6)
Total	18.0	23.0	25.2	37.4	33.5	39.8	46.9	51.3	64.8	90.8

Source: BNDES statistics, by modality, available on www.bndes.gov.br.

Review of BNDES finance by programme suggests the evolution of credit policies from 1995 through 2008. The three major programmes of direct finance, Financiamento a Empreendimentos (Business Finance, Finem), Mercado de Capitais (Capital Markets) and Export-Import finance remained between 50.5 per cent and 41.5 per cent of total BNDES lending, with the exception of 2002. Indirect lending through six broad programmes remained between 49.5 per cent and 58.5 per cent of total BNDES lending, with the exception of 2002. Indirect lending programmes include Finem business lending, Financiamento de Maquinas (Machine Finance, Fineme) with agricultural and leasing modalities, Export-Import financing and BNDES automatic lending provisions.

These trends suggest the realization of competitive advantages over private and foreign banks in Brazil. BNDES long term interest rates remained substantially lower than Selic benchmark overnight inter-bank interest rates throughout this period, while the lower cost of small staff and operations of the BNDES made lending at these rates viable. Another competitive advantage of the BNDES over private and foreign banks is the development bank's mandate as manager of funds from the forced savings fund Fundo de Amparo ao Trabalhador (Worker Asssistance Fund, FAT). Constitutionally mandated investments in productive activities (not government bonds) increased from R$3.1 billion in 2000 to R$10.1 billion in 2008, comprising 17.0 per cent of BNDES liabilities. This means that 17.0 per cent of BNDES finance and lending is based on long-term deposits that provide no liquidity risk. This provides a competitive advantage over private and foreign banks.

BNDES lending still focuses primarily on industry and infrastructure. Despite the adoption of second generation reforms that seek to free market forces and accelerate innovation and productivity through small and medium enterprises, BNDES lending still focuses on large scale industrial and long-term infrastructure finance. In this respect, the BNDES embodies a persistent need for state-led development banking along the lines emphasized by Lewis, Myrdal and development economists 50 years ago. This traditional sense of commanding heights thus still captures the role of the BNDES in Brazilian political economy. Despite more than two decades of privatizations, financial liberalization, bank reforms and a variety of fiscal, financial and economic reforms that have substantially modernized the domestic Brazilian economy and freed market forces, the BNDES remains the single most important source for long-term finance and credit. The capitalization of the Bovespa stock market in 2004–8, for the first time in Brazilian history, reduced the virtual monopoly of BNDES over long term finance.

Long-term investments have produced substantial profits at the BNDES. The bank has recorded profits each year since 1999, increasing from over R$600 million in 1999, over R$3.2 billion during 2005, reaching over R$7.3 billion in 2007. The long-term character of BNDES finance stands in stark contrast to policies at private banks. Contrary to strategy of private and foreign banks to trade and hold government paper described in chapter three, the BNDES suspended purchase and trading in government paper because of constitutional mandates to contribute to development and employment. Furthermore, the turn to capital markets at the BNDES has provided substantial returns since 2004.

However, this does not mean that BNDES lending protected unproductive industries. Instead of wasting resources to unnecessarily bail out firms or provide crony credit, high returns and strong profits at the BNDES suggest that lending was sound. Standard indicators of bank performance, asset quality and capital reserves against credit and capital risk provide empirical control. All these measures suggest that the BNDES weathered the period of adjustment and sustained counter-cyclical investment policies without placing resources at risk beyond Central Bank of Brazil regulations and BIS guidelines. And returns have increased since recovery in 2004. BNDES participation in the booming Bovespa stock market since 2003 has provided record returns.

Table 5.3: BNDES Financial Results, 2002–6.

	2002	2003	2004	2005	2006
Returns					
On Assets	0.42	0.68	0.95	1.89	3.49
On Liquid Assets	4.4	8.2	11.1	21.4	36.4
Asset Quality					
Past-Due Credit /Credit	0.5	3.1	0.6	0.8	0.7
Reserves / Past-Due Credit	836.0	146.0	571.0	450.0	422.0
Reserves / Credit	4.16	4.33	3.68	3.90	2.8
Capital Reserves					
Fixed Assets/Liq. Assets	90.7	113.0	106.5	93.5	86.0
Fixed Assets/Total Assets	7.42	9.55	9.17	8.4	8.7
Capital Adequacy					
Basel Index	11.5	14.3	15.3	16.7	23.1
Liquid/Total Assets	8.18	8.45	8.61	8.98	10.18

Source: BNDES, Annual Reports, 2002–6.

BNDESpar has also recorded strong returns during the period of economic growth and into the 2008 financial crisis. BNDESpar returns on liquid assets increased from 7.5 per cent in 2004 to 27.7 per cent in 2007, declining to 24.5 per cent in 2008. Average returns on assets and stock holdings also remained high, building the assets held by the BNDESpar subsidiary from 14.1–35.9 billion from 2005–8.

This increased participation of the BNDES in capital markets involves new relations and networks across government, private sector, labour unions, the private pension funds of government bank and government enterprise employees, and financial markets. By 2007, BNDES participation in stockholding and mutual funds reached across 261 firms and 25 mutual funds, totalling over R$91.0 billion. Furthermore, unlike the policy of private and foreign banks to trade and hold high interest rate paying short term government paper during the sudden stop of foreign finance and downturn in the Brazilian business cycle (2002–3) the BNDES expanded credit operations and reduced financial operations in secondary markets for indexed government paper. This countered the perverse impact of the liquidity preference among private and other government banks that increased market pressures and led to shorter terms and higher cost of Brazilian government debt.

The policy of averting government paper is due to a constitutional mandate to manage forced savings funds in ways that generate employment and income. As noted, a large part of BNDES resources (liabilities) are from domestic official savings programmes. The value of FAT resources increased from R$49.2 billion in 2003 to R$66.2 billion in 2005, while the PIS-Pasep fund remained at approximately R$20.0 billion. Foreign capital has also been channelled to the BNDES through multilateral agencies and foreign bond issues. Foreign loans to the BNDES have declined. Multilateral agencies provided R$7.0 billion in 2003, increased funding to R$12.9 billion during 2004 and continued to provide R$10.7 billion to the BNDES during 2005.

Comparison of BNDES structure and performance with development banks abroad suggests both the large scale and scope of BNDES operations and controls for mismanagement and political abuse of the bank. In 2007, BNDES assets reached almost double the value reported by the Inter-American Development Bank (IADB), over half the value of total assets held by the World Bank, and almost ten times the value of assets held by the French government development bank, CAF. Furthermore, profits and loans from the BNDES far exceeded all three institutions. The US$33.0 billion in loans reported by the BNDES far exceed the US$6.7 billion from the IADB, the US$11.0 reported by the World Bank and US$5.8 billion reported by the CAF. BNDES profits, returns on assets and return on liquid patrimony also far exceeded those reported by these three development banks that serve to control performance and policies at the BNDES. Finally, late loans at the BNDES remained at 0.11 per cent of total loans, well below levels reported by the World Bank, comparable to the 0.10 per cent reported by the IADB, while considerably above the 0.01 per cent reported by CAF.

The large scale of BNDES lending and finance make it possible for government policy to target counter-cyclical credit to avert or ameliorate economic downturns and substitute private and foreign credit shortages. In March 2009 testimony to Congress, BNDES President Coutinho described bank policy to reduce the cost and increase the supply of credit. Resources for counter-cyclical lending during 2008–2009 came from Treasury loans to BNDES released by provisional decrees 439 and 414 summing R$17.5 billion, transfer of R$6.0 billion in CVS funds, sale of FGTS Investment Fund and bank certificates summing R$17.0 billion. Furthermore, the third phase of conditional credit facility shared by Inter-American Development Bank and the BNDES provided the last tranche of a total US$6.0 billion for BNDES operations.

Two further means were used by the BNDES to infuse capital during the collapse of the stock market and shortage of credit during 2007–8. The counter-cyclical policies of the BNDES can also be seen in the over two-fold increase of BNDES holdings in private equity and investment funds. BNDES funds in private equity and mutual funds increased from R$403.8 million in 2007 to over R$1.0 billion in 2008. The capitalization of mutual funds and private equity firms by the BNDES also played an important counter-cyclical role.

BNDES par shareholding included the following percentile ownership and market value of shares at year end 2008:

América Latina Logística (10.6 per cent shares, R$638.6 million)
Aracruz (5.5 per cent shares/R$129.2 million)
Banco do Brasil (2.5 per cent shares, R$1.085.4 million)
Bom Gosto (34.5 per cent shares, R$245.8 million)
Brasil Telecom Participações (3.0 per cent shares, R$166.6 million)
Braskem (5.2 per cent shares, R$243.2 million)
Brenco (20.9 per cent shares, R$140.0 million)
CEG (34.5 per cent shares, R$140.6 million)
CESP (5.7 per cent shares, R$234.7 million)
Coteminas (10.3 per cent shares, R$134.0 million)
CPFL Energia (6.2 per cent shares, R$608.1 million)
Cia. Siderúrgica Nacional (3.6 per cent shares, R$151.3 million)
CVRD (4.0 per cent shares, R$1.50 billion)
ELETROBRÁS (11.8 per cent shares, R$2.24 billion)
EMBRAER (5.0 per cent shares, R$109.6 million)
Gerdau (3.5 per cent shares, R$153.3 million)
Independência (13.9 per cent shares, R$250.0 million)
JBS (13.0 per cent shares, R$1.47 billion)
Klabin (20.2 per cent shares, R$562.1 million)
Light (33.6 per cent shares, R$822.5 million)
Marfrig (14.6 per cent shares, R$817.6 million)
MPX Mineração (2.6 per cent shares, R$179.1 million)
Ouro Fino (20.0 per cent shares, R$105.7 million)
Paranapanema (17.5 per cent shares, R$125.2 million)
Petrobrás (7.6 per cent shares, R$1.02 billion)
Rede Energia S/A (25.3 per cent shares, R$263.3 billion)
Tele Norte Leste Participações (1.6 per cent shares, R$164.5 million)
Valepar (9.7 per cent shares, R$2.62 billion)
Subtotal, R$16.30 billion
Other firms, R$1.26 billion
Total, R$17.52 billion[72]

The BNDES also holds blocks of shares in many major Brazilian corporations through its participation subsidiary, BNDESPar. Comparing value of investments in 2007 and 2008 suggests that large purchases capitalized firms precisely as financial crisis and downturn in Bovespa stock market made it difficult for firms to find working capital

During the credit crunch and capital market downturn during 2008, the BNDES increased shareholding by over R$6.0 billion in 28 private Brazilian enterprises. Further temporary shareholding was held in five firms, (Bertin, 26.9 per cent; Brasiliana, 53.8 per cent; Copel, 23.9 per cent; Rio Polímeros, 25.0 per cent; Telemar, 31.3 per cent). Once again, the BNDES provided access to capital for firms caught in the sudden credit crunch and stock market collapse unable to meet obligations or raise funds through equity issues or commercial bank credit. This counter-cyclical role of government banks has been critical in Brazil since the nineteenth century.

BNDESPar private equity and investment fund participation at year end 2008 included the following holdings (managing enterprise in parentheses):

Brasil 21 (Dynamo) R$4.6 million
PROT (Mellon Financial Services) R$462.8 million
Logística Brasil (Bradesco) R$13.5 million
Fire (BrasilPrivate) R$26.9 million
FIPGG (Governança & Gestão Investimento) R$28.9 million
Opportunity Equity Partners (Mellon Financial Services) R$104.6 million
Brasil Energia (Bradesco) R$118.4 million
InfraBrasil (ABN-Amro) R$67.7 million
Rio Bravo Cinema (Rio Bravo) R$11.6 million
Brascan Petro & Gás Bank (Brascan) R$13.6 million
AG Angra Infra-Estrutura (Bradesco) R$38.0 million
São Paulo Metro Fund (Bradesco) R$79.1 million
Other Funds R$65.3 million
Total R$1.03 billion[73]

Finally, Brazilian federal government triennial plans include investment targets by the BNDES. If current plans are compared to 2004–7 investments, several structural changes in BNDES lending appear.[74] First, BNDES plans for Oil and Petroleum production reveal a profound change for Brazilian political economy. In 1990, roughly 45 per cent of oil consumed in Brazil was imported. In 2007, before oil price increased reversed the balance, Brazil reported domestic production levels sufficient to meet domestic consumption. Furthermore, discoveries of substantial deep sea oil reserves have led the BNDES to plan massive investments involving Petrobras and other global petroleum firms. Planned investments for 2009–12 include, in petroleum and gas (R$269.7 billion), Petrochemicals (R$23.7 billion), and Ethanol (R$19.7 billion) summing over R$313.0 billion.

The BNDES also retains a presence in government projects by providing management assistance. During 2008, BNDES staff provided management support for implementation of 192 projects involving R$71.0 billion of total R$142 billion PT government growth acceleration projects. BNDES staff also participated in the design, management and implementation of President Lula's Política de Desenvolvimento Produtivo (Policy for Production Development) involving R$210.0 billion targeting production chains designed to maximize employment and regional development benefits. Finally, the BNDES was also charged to create and co-manage a Fundo Amazonia with the Ministry of Environment to provide incentives to reduce deforestation of the Amazon region. BNDES Plans for 2009 include completion of concession for construction of high speed train line and service for Rio de Janeiro-São Paulo corridor, two blocks of highway concession sales involving three major highways in each block of sales, sale of management concessions for regional airports, and the reorganization of INFRAERO federal government airport management company.

These policies reflect the goal of BNDES policy to launch firms on the stock market rather than maintain direct credit and finance. Exceptions during 2008 involve Auto and Ethanol industries, both for strategic and broader policy reasons. Given the sharp downturn in auto sales during fourth quarter 2008, the BNDES provided significant lending to avert further downsizing or failure of auto companies in Brazil. Given the current global redistribution of automobile production, BNDES policies are designed to help the Brazilian operations of major auto firms through the period of adjustment and increase the attractiveness of domestic operations in global production strategies of multinational auto companies. Ethanol production also received massive funds to sustain an industry seen as critical for alternative and sustainable fuel source capable of replacing petroleum: Ethanol reached over 50 per cent of automotive fuel sales in 2007.

Under the Lula government, the BNDES has also resumed lending to state and municipal governments. Since the renegotiation of municipal and state government debts in the late 1990s, states and municipalities have been largely prohibited from taking on debt. This was emblematic of the recentralization required to control fiscal excesses during military rule and the prolonged period of transition to democracy. Policies during the 1990s were designed to avert overspending seen as critical to maintain price stability under the Real Plan (1994). In 2000, the Lei de Responsibilidade Fiscal (Fiscal Responsibility Law) largely prohibited credit and finance to state and municipal governments. Since 2000, municipalities and states have been required to submit detailed budget statements that, in turn, have been the basis for a gradual return to sub-national government finance. In August 2006, central bank and Treasury regulations freed municipalities to take on credit up to 120 per cent of liquid receipts. Since then, the BNDES has led in terms of credits and finance to sub-national governments through a Programa Especial de Financiamento aos Estados e Distrito Federal (Special Programme for State and Federal District Finance).

The BNDES also developed the first system in Brazil for risk analysis of municipal governments and has led in the market for municipal credit freed by August 2006 procedures for approval at Treasury, the Central Bank and Conselho Monetário Nacional (National Monetary Council). Prosecution of mayors and firms charged with managing municipal credits with the BNDES revealed fraudulent practices. These funds for sub-national public finance also became critical mechanisms to counter severe budget shortfalls caused by financial crisis during 2008. Given that municipal and state government tax bases are shallow and that federal government transfers provide the bulk of sub-national government resources, the Lula administration allocated R$ 4.0 billion to the Fundo de Participação dos Estados (State Participation Fund) through a Programa Emergencial de Financiamento (Emergency Finance Fund), administered by the BNDES.

In sum, the BNDES expanded credit and finance operations substantially during four years of sustained growth from 2004–7. And having helped underwrite the stock market boom and capitalized Brazilian firms directly and indirectly through credit, finance, mutual funds and private equity funds, the BNDES retained sufficient scale, scope, and capital base to provide counter cyclical credit and finance to help firms adjust to financial crisis and credit shortage during 2008. In retrospect, the growth of the BNDES since liberalization and privatizations of state government banks in the 1990s suggest the comparative advantages of development banking. BNDES credit and finance fell to 5.2 per cent of fixed capital formation in 1995. Since then, the turn to neo-developmentalism and a period of sustained economic growth during the Lula administration increased the BNDES share of total fixed capital formation during 2006 and 2007 to 12.6 and 14.1 per cent. Critics charge that monopoly over FGTS and PIS-PASEP official savings funds as liabilities provide the BNDES with unfair competitive advantage over private banks. In 2008, forced savings funds summed to only 17 per cent of BNDES liabilities (resources). The BNDES does not rely exclusively on forced savings for competitive advantage. Instead, market-oriented policies, joint-ventures with private mutual funds, investment funds, private equity firms, large blocks of shareholding in Brazilian firms, and massive amounts of credit and investment to the private sector at below market but still profitable long term interest rates of 6.25 per cent suggest that the large scale and scope of BNDES operations provide institutional foundations of comparative advantage over private and foreign banks.

Conclusion

Since 1952, the BNDE(S) has provided policy options and retained powerful competitive advantages over private and foreign banks in Brazil. Far from impeding private sector development, BNDES policies have subsidised the private sector, helped banks underwrite and firms issue stock and contributed to the capitalization of the Bovespa stock exchange and private banking through indirect finance and interbank loans and investments. This case study confirms the apparent anomaly for liberal theory. Since liberalization of Brazilian banking and privatization of state owned enterprises in the 1990s, the BNDES has reasserted a predominant role in long term finance. Privatizations in the 1980s and '90s modernized BNDES policies and networks in state and society. Since liberalizations and privatizations in the 1990s, the BNDES has helped globalize major Brasilian enterprises, transform the BMF-Bovespa into one of the world's largest capital markets, and led investment strategies that transformed Brazil from an oil importing country (50 per cent of consumption in 1990) into major petroleum producing and exporting country.

This case study reveals how the BNDES provides policy alternatives and exercises competitive advantages. The BNDE evolved as a centrepiece of developmentalism during the 1950s until the breakdown of democracy in 1964. Under military rule, the bank channelled vast resources from abroad (and forced savings at home) through financial markets to private and state owned enterprises. Reforms in the 1960s sought to free market forces, private banking and capital markets. Instead, during the 1970s the BNDE became principal intermediary between foreign investors, forced savings and state-led policies designed to complete import substitution industrialization by installing capital goods production. State led strategies ended in 1982 when foreign debt crisis and fiscal imbalances reduced state capacity and BNDES resources. The BNDES shifted policies toward privatization, liberalization and the private sector. During the 1990s, the BNDES became auctioneer for privatization of state owned enterprises and sought to maximize the gains of liberalization and private investments.

Liberalization and privatizations during the 1990s thereby *modernized* the BNDES. This endowed President Lula's PT coalition government with an agile, centralized development bank able to compete (and cooperate and collaborate) with private and foreign banks and provide policy alternatives for long term investments and development strategies. Since 2003, the BNDES has sought to reassess developmentalism, shift toward micro-, small- and medium enterprises, and help modernize domestic firms. The BNDES has remained at the centre of Brazilian political networks, government policy options, corporate governance modernization, and financial development.

Indicators of banking performance suggest the BNDES is not a financial black hole that protects unproductive industry and bails out large conglomerates. And like the Banco do Brasil and Caixa, the problems of development banks emphasized by critics occurred largely during military rule and prolonged transition, not democracy. The secretive politics of BNDES finance under military government in the 1960s and 70s, and the chaotic conditions of inertial inflation and seven anti-inflation packages during the late 1980s and early 1990s, remain opaque and require further study. However, the BNDES has emerged from the politicization of finance under military rule and new challenges after the downsizing of the Brazilian state through privatizations. Charges of misconduct involving inside information and phone tapping among BNDES officials responsible for privatizations led to resignation of BNDES President André Lara Resende in 1998. However, the bank's trajectory of growth during the 2000s and the ability of the BNDES to provide counter-cyclical credit and finance during the sudden stop of foreign capital inflows from 2001–3 (and during the 2008 financial crisis) suggest that this federal government development bank retains competitive advantages and provides policy alternatives.

Theories of financial repression and grabbing hand overstate problems with development banks. The absence of transparency, accountability, congressional oversight and judicial review, and the realities of censorship, intimidation and institutional decay under military rule suggest that problems during the 1960s and 70s had to do with authoritarianism not development banking. After return to civilian rule, the BNDES became primary agent of privatizations and financial, fiscal and administrative reforms during the 1990s. This endowed the PT coalition government under President Lula with a very large development bank able to pursue new policies despite capital flight, perceptions of political risk among foreign investors and lack of confidence in private finance and banking early in his administration. The BNDES has thereby returns to where it began, in search of collaboration between public and private sector and domestic and foreign capital to overcome constraints on economic growth. The evidence since 1952 suggests that the BNDES responded with credit and finance when markets collapsed, capital fled and private banks refused to provide long-term loans. Suggesting that the BNDES reproduces financial repression and underdevelopment misrepresents this causal sequence.

CONCLUSION

'The profit of a public bank has been a source of revenue to more considerable states ... not only to Hamburgh, but to Venice and Amsterdam. Revenue of this kind has even by some been thought not below the attention of so great an empire as that of Great Britain ... The orderly, vigilant and parsimonious administration of such aristocracies as those of Venice and Amsterdam, is extremely proper, it appears from experience, for the management of a mercantile project of this kind. But whether such a government as that of England, which, whatever may be its virtues, has never been famous for good oeconomy; which, in time of peace, has generally conducted itself with the slothful and negligent profusion that is perhaps natural to monarchies and in time of war has constantly acted with all the thoughtless extravagance that democracies are apt to fall into; could be safely trusted with such a project, must at least be a good deal more doubtful.'

A. Smith, *The Wealth of Nations* (1776), p. 880

Since Adam Smith, liberal economists have remained sceptical about government banking. Smith rejected government banks as a source of public revenue, but his arguments anticipate those of recent critics. Government banks are mercantilist and interfere with free market relations. Government banks are subject to mismanagement ranging from 'slothful and negligent profusion' under monarchies in times of peace to 'thoughtless extravagance' under democracies in times of war. For Smith, risks of government banking outweigh possible benefits such as retaining profits for public policy. For liberal economists, finding that federal banks remain among the largest financial institutions and account for over a third of credit in twenty-first-century Brazil is an anomaly. Configurations of domestic banking often appear exceptional, but the persistence of federal banks in a country wracked with terrible income distribution and low growth for over twenty years assumes a large burden of proof. Critics of state intervention warn about rent seeking, crony credit, corporatism and financial repression. However, the persistence of underdevelopment is not *prima facie* evidence in favour of free markets. To the contrary, theories from comparative political economy, public policy, banking and financial economics suggest that public banking and government intervention are far from necessarily detrimental.

Banking theory, comparison of bank performance in Brazil since liberalization of the industry in the 1990s and three case studies suggest that critics tell only half the story. They emphasize risks but ignore opportunities. Government banks in Brazil and abroad have modernized to provide policy alternatives and realize competitive advantages over private and foreign banks. Federal banks in Brazil have converged toward levels of performance achieved by the best private and foreign banks operating in the country. Since 1994, Brazilian federal banks have adjusted to price stability, pursued new business strategies and helped implement new public policies amidst greater transparency, accountability, central bank supervision and democratization. During the 1990s, these institutions helped stave off the return of inertial inflation, restore confidence in the private banking system and induce sub-national governments to adjust accounts to price stability. Federal banks also provided countercyclical lending during the financial crises that wracked the country after transition from military rule (Mexico, 1994–5; Asia, 1997; Russia, 1998; Brazil, 1999; Argentina, 2001; Brazil, 2002–3; US, 2007). And from recovery in 2004 until the global crisis hit Brazil in 2008, federal banks led in correspondent banking, popular credit, payroll lending, investment banking and underwriting the globalisation of large Brazilian firms and stock launches on the Bovespa and abroad. During 2008–9, the big three federal banks once again provided counter cyclical credit and lending of last resort to firms and private banks amidst a credit crunch and steep fall in the Bovespa stock market.

For ideologies on the left that see the nationalisation of banks as sure means to reach socialism, federal bank policies under President Lula and PT coalition government surely appear disappointing. Soon after taking office in 2003, President Lula called on federal banks to increase lending, avert recession and spur growth. The cautious responses of federal bank executives (emphasizing regulatory constraints and credit risk) illustrate the independent logic of these institutions and the realities of banking during downturns. Their caution reflects tensions between policy mandates, the realities of market-based credit and finance decisions and central bank regulations of banking. Difficulties at the newly formed Banco Popular do Brasil (a subsidiary of the Banco do Brasil closed in 2008) also demonstrate that federal banking is not a guaranteed success. High levels of late and non-paying loans ate into working capital and forced management first to downsize staff and reform internal procedures, then to close operations when reforms failed to improve results. The success or failure of government banking is not predetermined. Government banks must respect core realities of banking if they are to provide policy alternatives and realize competitive advantages. In this sense, critics of government banking should be taken seriously, alongside core ideas from banking theory and corporate governance about control, information, credit analysis and the complexities of managing large firms, especially government banks that operate at the vortex of politics, society and policymaking to authoritatively allocate resources, multiply money and create assets.

Brazilian federal banks are commanding heights that have begun to provide depth. These institutions are just emerging from centralisation and mismanagement under military rule and the last dance of traditional elites that prolonged transition. They have the scale and scope to both compete with private and foreign banks and perform policy functions. Brazilian federal banks still pale before institutions in advanced economies such as decentralised local and regional government savings banks and sophisticated development banks able to modernize industry toward green production. Liberal critics are right in the sense that federal banks may undercut development and democracy unless they respect sound credit practices, prudent banking, economic constraints and environmental imperatives. But far from Leninist conceptions that see banks as means to capture state and corporate power, the Brazilian experience confirms the importance of pluralist statecrafting. Statecrafting emphasizes how policies may recast existing institutions and markets during the large windows of opportunity provided by critical junctures. Price stability and democratization in Brazil since 1994 have provided a critical juncture. Brazilian statism and developmentalism have changed. Liberalization and privatizations have modernized banking, finance and many other industries in Brazil. Private domestic and foreign banks have expanded their leadership and market shares. However, federal banks have also modernized, increased market shares, led the deepening of banking and finance *and* provided policy alternatives for adjustment, recovery and shaping growth in manifold ways.

This is an anomaly for neo-liberal theory. It also reverses recent relations between economics, political science, sociology and public policy. Case studies and comparisons suggest that political and social forces provide competitive advantages in banking. Brazilian federal banks provide important alternatives for public policy. This reverses relations between politics and banking as ascribed by neoclassical economics and the self declared 'new' political economy. It is now widely accepted that *politics* often determines the success of liberalization and privatization policies. During the last decades, many protected industries were opened to competition to benefit consumers. Many state monopolies were privatized or split to encourage competition and free market forces. Political entrepreneurship, leadership and coalition building can make or unmake reforms. These findings reinforced the neo-liberal paradigm.

Banking is different. Banking belies the idea of a universal trend toward and causal nexus between *liberalization* in the sense of removing barriers to competition and *privatization* in the sense of selling state-owned enterprises. Opening the Brazilian banking industry to foreign competition led *not* to the replacement of public by private banking but to the reform, modernization and realization of competitive advantages by federal banks. This is the anomaly for liberal theory. Scholars of Continental Europe have developed models of coordinated capitalism and concepts of social economy to describe how alternative banking and complementarities across their institutions and markets help sustain social inclusion. Brazilian scholars and policymakers were not so sure. Epistemic communities in Brazil during the 1990s groped for alternative approaches that paled in the face of reams of research from international financial institutions, think tanks and universities that upheld privatization, deregulation and a single model for markets. Nonetheless, an economic policy team trained in neoclassical economics, wedded to financial markets and determined to privatize several sectors in the closed and state-centred Brazilian economy chose *not* to privatize federal banks. This indicates the greater frailty of policy ideas and epistemic communities in developing countries. This also inaugurated a series of policy innovations, reactions to circumstances and unexpected consequences typical of statecrafting and political economy.[1]

Like Brazilian policymakers, this book reflects a struggle to understand federal banks. It began with surprise that the reformist government of President Cardoso chose to capitalize and reform rather than privatize these state owned enterprises. Case studies revealed three different institutional histories and corporate strategies. The Caixa has maintained the classic functions of a savings bank and urban development bank while attempting to modernize, streamline management and reverse the centralisation of corporate governance under military rule. In historical perspective, the policies and competitive advantages of the Banco do Brasil help explain the fundamental anomaly of Brazilian development - that imperial statecraft defeated liberal, republican and regional forces to maintain monarchy and slavery until 1888–9. The Banco do Brasil also housed a veto coalition against orthodox money and banking reforms for most of the twentieth century. This helps explain another anomaly of Brazilian development - the very late creation of a central bank in 1965. Since 1945, the Banco do Brasil gradually relinquished control over monetary policy, central banking and government accounts to adopt corporate governance standards from private banking in the 1990s, float shares on the Bovespa stock market and realize powerful competitive advantages in commercial and investment banking. The BNDES also changed from a developmentalist stronghold in the 1950s and 1960s into an agent (after politicization under military rule) for both privatization of state owned enterprises during the 1990s and neo-developmentism in the 2000s. Case studies provide new perspectives on Brazilian political economy and confirm the risks and opportunities of government banking. However, the evidence from comparisons and case studies is compelling. Instead of privatizations and liberalization producing convergence toward private banking, the modernization of federal banks and the importance of their new policies stand out as central features of Brazilian development and democracy.

Theories from political economy first helped explain this apparent anomaly. The varieties of capitalism approach and the commanding heights tradition helped clarify how government banks provide policy alternatives. Banking theory helped describe how federal banks can do more for less in terms of government budget lines and policy implementation. Instead of handing over cash, federal banks hold deposits in reserve against loans that create money and assets. As banks, they also monitor creditors to increase public control over policy implementation. Federal banks retain competitive advantages over private and foreign banks because they remain at the centre of political webs and social networks that cross government, society, labour unions, political parties, financial markets, pension and mutual funds and coalition governments.

Theories from political economy and banking reinforced case studies and comparisons. This iterative process trespassed from politics and sociology into economics, finance, banking and public policy. Controlling for economic variables and alternative explanations often seemed impossible. Flaws of theory, logic and inference may remain. However, the large quantity of evidence provides a safe margin for error and tips the scale toward our conclusion. Brazilian federal banks remain competitive financial institutions and valuable policy instruments over fifteen years after opening the industry and privatization of most state government banks.

This places politics at the centre of concerns about economics and banking. If Brazilian federal banks retain competitive advantages over private and foreign banks, then the autonomy of economics as a discipline describing free markets is called into question. If federal banks provide policy alternatives, then state intervention overrides core ideas about the ability of free markets to maximize welfare. If consumers place greater trust in federal banks and choose to become or remain clients at these institutions over private or foreign banks, then government and politics become embroiled with core questions about resource allocation. Liberal theory implies both government as guarantor of private property and the autonomy of free markets from politics as the terrain of economics. Government banking fuses questions of money, credit, politics, investment, growth and welfare that have been separated since liberal classics of the eighteenth century. This does not imply an easy return to pre-economic political analysis. Nor does this ascribe moral status to government banks. To the contrary, this study has taken critics seriously, controlled for economic variables and searched for abuse of these institutions. The evidence is overwhelming. Government banks in Brazil and abroad are rarely responsible for unbridled politicization that reproduces underdevelopment. Indeed, politicization of government banks in Brazil occurred most notably under military rule and monarchy in the past.

Critics of government banking are wrong to reaffirm the divide between economics and politics. For critics, government banks waste resources, reproduce inequalities and cause bad equilibrium. In opposition, theories from banking studies, political and social economy, public policy, late development and the varieties of capitalism approach suggest that government banks provide important advantages for public policy, political leaders, social forces, firms and consumers of banking products and services. Government banks retain competitive advantages over private commercial and investment banks *and* provide broader and more secure access to banking services. Government savings banks help preserve social networks and sustain small enterprises, communities and organizations. In Brazil, federal banks provided policy alternatives for economic adjustment, reform and the alleviation of poverty. Brazilian federal banks have led in the introduction of new correspondent banking practices and popular savings and credit programmes that have attracted widespread attention from international financial institutions and other emerging and developing nations.

These findings may affront liberals and puzzle residents of liberal market economies without government banks. However, Brazil is not the outlier. The Caixa case study chapter begins with examples of savings bank modernization and reform across Europe and other developing, emerging and transition countries. The Chilean government savings bank BancoEstado is a compelling example from a country often cited as liberal paradigm. Liberalization policies have internationalized and deepened banking and finance in Chile. However, the federal government savings bank, BancoEstado, retained over *ninety* per cent of domestic savings accounts in Chile in 2005. In many other countries, liberalization has induced (mostly government owned) savings banks to modernize and successfully compete against private and foreign banks. Convergence toward private banking and equity markets has been less pervasive. This counters theories, since Adolf Bearle and Gardiner Means, that expect liberalization and privatizations to produce convergence toward private banking and market centred financial systems.[2] Theories of institutional foundations of competitive advantage and relational banking provide a promising alternative to help explain the unexpected paths of bank change in Brazil and beyond.

Since John Zysman's landmark work almost thirty years ago, research has clarified how bank-centred and market-centred financial systems work. And rather than rigid systems or types, studies of Continental Europe and developing countries after liberalization during the 1980s and '90s emphasize the cohabitation of alternative banking and government control and regulation alongside private banking and capital markets. Liberalization and deregulation inspired concern about the viability of traditional patterns of household savings and banking. The collapse of savings and loan institutions in the US during the 1980s and early 1990s was a fiasco. Great Britain also simply privatized savings banks. However, most domestic banking systems appear to have retained and reinforced traditional institutions of alternative banking such as cooperatives, mutual societies and savings banks. Financial markets have developed in traditional bank-centred financial systems such as Germany. Other state and bank-centred systems such as France and Italy have privatized and liberalized substantially. Understanding the diversity of bank change requires further research. However, one observation seems sure. Alternative banking and private banks and financial markets coexist after liberalization. Banking has *not* converged toward private commercial and investment firms and equity markets along the lines of the US and UK. Indeed, scholars of the US and UK emphasize the importance of new developments such as private equity and bank lending that indicate a shift away from the traditional Berle and Means paradigm of dispersed public stock ownership, liquid trading of equities on financial markets and shareholder control of corporate governance. The UK government has called for reassessment of alternative banking.[3]

Further research is needed because government and alternative banking tap deep differences. Theories of financial repression see state banking as responsible for reproducing underdevelopment and privatization and liberalization as necessary to free market forces. Theories of institutional foundations of competitive advantage, relational banking and public and social banking insist, to the contrary, that long-term relations between alternative banks, local communities, political forces and firms are necessary to realize the gains of investments and social policies. That these relations be sheltered from market forces is fundamentally at odds with core ideas about financial markets. Perhaps the central difference turns on liquidity. Advocates of markets suggest that liquidity, transparency, competition and market prices produce higher levels of welfare. Advocates of relational banking and government coordination value patient capital, political networks, social policies and institutions that, in the long-run, ensure higher rates of growth and welfare.

Evidence from Brazil suggests that combining these perspectives may maximize welfare. Finding that government banks *and* markets have increased welfare in Brazil is consistent with research in comparative political economy and financial economics. If financial development is determined more by legal systems than whether banks or markets predominate, it follows that government banks are not necessarily detrimental. Instead of a single market-centred model for development, recent research has been described as a financial services view, one that stresses particular configurations of banking and the complexity of complementarities that link institutions and markets. This also counters strong claims against government banking. Indeed, recent studies in finance and banking return to core ideas in classics such as Shonfield and Polanyi. If particular configurations determine best policies, then it follows that single models based on privatization may well not apply. The challenge is to adapt policies to domestic settings.

This approach also averts errors of formal dichotomies and the fallacy of aggregation. This study was inspired by Hall and Soskice's call to study firms and Lijphart's dictum for adopting case studies. Hall and Soskice argue for bringing the study of particular firms back into political economy. Case studies of the big three Brazilian federal banks suggest the value of keeping close to empirical evidence when questions of theory are so contested. Scholars in the disciplines of financial economics, political economy, business administration and comparative politics and public policy agree with this research strategy. Case studies and focused comparisons are needed to avert the fallacy of aggregation that haunts cross-national data analysis. Since John Stuart Mill, social scientists have turned to case studies and focused comparisons when statistical analysis or experiments fail. Government banking fits Lijphart's dictum. Phenomena that present too few cases and too many variables require case studies. Aggregate cross national comparisons fail to reveal the causes and consequences of government banking. Whether government banks provide institutional foundations for policy making and competitive advantage or, to the contrary, are simply used by politicians and organized interests to capture policies, divert resources, feed inflation and produce bad equilibrium depends on too many variables and circumstances to be emphatically for or against these institutions.

This is important because differences about banking and finance often coincide with fundamental disagreements between nations. Foreign policy and international relations haunt these matters already interdisciplinary and deeply contested. Differences between nations parallel differences described by the varieties of capitalism approach (liberal- and coordinated market economies) and financial economists (bank- and market-centred financial systems). However, labelling different domestic policy traditions as non-liberal is excessive. The non-liberal label captures differences between early and late development. And past failures of liberalism and democracy in Germany, Japan, Italy and Brazil certainly provide grounds for caution. But this does not warrant ceding the liberal tradition to neoclassical economics. Non-liberal economic policies are not necessarily non-liberal in terms of politics or society. Although far from this study, the work of John Rawls provides a useful analogy. Communitarian (or other alternative) perspectives in political theory need not assume they are outside the liberal tradition. From this perspective, Rawl's *Political Liberalism* attempted to recuperate the political dimension of liberalism and shift the terms of debate back to level ground.[4] A similar conceptual shift may be needed to understand federal banking in Brazil. These institutions may stray from assumptions about free markets that remain inextricably associated with liberalism for many economists. This seems fundamentally wrong. Brazilian policymakers and political and social forces intuitively ignored these assumptions and resisted recommendations to privatize. Brazilians chose instead to capitalize, reform and modernize federal banks, a strategic and intuitive choice that nonetheless resonates with and remains grounded in liberal and democratic politics, liberal social policies and sound policies for financial development.

In terms of politics, this is more mainstream than it may appear. Political science has long focused on the incorporation of social classes into political institutions during modernization. Brazilian federal banks remain agents of *political* development. These institutions helped incorporate those left behind in Brazil, precisely while aspirations were raised by social mobilization since transition from military rule. Political development theory holds that social inclusion is independent from economic growth. Waiting for economic growth to resolve questions of democracy and social inclusion is mistaken. This book thus deals with the questions raised by Robert Dahl, Giovanni Sartori, Seymour Martin Lipset, Stein Rokkan, Samuel Huntington, Charles Tilly and many others that attempted to understand how social classes are, or are not, incorporated into political institutions during modernization.[5] This also draws attention to the unfinished business of political development and social inclusion in Brazil. It is precisely the dramatic distribution of Brazilians in terms of IBGE social classes (more simply, the persistence of poverty) that suggests the importance of price stability and government banking for social inclusion in the still new Brazilian democracy. Normative questions aside, social classes C, D and E (those earning less than R$760.00/US$390.00 per month) form an immense majority of Brazilian voters. Federal bank policies have implemented policies, allocated resources and incorporated voters into the new institutions of Brazilian democracy and market economy. This has reinforced the record popularity of President Lula (over 82 per cent after eight years in office).

Critics of government banking warn that these institutions may abuse public trust and reproduce underdevelopment. Brazilian federal banks are so large that their future will determine, to an important degree, the future of Brazilian development and democracy. Case studies reveal both mismanagement in the past and progress since transition from military rule. These banks provided policy alternatives for economic management, reform and social inclusion. Gains were not easy. Nor are they permanent. Like liberty, government banks require eternal vigilance. If organized interests capture credit and finance, or bailouts simply increase moral hazard and lead to poor investments, then future policies may erode recent gains. However, the record to date is clear. Brazilian federal banks remain commanding heights fifteen years after liberalization and reforms under democracy that have transformed the statism of Brazilian banking and political economy. These banks breach the organizational level of analysis. Their large size, broad networks, and competitive advantages require rethinking assumptions about states, societies, markets and politics.

Advances in banking have transformed economic constraints to change. In 1975, David Gold, Clarence Lo and Erik Olin Wright wrote that Marxist views of state-society relations had developed from instrumental through functional to structural conceptions.[6] Most research in comparative political economy since describes markets as the sum of individual agents allocating resources. This still holds. Overspending by governments still creates fiscal deficits that require tax increases that drag the economy by reducing private investment. This further reduces growth, tax revenue and investment. This syndrome describes the macroeconomics of populism and barriers to change encountered by socialist and populist governments in Latin America 30–40 years ago. Federal banking in twenty-first-century Brazil is fundamentally different. Federal bank policies for social inclusion work within a new regulatory framework based on profound advances in monetary economics, banking theory and policy and information technology. Concepts such as the credit channel and advances in bank regulation, financial reporting standards and transparency provide a new context for policies and state-society relations. The microeconomics of popular credit and savings today differ from confrontational policies in the past such as large increases in the minimum wage, nationalisation of industries and government overspending to heat the economy. In Brazil, the microeconomics of social inclusion have replaced the macroeconomics of populism.

Theory and evidence suggest Brazilian federal banks retain competitive advantages and provide policy alternatives. Government banks can direct credit to manage industrial change. Government banks can direct credit downmarket to accelerate social inclusion. Government banks provide policy alternatives for economic adjustment and public sector reform. They make the most of taxes by leveraging budget lines and multiplying money for public policy. Government banks increase accountability, control and supervision over policy implementation because their loans provide contractual control over projects to ensure returns on public investments. Brazilian federal banks survived centralisation and mismanagement under military rule in the 1960s and 70s and further abuse during the last dance of traditional elites that prolonged transition and fed inertial inflation during the 1980s and early 1990s. Democratization changed the story. Since transition from military rule in Brazil, three large federal banks helped private banks and the public sector adjust to price stability amidst a seemingly endless series of financial crises. After capitalization in 2001, the Banco do Brasil, Caixa and BNDES helped avert recession during 2002–3 (and once again in 2008–9) by providing counter-cyclical credit. After adjustment, downsizing and liberalization under President Cardoso during the 1990s, these institutions helped accelerate social inclusion, recovery and growth under President Lula in the 2000s. Federal banks helped deepen Brazilian banking, finance and democracy.

NOTES

1 Government Banking Theory

1. Regional development banks, Banco do Nordeste (Bank of the Northeast, BNB), Banco da Amazonia (Bank of Amazonia, Basa) and the Central Bank of Brazil remain beyond the scope of this study.
2. Central Bank of Brazil, 'Top 50 Banks', September 2009. Available on http://www4.bcb. gov.br/top50/ingl/top50–i.asp [accessed 27 March 2010].
3. On these biases, see: G. O'Donnell, 'Illusions about Consolidation, '*Journal of Democracy*, 7:2 (1996), pp. 34–51 and L. Armijo, P. Faucher and M. Dembinska, 'Compared to What? Assessing Brazil's Political Institutions', *Comparative Political Studies*, 39:6 (2006), pp. 759–86.
4. On state government banks, see: A. Moura, 'Bancos Públicos Estaduais e Políticas Macroeconômicas', in A. C. Pinheiro and L. C. Oliveira Filho (eds), *Mercado de Capitais e Bancos Públicos: Análise e Experiências Comparadas* (Rio de Janeiro: Contra Capa-ANBID, 2007), pp. 305–18: H. M. Makler, 'Bank Privatization in Brazil: is the End of Financial Federalism in Sight?', Centre for Brazilian Studies Working Paper 8, University of Oxford (1999), J. P. P. Paes, 'Bancos Estaduais, 'Criação' de Moeda e Ciclo Político' (Masters Dissertation, EAESP-FGV, São Paulo, 1996) and S. Werlang and A. Fraga, 'Os Bancos Estadais e o Descontrole Fiscal: Alguns Aspectos', *Revista Brasileira de Economia*, 49:2 (1995), pp. 165–75.
5. For example, the São Paulo state government savings bank, Nossa Caixa, received the *Conjuntura Econômica* award for public enterprise turnaround in 2002.
6. L. Sola and L. Whitehead (eds), *Statecrafting Monetary Authority, Democracy and Financial Order in Brazil.* (Oxford: University of Oxford Centre for Brazilian Studies, 2006).
7. Critics emphasize abuse of state government banks during the electoral campaigns of 1982 and 1986. However, Juan Linz described Brazilian politics in this period as a situation of 'diarchy' because of the unprecedented combination of military control over the federal government alongside the holding of gubernatorial and legislative elections. The 1986 election was also held (without the presidency) in the first year of civilian government shaped by a price and wage freeze and before the 1988 Constitution. See P. Arida, 'Prefácio', in A. C. Pinheiro and L. C. O. Filho, *Mercado de Capitais e Bancos Públicos* (Rio de Janeiro: Contra Capa, 2007), p. 11.
8. Last dance (*último baile*) is an idiomatic expression referring to the last royal ball in Rio de Janeiro on 14 November 1889, the night before a military coup ended monarchy. It captures the behavior of traditional elites on the verge of major change – a central con-

cern during the prolonged transition from military rule in the country during the 1980s and 90s.

9. Epitomized by Polany and Shonfield, this tradition includes J. Zysman, *Governments, Markets and Growth: Financial Systems and the Politics of Industrial Change* (Ithaca, NY: Cornell University Press, 1983), P. Gourevitch *Politics in Hard Times: Comparative Responses to International Economic Crises* (Princeton, NJ: Princeton University Press, 1986), P. A. Hall and D. Soskice (eds), *Varieties of Capitalism: The Institutional Foundations of Comparative Advantage* (Oxford: Oxford University Press, 2001), C. Conaghan and J. Malloy, *Unsettling Statecraft: Democracy and Neoliberalism in the Central Andes* (Pittsburgh, PA: University of Pittsburgh Press, 1994) and Sola and Whitehead (eds), *Statecrafting Monetary Authority*; P. Kingstone, *Crafting Coalitions for Reform: Business Preferences, Political Insitutions and the Politics of Neoliberal Reform in Brazil* (University Park, PA: Pennsylvania State University Press, 1999), C. Kearney, 'The Comparative Influence of Neoliberal Ideas: Economic Culture and Stabilisation' (Doctoral Dissertation, Brown University Department of Political Science, 2001); K. Eaton and J. T. Dickovick, 'The Politics of Recentralisation in Argentina and Brazil', *Latin American Research Review*, 39:1 (2004), pp. 90–122 and D. Samuels, 'Fiscal Straightjacket: The Political Economy of Macroeconomic Reform in Brazil, 1995–2002', *Journal of Latin American Studies,* 35 (2003), pp. 1–25 all explore *political* determinants of economic policies in Brazil.

10. Claus Offe describes this as a sociological approach to political economy that focuses on how social interests, organizations and political coalitions sustain economic policies. C. Offe, 'Political Economy: Sociological Perspectives' in R. E. Goodin and H.-D. Klingemann (eds), *A New Handbook of Political Science* (Oxford: Oxford University Press, 1998), pp. 675–90. Comparative financial economics also emphasizes politics. See: F. Allen and A. Gale, *Comparing Financial Systems* (Cambridge, MA: MIT press, 2000) and R. Rajan and L. Zingales, 'The Great Reversals: The Politics of Financial Development in the Twentieth Century. '*Journal of Financial Economics*, 69:1 (2003), pp. 5–50.

11. Compare Lenin: 'Without big banks, socialism would be impossible. The big banks are the 'state apparatus' which we need to reach socialism and which we take ready-made from capitalism. (V. I. Lenin, *Selected Works*, Moscow, 2001 (1st edition, 1895), p. 365) to Shonfield: 'How much more profound was this Keynesian vision of control through a combination of financial pressure and improved economic information, than the socialist formula, which guided the dominant movement for reform for close on half a century, of capturing the 'commanding heights' of the economy' (A. Shonfield, *Modern Capitalism: The Changing Balance of Public and Private Power* (Oxford: Oxford University Press, 1965), p. 224).

12. Three examples from Shonfield's *Modern Capitalism*: 'Postwar French planning can be regarded as a device that mobilized a number of instruments of public enterprise and pressure, which had been lying around for some time and pointed them all in the same direction.' (p. 85) 'Through a series of accidents starting with a desperate piece of salvage by the Fascist Government, the Italians arrived at an alternative formula.' (ibid. p. 189) 'A body of nationalized undertakings as extensive and varied and as haphazardly put together as the Italian, is Austria (ibid., p. 192).

13. 1) 'the vastly increased influence of the public authorities', i. e., banks, state-owned or mixed enterprises: 2) economic policy on the continent remained anchored in social welfare and income policies: 3) policies tamed the 'violence' of the market both in terms of averting recessions and reducing competition so firms could invest in the long-term: 4)

sustained real income increases across all social classes also sustained growth: 5) advances in economic policy and theory enabled governments to plan in collaboration with the private sector and reduce the peaks and troughs of business cycles 'with a lighter touch' to increase growth. Shonfield, *Modern Capitalism*, pp. 66–7.

14. M. Aoki and H. Patrick (eds), *The Japanese Main Bank System: Its Relevance for Developing and Transforming Economies* (Oxford: Oxford University Press, 1995), p. 524.

15. Hall and Soskice, *Varieties of Capitalism*.

16. C. Johnson, *MITI and the Japanese Miracle: the Growth of Industrial Policy, 1925–1975* (Stanford, CA: Stanford University Press, 1982), p. 18.

17. S. Berger (ed.), *Organizing Interests in Western Europe: Pluralism, Corporatism and the Transformation of Politics* (Cambridge: Cambridge University Press, 1981) and P. Schmitter, 'Still the Century of Corporatism', *Review of Politics*, 36 (1974), pp. 85–131.

18. J. L. Campbell, J. R. Hollingsworth and L. N. Lindberg, *Governance of the American Economy* (Cambridge: Cambridge University Press, 1991), R. P. Dore, *Flexible Rigidities: Industrial Policy and Structural Adjustment in the Japanese Economy, 1970–80* (Stanford, CA: Stanford University Press, 1986), C. Edquist, *Systems of Innovation: Technologies, Institutions and Organizations* (London: Pinter, 1997), J. R. Hollingsworth and R. Boyer, *Contemporary Capitalism: The Embeddedness of Institutions* (Cambridge: Cambridge University Press, 1997), W. Lazonick, *Business Organization and the Myth of the Market Economy* (Cambridge: Cambridge University Press, 1991), R. R. Nelson, *National Innovation Systems: A Comparative Analysis* (Oxford: Oxford University Press, 1993), P. Schmitter and W. Streek, *Private Interest Government: Beyond Market and State* (London: Sage, 1985) and R. Whitley, *Divergent Capitalisms: The Social Structuring and Change of Business Systems* (Oxford: Oxford University Press, 1999).

19. J. Kirschner (ed.), *Monetary Orders: Ambiguous Economics, Ubiquitous Politics.* (Ithaca, NY: Cornell University Press, 2003).

20. Conaghan and Malloy, *Unsettling Statecraft.*

21. S. Hoffmann, *Politics and Banking: Ideas, Public Policy and the Creation of Financial Institutions* (Baltimore, MD: Johns Hopkins University Press, 2001).

22. H. Laurence, *Money Rules: The New Politics of Finance in Britain and Japan* (Ithaca, NY: Cornell University Press, 2001).

23. S. Pérez, *Banking on Privilege: The Politics of Spanish Financial Reform* (Ithaca, NY: Cornell University Press, 2003).

24. S. Maxfield, *Governing Capital: International Finance and Mexican Politics* (Ithaca, NY: Cornell University Press, 1990).

25. J. E. Woo, *Race to the Swift: State and Finance in Korean Industrialization* (New York: Columbia University Press, 1991).

26. On a veto coalition against reforms centred in the Banco do Brasil, see: M. Nobrega and G. Loyola, 'The Long and Simultaneous Construction of Fiscal and Monetary Institutions', in Sola and Whitehead, *Statecrafting Monetary Authority.* pp. 57–84.

27. S. Haggard, C. Lee and S. Maxfield (eds), *The Politics of Finance in Developing Countries* (Ithaca, NY: Cornell University Press, 1993), W. Novaes Filho and S. Werlang, 'Inflationary Bias and State Owned Financial Institutions', *Journal of Development Economics*, 47 (1995), pp. 135–54, M. Boycko, A. Shleifer and R. W. Vishny, 'A Theory of Privatization', *Economic Journal*, 106:435 (1996), pp. 309–19, A. Schleifer and R. W. Vishney, *The Grabbing Hand: Government Pathologies and their Cures* (Cambridge: Harvard University Press, 1998), M. Woo-Cummings (ed), *The Developmentalist State* (Ithaca, NY: Cornell University Press, 1999), R. La Porta, F. Lopez-de-Silanes and A. Schleifer, 'Gov-

ernment Ownership of Banks', *Journal of Finance*, 57:1 (2002), pp. 265–301, S. I. Dinç, 'Politicians and Banks: Political Influences on Government-Owned Banks in Emerging Markets', *Journal of Financial Economics*, 77 (2005), pp. 453–79, M. Nakane and D. B. Weintraub, 'Bank Privatization and Productivity: Evidence for Brazil', *Journal of Banking and Finance*, 29 (2005), pp. 2259–89, Pinheiro and Filho, *Mercado de Capitais e Bancos Públicos*.

28. B. Bortolotti and D. Siniscalco (eds), *The Challenges of Privatization: An International Analysis* (Oxford: Oxford University Press, 2004) and K. C. Lavelle, *The Politics of Equity Finance in Emerging Markets* (Oxford: Oxford University Press, 2004).

29. W. Coleman, 'Policy Convergence in Banking: a Comparative Study', *Political Studies*, 42 (1994), pp. 274–92, J. P. Krahnen and R. H. Schmidt, *The German Financial System* (Oxford: Oxford University Press, 2006), Allen and Gale, *Comparing Financial Systems*, T. Beck and R. Levine, 'New Firm Formation and Industry Growth: Does Having a Market- or Bank-Based System Matter?', *World Bank Working Paper* 2383, 2000.

30. La Porta, Lopez-de-Silanes and Schleifer, 'Government Ownership of Banks', A. Shleifer and R. W. Vishny, 'Politicians and Firms', *Quarterly Journal of Economics*, 109:4 (1994), pp. 995–1025.

31. On financial repression, see: R. McKinnon, *Money and Capital in Economic Development* (Washington, DC: Brookings Institution, 1973) and E. S. Shaw, *Financial Deepening in Economic Development* (Oxford: Oxford University Press, 1973).

32. Replication of La Porta, Lopez-de-Silanes and Schleifer's regression of government bank ownership on GDP growth for 1995–2004 (they used average growth from 1960–95) produced *opposite* regression results, i.e. government bank ownership correlated positively with higher levels of economic growth. See: K. von Mettenheim and L. Gonzalez, 'Government Ownership of Banks Revisited. 'São Paulo, FGV-EAESP, 2007 (memo).

33. On more focused comparisons, see: H. Brady and D. Collier (eds), *Rethinking Social Inquiry: Diverse Tools, Shared Standards* (Lanham, MD: Rowman & Littlefield, 2004).

34. M. Pagano and P. Volpin, 'The Political Economy of Finance', *Oxford Review of Economic Policy*, 17:4 (2001), pp. 502–19, T. Boeri, M. Castanheira, R. Faini, V. Galasso, G. B. Navaretti, C. Stéphane, J. Haskel, G. Nicoletti, E. Perotti, C. Scarpa, L. Tsyganok and C. Wey (eds), *Structural Reforms Without Prejudices* (Oxford: Oxford University Press, 2006), and the journal *New Political Economy*.

35. Studies of Japanese banks also emphasize these attributes. Hoshi argues: 'Past empirical studies suggest four important benefits of ... the main bank system in Japan: (1) implicit insurance (2) alleviation of the information problem (3) reduction in the cost of financial distress and (4) effective corporate monitoring.' T. Hoshi, 'Back to the Future: Universal Banking in Japan', in A. Saunders and I. Walter (eds), *Universal Banking: Financial System Design Reconsidered* (Chicago, IL: Richard Irwin, 1996), p. 210. See also: T. Hoshi, *Corporate Finance and Governance in Japan* (Cambridge, MA: MIT Press, 2004).

36. R. G. King and R. Levine, 'Finance and Growth: Schumpeter Might be Right', *Quarterly Journal of Economics* 108:3 (1993), pp. 717–37.

37. M. Hellwig, 'On the Economics and Politics of Corporate Finance and Corporate Control', in X. Vives (ed.), *Corporate Governance: Theoretical and Empirical Perspectives* (Cambridge: Cambridge University Press, 2000), pp. 95–134, R. Rajan and L. Zingales, 'Financial Dependence and Growth', *American Economic Review*, 88:3 (1998), pp. 559–86.

38. D. E. Weinstein and Y. Yafeh, 'On the Costs of a Bank-Centreed Financial System: Evidence from the Changing Main Bank Relations in Japan', *Journal of Finance*, 53 (1998), pp. 635–72.

39. Hellwig, 'On the Economics and Politics of Corporate Finance and Corporate Control'.

40. J. Stiglitz and A. Weiss, 'Credit Rationing in Markets with Imperfect Information', *American Economic Review*, 71 (1981), pp. 353–76.

41. For Beck and Levine, four theories have been pursued: bank-based, market-based, financial services and law and finance, with the latter two currently in favour and, we suggest, consistent with this third 'government banks and markets' theory of change. Beck and Levine, 'Industry Growth and Capital Allocation'. See also: T. Beck, R. Levine and E. Loayza, 'Finance and the Sources of Growth', *Journal of Financial Economics*, 58:1–2 (2000), pp. 261–300, R. Rajan and L. Zingales, 'Financial Dependence and Growth', R. Levine, 'Financial Development and Economic Growth: Views and Agenda', *Journal of Economic Literature*, 35 (1997), pp. 688–726, R. King and R. Levine, 'Finance, Entrepreneurship and Growth: Theory and Evidence', *Journal of Monetary Economics*, 32 (1993), pp. 513–42. The classic contribution is: R. Goldsmith, *Financial Structure and Development* (New Haven, CT: Yale University Press, 1969).

42. For example, from time series analysis of five advanced economies, Arestis, Demetriades and Luintel conclude: '... while stock markets may be able to contribute to long-term output growth, their influence is, at best, a small fraction of that of the banking system. Specifically, both stock markets and banks seem to have made important contributions to output growth in France. Germany and Japan, even though the former's contribution has ranged from about one-seventh to around one-third of the latter. Finally, the link between financial development and growth in the United Kingdom and the United States was found to be statistically weak and, if anything, to run from growth to financial development. Thus, our findings are consistent with the view that bank-based financial systems may be more able to promote long-term growth than capital-market-based ones.' P. Arestis, P. O. Demetriades and K. B. Luintel, 'Financial Development and Economic Growth: The Role of Stock Markets', *Journal of Money, Credit and Banking*, 33:1 (2001), p. 37.

43. A. Demirgüç-Kunt and R. Levine (eds), *Financial Structure and Economic Growth: A Cross-Country Comparison of Banks, Markets and Development* (Cambridge, MA: MIT Press, 2004).

44. This conclusion was also reached by R. Ayadi, R. H. Schmidt and S. C. Valverde, *Investigating Diversity in the Banking Sector in Europe: The Performance and Role of Savings Banks* (Brussels: Centre for European Policy Studies, 2009).

45. L. C. Bresser Pereira, *Globalization and Competition* (Cambridge: Cambridge University Press, 2010).

46. A. Amsden, 'Editorial: Bringing Production Back In: Understanding Government's Economic Role in Late Industrialization', *World Development*, 25:4 (2003), pp. 469–80 and A. Amsden, *The Rise of the Rest: Challenges to the West from Late Industrializing Economies* (Oxford: Oxford University Press, 2001).

47. H. J. Chang, *Kicking Away the Ladder? Policies and Institutions for Economic Development in Historical Perspective* (London: Anthem Press, 2002), P. Evans, *Embedded Autonomy: States and Industrial Transformation* (Princeton, NJ: Princeton University Press, 1995).

48. '... where investors are linked to the firms they fund through networks that allow for the development of reputations based on extensive access to information about the internal

operations of the firm ... investors will be more willing to supply capital to firms on terms that do not depend entirely on their balance sheets.' Hall and Soskice, *Varieties of Capitalism*, p. 10.

49. Amable also includes differences across financial systems as one of five central dimensions that determine the diversity of modern capitalism. B. Amable, *The Diversity of Modern Capitalism* (Oxford: Oxford University Press, 2003).

50. Conaghan and Malloy, *Unsettling Statecraft* and J. Nelson (ed.), *A Precarious Balance: Democracy and Economic Reforms in Latin America* (Washington, DC: Overseas Development Council, 1994).

51. Y. Altunbas, L. Evans and P. Molyneux. 'Bank Ownership and Efficiency', *Journal of Money, Credit and Banking*, 33:4 (2001), pp. 926–54.

52. Note Abraham Lincoln's fiscal arguments for a national bank: 'Of the subTreasury, then, as contrasted with a national bank for the before-enumerated purposes, I lay down the following propositions, to wit: (1) It will injuriously affect the community by its operation on the circulating medium. (2) It will be a more expensive fiscal agent. (3) It will be a less secure depository of the public money.' *The Writings of Abraham Lincoln*, Gutenberg Project Centennial Edition, p. 98.

53. Campos served as President of the Brazilian National Develpment Bank from August 1958–July 1959. Roberto Campos, Interview, BNDES Depoimentos, 1982.

54. Data from Federação Brasileira de Bancos (Brazilian Bank Federation, FEBRABAN), Central Bank of Brazil and Associação Brasileira das Entidades de Crédito Imobiliário e Poupança (Brazilian Association of Home Loan and Savings Entities).

55. T. Beck, A. Demirgüç-Kunt and R. Levine, 'Finance, Inequality and the Poor', *Journal of Economic Growth*, 12:1 (2007), pp. 27–49.

56. IBGE, *Pesquisa Nacional de Amostra de Domicílios* (National Household Sample Survey, PNAD) and Centre for Social Policy, FGV. Misery = <R$121.0 monthly per capita household income. Extreme poverty = <US$1.0 PPP per day income.

57. A. Przeworski, *Social Democracy as a Historical Phenomena* (Cambridge: Cambridge University Press, 1979).

58. J. Gurley and E. Shaw, 'Financial Aspects of Economic Development', *American Economic Review*, 45:4 (1955), pp. 515–38.

59. E. Fama, 'Banking in the Theory of Finance', *Journal of Monetary Economics* 6 (1980), pp. 39–57 and M. Klein, 'A Theory of the Banking Firm', *Journal of Money, Credit and Banking*, 3 (1971), pp. 205–18.

60. J. Tobin, 'The Commercial Banks as Creators of 'Money', in *Essays in Economics*, 3 vols (Cambridge, MA: MIT Press, 1982–7), vol. 1, p. 279) and J. Tobin, 'The Commercial Banking Firm: A Simple Model', *Scandanavian Journal of Economics* 84:4 (1982), pp. 495–530.

61. A. M. Santomero, 'Modeling the Banking Firm', *Journal of Money, Credit and Banking*, 16:4 (1984), pp. 576–602 and E. Baltensperger, 'Alternative Approaches to the Theory of the Banking Firm', *Journal of Monetary Economics*, 6 (1980), pp. 1–37.

62. M. O'Hara, 'A Dynamic Theory of the Banking Firm', *Journal of Finance*, 38:1 (1983), pp. 127–40.

63. G. A. Dymski, 'A Keynesian Theory of Bank Behavior', *Journal of Post Keynesian Economics* 10:4 (1988), pp. 499–526.

64. R. Studart, *Investment Finance in Economic Development* (London: Routledge, 1995), p. 1.

65. D. Diamond and R. G. Rajan, 'A Theory of Bank Capital', *Journal of Finance* 55:6 (2000), pp. 2431–465.

66. D. Diamond and R. G. Rajan, 'Liquidity Risk, Liquidity Creation and Financial Fragility: A Theory of Banking', *Journal of Political Economy* 109:2 (2001), pp. 287–327.
67. J. Hawkins and M. Dubravko, 'The Banking Industry in the Emerging Market Economies: Competition, Consolidation and Systemic Stability – An Overview' (Basel: Bank for International Settlements, 2001), p. 11 and S. Claessens, T. Glaessner and D. Klingebiel, 'Electronic Finance: Reshaping the Financial Landscape Around the World', *Journal of Financial Services Research*, 22:1–2 (2002), pp. 29–61.

2 Bank Change in Brazil

1. On Brazilian banking and finance before 1994, see: F. A. Lees, J. M. Botts and R. P. Cysne, *Banking and Financial Deepening in Brazil* (Basingstoke: Macmillan, 1990) and Studart, *Investment Finance in Economic Development*.
2. On foreign bank entry, see: L. F. Rodrigues de Paula, *The Recent Wave of European Banks in Brazil: Determinants and Impacts* (Oxford: Centre for Brazilian Studies, 2001).
3. I. Goldfajn, K. Henning and H. Mori, 'Brazil's Financial System: Resilience to Shocks, no Currency Substitution, but Struggling to Promote Growth', Central Bank of Brazil Working Paper 75 (2003), p. 5.
4. J. Zysman, 'How Institutions Create Historically Rooted Trajectories of Growth', *Industrial and Corporate Change*, 3:1 (1994), pp. 243–83.
5. On PROER, see: W. Baer and N. Nazmi, 'Privatization and Restructuring of Banks in Brazil'. *Quarterly Review of Economics and Finance*, 40:1 (2000), pp. 3–24, E. McQuerry, 'Managed Care for Brazilian Banks', *Federal Reserve Bank of Atlanta Review*, 86:2 (2001), pp. 27–44.
6. On PROES, see: T. Beck, J. M. Crivelli and W. Summerhill., 'State Bank Transformation in Brazil: Choices and Consequences', *Journal of Banking and Finance*, 29:8–9 (2005), pp. 2223–57, Samuels, 'Fiscal Straightjacket' and S. Cleofas, 'Bancos Estaduais: dos problemas crônicos ao PROES' (Brasilia: Central Bank of Brazil, 2004).
7. On deposit insurance funds, see: C. Calomiris, *The Postmodern Bank Safety Net: Lessons from Developed and Developing Countries* (Washington, DC: AEI Press, 1997).
8. On timing and politics of federal interventions, see: L. Sola and E. Kugelmas, 'Crafting Economic Stabilization: Political Discretion and Technical Innovation in the Implementation of the Real Plan', in Sola and Whitehead, *Statecrafting Monetary Authority*, pp. 85–116.
9. On federalism in transition from military rule, see: F. Abrucio, *Os Barões da Federação* (São Paulo: Edusp, 1999). On recentralization, see: Eaton and Dickovick, 'The Politics of Recentralisation in Argentina and Brazil'.
10. Vidotto summarizes goals of reforms and the 1988 World Bank International Finance Corporation agreement as follows: '1) to eliminate government interference in credit markets and develop private capital markets and long term lending instruments 2) to equalize reserve requirements for all instruments and all financial institutions ... 3) to strengthen the operating environment by increasing competition between banks and introducing a deposit insurance scheme 4) to support institutional reforms at the central bank to restructure the state bank system through liquidation or privatization of state government banks and 5) to reform the housing finance system through elimination of directed credits and development of private resources in the market.' C. A. Vidotto, 'O Programa de Reestruturação dos Bancos Federais Brasileiros nos Anos Noventa: Base Doutrinária e Afinidades Teóricas', *Economia e Sociedade*, 14:1 (2005), pp. 58–9.

11. On the 1999 crisis, see: W. C. Gruben and J. H. Welch, 'Banking and Currency Cri-
    sis Recovery: Brazil's Turnaround of 1999', *Economic and Financial Review* (2001), pp.
    12–23.
12. Vidotto, 'O Programa de Reestruturação dos Bancos Federais Brasileiros nos Anos
    Noventa', pp. 57–84.
13. E. Lundberg, 'Bancos Oficiais: Problema de Finanças Públicas ou Sistema Financeiro',
    Informações FIPE, 148 (1993), pp. 6–9.
14. Werlang and Fraga, 'Os Bancos Estaduais e o Descontrole Fiscal'.
15. Executive Secretary, Ministry of Finance (Secretaria Executiva, Ministério da Fazenda),
    'Nota Técnica 020', 23 July 1995.
16. '... the financial agents of the federal government, in the current context and foreseeable
    future, are justified as instruments for credit policy and agents of the federal Treasury, as
    complements to the financial system for strategic security.' ibid, p. 1.
17. Booz-Allen – FIPE (Fundação Instituto de Pesquisas Econômicas, Institute for Eco-
    nomic Research Foundation, Universidade de São Paulo). 'Relatório de Alternativas para
    a Reorientação Estratégica do Conjunto das Instuições Financeiras Públicas Federais.'
    Posted on http://www. fazenda. gov. br accessed in August 2000. Costa notes that this
    report lacks references to data sources and methods used to forecast profits/losses for
    Brazilian federal government banks. Indeed, the report's prediction that Brazilian fed-
    eral banks would sustain losses in 1999 and 2000 proved wrong. Use of 1994–5 data was
    also problematic because of use, during these years, of federal banks to cushion adjust-
    ment to price stability. F. N. Costa, 'Por uma alternativa para a reorientação estratégica
    das institutioções financeiras públicas federais: uma crítica construtiva ao Relatório
    Booz Allen & Hamilton – FIPE/USP submetida à audiência pública' (Campinas: UNI-
    CAMP, Instituto de Economia, memo, 2000).
18. The Brazilian federal government Asset Management Firm (Empresa Gestora de Ativos,
    Emgea) was created in 2001 to liquidate (recover and sell) problematic assets from
    federal government banks. Caixa liabilities to the FGTS, FDS and FAHRE were also
    transferred to the EMGEA. Subsequent injections of Itipu receivables (R$5.8 billion)
    and Caixa mortgage contracts (R$4.3 billion) increased Emgea capital in 2002 and 2003.
    The 2006 EMGEA financial statements report R$26.8 billion assets and R$11.0 billion
    losses accumulated since formation of the asset management company in 2001. Further
    costs reported by federal government since the 2001 capitalization of federal govern-
    ment banks include transfer of a further R$551.0 million mortgage contracts from the
    Caixa to EMGEA and R$20.5 million reported in 2006 budget for cost of acquiring
    credits under PROEF programme.
19. Estimates from: G. Hoggarth, R. Reis and V. Saporta, 'Costs of Banking System Instabil-
    ity: Some Empirical Evidence', *Journal of Banking & Finance*, 26:5 (2002), pp. 825–55.
20. On consolidation of sub-national debts in 1997, see: Central Bank of Brazil, 'Programa
    de Refinanciamento das Dívidas Públicas Municipais Relatório das Operações Realiza-
    das (Resolução n° 37, de 17/09/1999, do Senado Federal – art. 4°)' (Brasília: Central
    Bank of Brazil, 2000). On the evolution of municipal debt since 1997, see: Treasury
    Secretary, Ministry of Finance (Ministério da Fazenda, Secretaria do Tesouro Nacional),
    'Perfil e Evolução das Finanças Municipais, 1998–2003' (Brasília: Finance Ministry,
    Treasury Secretary, 2004).
21. On the Home Finance System, see: J. M. Aragão, *Sistema Financeiro da Habitação*
    (Curitiba: Juruá, 2006). A. M. Castelo, 'Sistema Financeiro da Habitação. 'Pesquisa e
    Debate 8:10 (1997), pp. 169–92.

22. On the BNH, see pp. 126–8 above and: C. Faro, *Vinte anos de BNH – a evolução dos planos básicos de financiamento para a aquisição da casa própria no BNH: 1964–84* (Niterói, RJ: EDUFF & Editora FGV, 1992).

23. Data from the Central Bank separates types of consumer credit during the period of recovery 2003–6. The largest increase in consumer credit comes from payroll loans that rose from R$9.7–R$48.1 billion 2003–6, followed by auto loans (R$30.0 billion– R$63.5 billion, 2003–6 and personal credit (R$30.5 billion–R$79.9 billion, 2003–6). Central Bank of Brazil, 'Relatório de Economia Bancária e Crédito' (Brasília, 2006).

24. Central Bank of Brasil, *Financial Stability Report*, 2005, p. 100. See also: E. Diniz, 'Correspondentes Bancários e Microcrédito no Brasil: Tecnologia Bancária e Ampliação dos Serviços Financeiros para a População de Baixa Renda' (São Paulo: FGV-EAESP, GVpesquisa Report, 2007) and A. Kumar, A. Parsons and E. Urdapilleta, 'Expanding Bank Outreach through Retail Partnerships: Correspondent Banking in Brazil', World Bank Working Paper 85 (2006). The reported monthly salary of correspondent bank clients suggest that these new points of banking services have reached lower income groups in Brazil. Of correspondent bank clients surveyed by the World Bank during 2005, 47.9 per cent of Caixa and 58.0 per cent of Bradesco (Banco Postal) clients reported earning less than R$200.0 (US$100.00) per month, while a further 39.2 per cent and 15.0 per cent respectively reported earning between R$200.00 and R$400.00.

25. Kumar, Parsons and Urdapilleta, 'Expanding Bank Outreach through Retail Partnerships'.

26. Ministry of Finance Brazil, Presentation 'Micro-credit and Micro-fiance under the Lula Government' (Brasilia: Finance Ministry, 2006).

27. Central Bank of Brazil, *Financial Stability Report* (Brasilia: Central Bank of Brazil, 2002).

28. Central Bank of Brazil, *Financial Stability Reports* (Brasilia: Central Bank of Brazil, 2002–6).

29. *Bankscope* cited in Central Bank of Brazil. *Financial Stability Report*. November 2008, p. 56 and Central Bank of Brazil, *Financial Stability Reports*, 2004–7.

30. Central Bank, *Financial Stability Reports*, 2002–6.

31. Central Bank, *Financial Stability Report*, November 2008, p. 56.

32. Central Bank, *Financial Stability Report*, 2006–8.

33. World Bank, 'Brazil: The Industry Structure of Banking Services' (Brasília: 2007).

34. Central Bank of Brazil, *Financial Stability Report*. November 2008, p. 56.

35. World Bank, 'Brazil: The Industry Structure of Banking Services'.

36. J. Boudoukh, M. Richardson, R. Stanton and R. Whitelaw, 'MaxVaR: Long Horizon Value at Risk in a Mark-to-Market Environment', *Journal of Investment Management*, 2:3 (2004), pp. 14–19.

37. Central Bank of Brazil, *Financial Stability Reports*, 2002–6. Basel Index = Measure of capital risk adequacy from Bank for International Settlements Basel Committee that calculates Base Capital as a percentage of total assets weighted by risk. Central Bank of Brazil minimum requirements of eleven remain above BIS recommendation of 8.0 per cent.

38. Survey of seventy-five Federal Deputies in 2002 by FAPESP Thematic Research Project, 'The Construction of Monetary Authority and Democracy: The Brazilian Experience in the Context of Global Economic Integration'.

3 The Banco do Brazil

1. Banco do Brasil assets at year end 2009 reached R$708.5 billion (after acquisition of the São Paulo state government savings bank, Nossa Caixa, and Votorantim Bank), once again displacing Itaú-Unibanco (R$608.3 billion assets) as the largest financial institution in Brazil and Latin America. The Banco do Brasil reported record profits for 2009, up 36 per cent over 2008 with 33.8 per cent increase in value of credit.

2. See Cysne's calculation of value transferred to banks under inflation. R. P. Cysne and P. C. C. Lisboa, 'Imposto Inflacionário e Transferências Inflacionárias no Brasil: 1947–2003', Rio de Janeiro: EPGE-FGV Ensaios Econômicos, 539 (March 2004).

3. British government debt increased from 247 million pounds sterling before continental war (1793) to 861 million pounds sterling after 1815. Given the shallow tax base of an estimated 70 million pounds sterling per year, the Bank of England is widely recognized as a comparative advantage for British policy and war.

4. D. T. Vieira, *Evolução do Sistema Monetário Brasileiro*, p. 68.

5. J. J. Sturz, *A Review, Financial, Statistical, and Commercial, of the Empire of Brazil and its Resources* (London: Effingham Wilson, Royal Exchange, 1837), p. 5.

6. J. R. Dunlop, *Curso Forçado*, 2nd edn (Rio de Janeiro: Laemmert, 1888).

7. 'I am convinced that of all the public delapidations that have occured in the Finance Ministry, none compare to the great robbery of the Banco do Brasil. They (shareholders and directors), have, for their personal interest, sacrificed the entire nation. Until this company is dissolved, I will not vote for one penny of loans. This company has robbed Treasury. Call me revolutionary, I shall call them thieves.' Odorico Mendes, cited in J. Lyra Filho, *O Estado Monetário: Introdução à História das Caixas Econômicas Brasileiras* (Rio de Janeiro: Irmãos Pongetti, 1948), p. 33.

8. 'Monetary chaos' is taken from C. A. Souza, *A Anarquia Monetária e suas Conseqüências* (São Paulo, Monteiro Lobato, 1924). Demand for copper coins, especially in the north, encouraged contraband copper coin from the US and neighbouring states.

9. Finance Ministry Report, 1832, p. 66.

10. Mauá then founded the private bank Mauá-MacGregor. See: J. Caldeira, *Mauá: Empresário do Império* (São Paulo: Companhia das Letras, 1995).

11. A. Vilella, 'The Political Economy of Money and Banking in Imperial Brazil, 1850–1870' (London: London School of Economics and Political Science, doctoral dissertation, 1999).

12. The failure of Overend, Gurney & Co. in England in 1866 also led to a run on deposits of the London & Brazilian Bank and request for support from the Banco do Brasil. The Director of the Banco do Brasil notes: '[for] fifteen days they were called upon to pay upwards of one million in pounds sterling in deposits.' Vilella, 'The Political Economy of Money and Bankin in Brazil', p. 262.

13. Ibid., p. 164.

14. G. D. Triner, 'Banking, Economic Growth and Industrialisation: Brazil, 1906–30', *Revista Brasileira de Economia,* 50:1 (1996), pp. 141.

15. From 26 November to 27 December 1889, the provisional government granted permission to print currency to: Banco Mercantil de Santos, Crédito Real do Brasil, Banco Comercial do Rio, Banco Mercantil da Bahia, Banco de Pernambuco, Banco Comerical Pelotense, Banco União da Bahia, and Banco Sociedade Comércio da Bahia.

16. J. P. Calogeras, *La Politique Monétaire du Brésil* (Rio de Janeiro, Editora Nacional, 1910), pp. 225–6.

17. 1892 Ministry of Finance report, Calogeras, *La Politique Monétaire du Brésil*, p. 245.
18. S. Topik, *The Political Economy of the Brazilian State, 1889–1930* (Austin: University of Texas Press, 1987), p. 31.
19. Ibid., p. 34.
20. N. L. Vilela (ed), *Idéias Econômicas de Joaquim Murtinho* (Brasília: Senado Federal/ Fundação Rui Barbosa, 1980).
21. Shareholders recovered losses when bank reopened at 30 per cent of pre-crisis.
22. Topik, *The Political Economy of the Brazilian State*, p. 40.
23. The Caixa de Conversão attempted to stabilize the foreign exchange rate at 15 pence by receiving gold coin and printing only currency convertible to gold.
24. On Celso Furtado's analysis of cost socialization, see: L. C. Bresser Pereira and J. M. Rego (eds), *A Grande Esperança em Celso Furtado* (São Paulo: Editora 34, 2001), pp. 228.
25. Decline of world coffee prices in 1920 led producers to appeal for emergency credits and new mechanisms to stock coffee along the lines of the 1906 accord. After Congress refused to purchase coffee stocks through emission of Treasury bills, the creation of the Carteira de Emissão (Emissions Portfolio) in October 1920 responded to these pressures for liquidity.
26. Topik estimates that domestic ownership requirements for rediscount operations increased market share of domestic banks from 50–70 per cent. Topik, *The Political Economy of the Brazilian State*, p. 36.
27. The treasury supplied the bank with notes, paid over 40,000 contos in interest rates on those notes, and permitted trading all the while taking loans out from the bank. Receipts from these operations were distributed 30 per cent to the bank, 20 per cent to the Treasury, 3 per cent to Carteira de Redescontos reserves, and 20 per cent to purchase gold reserves for paper money.
28. During this period of tight money and recovery, the São Paulo state government bank, Banespa, also became a critical player in domestic banking. Banespa implemented yet another scheme to stock coffee and support producers, facilitated in part by the eagerness of London banks without previous experience in Brazil to enter the market.
29. R. Thorp (ed), *Latin America in the 1930s* (London: Palgrave, 1984).
30. Coffee blooms provided accurate crop forecasts and set futures prices.
31. Law n°. 21.499, 9 June 1932.
32. 'The Fund would extend loans to banks according to assets. In turn, loans could not be used for other upcoming bank operations: the resources received from the Fund would only be used for operations linked to the active assets that were shown to the Fund. The loans could be extended for up to 5 years.' A. Villela and W. Suzigan, *Política do Governo e Crescimento da Economia Brasileira, 1889–1945* (Rio de Janeiro: IPEA, 1973), p. 182.
33. 'In December 1931, the rediscount portfolio of the Banco do Brasil was given the right by the Federal government to increase its operating capital to 400 thousand contos. At the same time the Carteira was given the right to discount the bonds of the Conselho Nacional do Café (National Coffee Council), basing this change on the '10 shillings tax'. Later, the Counsel shifted to depositing the income from that tax in the Banco do Brasil', Villela and Suzigan, *Política do Governo e Crescimento da Economia Brasileira*, p. 195.
34. D. T. Vieira, *Evolução do Sistema Monetário Brasileiro*, 1962, p. 272.
35. Law n°. 20.695, 20 November 1932.
36. Villela and Suzigan, *Política do Governo e Crescimento da Economia Brasileira*, p. 352 from Banco do Brasil Annual Reports.

37. Decree 1201, 8 April 1939.
38. Nobrega and Loyola, 'The Long and Simultaneous Construction of Fiscal and Monetary Institutions', p. 61.
39. CACEX was founded in December 1953. In response to accusations of corruption and abuse, the government later substituted it with the Carteira de Exportação e Importação (Import Export Facility).
40. Law 1807, January 1953.
41. The Banco do Brasil was authorized to buy foreign currency at a fixed rate with repayment due in up to ninety days. Banco do Brasil gains from swap and short term bank credits were not classified as returns on capital because the period (ninety days) remained below that in law.
42. For purchase of PVCs at auction, it was necessary to pay for an exchange certificate and receive an import licence. With the PVC and licence in hand, firms could purchase foreign exchange in banks at the official rate. Licenses and PVA prices were set according to five categories scaled by importance of imports for the economy.
43. Government spending increased because of public works, policies to alleviate drought in the Northeast, payment of a bonus for public employees and Banco do Brasil coverage of overdue payments from São Paulo state government.
44. 'Records show that the Banco do Brasil played a crucial role in the expansion of the currency stock through its various funds. Paper-money issued through rediscounting reached 5.3 billion cruzeiros. Of this total, the Banco do Brasil Rediscount Account absorbed 4.8 billion: the rest of the banking sector 0.5 billion. Of the total increase in credit, the Banco do Brasil was responsible for 68.6 per cent, summing to 17 billion cruzeiros for government projects and three billion for the private sector.' C. M. Peláez and W. Suzigan, *História Monetária do Brasil* (Brasilia: UNB, 1981), p. 247.
45. 'Finance Minister Aranha's attempt to control credit aroused protests from São Paulo businessmen, who petitioned the minister in July (1954) to use the large money reserves which the Bank of Brazil had accumulated from the profits of its auction sale of foreign exchange under the regulations introduced the preceding October.' T. Skidmore, *The Politics of Brazil, 1930–1964 An Experiment in Democracy* (New York: Oxford University Press, 1967), p. 135.
46. Sumoc Instruction 113 (27 January 1955) authorized CACEX to release import licences without exchange rate coverage for equipment listed as import priority. For Brazilian firms without access to foreign credit, this became an attractive option.
47. Increases of 30 per cent in M1 and 28.0 per cent in M2, Peláez and Suzigan, *História Monetária do Brasil*, p. 254.
48. Foreign investment under Law nº 4131, 1962 increased capital inflows during the following decade. Resolution nº 63, 1962 also allowed Brazilian banks to raise capital abroad to increase credit and finance of domestic firms unable to tap foreign markets.
49. A. Fishlow, 'Thirty Years of Combating Inflation in Brazil: from the PAEG (1964) to the Plano Real (1994)', University of Oxford Centre for Brazilian Studies, Working Paper 68, 2005.
50. On orthodox economic policy and military rule, see: G. O'Donnell, *Modernization and Bureaucratic Authoritarianism* (Berkeley, CA: University of California Institute for International Studies, 1973), A. Foxley, *Latin American Experiments in Neo-Conservative Economics* (Berkeley, CA: Univesity of California Press, 1983) and H. Shamis, 'Reconceptualizing Latin American Authoritarianism in the 1970s: From Bureaucratic-Authoritarianism to Neoconservatism', *Comparative Politics*, 23:2 (1991), pp. 201–20.

51. Bank Reform Law 4595.
52. M. C. Tavares, *Da substituição de importações ao capitalismo financeiro: ensaios sobre economia brasileira* (Rio de Janeiro: Zahar Editores, 1978).
53. A. A. Zini Jr, 'Uma avaliação do setor financeiro no Brasil: da reforma de 1964/65 à crise dos anos 80' (Campinas, DEPE-UNICAMP, masters dissertation, 1990), p. 45.
54. Indexed bonds remained beneficial through the 1970s. However, foreign debt and fiscal crises transformed government bond issues and interest rate policies into motor of inertial inflation. L. C. Bresser Pereira and Y. Nakano, *The Theory of Inertial Inflation* (Boulder, CO: Lynn Reiner, 1987).
55. L. A. C. Lago, 'A retomada do crescimento e as distorções do 'milagre': 1967–1973', in M. Abreu (ed.), *A Ordem do Progresso: Cem Anos de Política Econômica Republicana. 1889–1989* (Rio de Janeiro: Campus, 1990), pp. 233–94.
56. On IMF-Brazil relations, see: Kugelmas, 'Difícil Hegemonia: Um Estudo sobre São Paulo na Primeira República' (Doctoral Dissertation, Universidade de São Paulo Department of Political Science, 1986).
57. In 1984, an international commission recommended the transfer of budget execution from the Banco do Brasil to the Ministry of Finance. However, 'Twelve federal Congressmen were permanent [Banco do Brasil] employees, including the House majority leader ... The president of the Federal Accounting Court was against the measures ... Being also a bank employee, he later declared, with pride, that he was the leader of the group pushing for cancellation of the reform. The Minister of Agriculture, a former president of the Banco do Brasil, also publicly condemned the measures.' Nobrega and Loyola. 'The Long and Simultaneous Construction', pp. 69–70.
58. M. C. Tavares, 'O rombo do Banco do Brasil', *Correio Braziliense* (14 April 1996).
59. Folha de S. Paulo, 17 August 1994, B1.
60. Folha de S. Paulo, 14 February 2001.
61. Folha de S. Paulo, 25 July 1995, B1.
62. Previ, the Banco do Brasil employee pension fund has become one of the central players in Brazilian political economy: with assets summing over R$116.0 billion at year end 2008. See www.previ.com.br.
63. On agricultural credit, see: J. G. Gasques and C. M. Villa Verde, 'Gastos Públicos na Agricultura, Evolução e Mudanças', Brasília, IPEA Discussion Paper 948 (2003).
64. Ibid., p. 15
65. For example, see O Estado de S. Paulo economy columnist C. Ming, 'O Lucro do Banco do Brasil', 27 February 2010, B2.
66. Central Bank of Brazil, *Relatório de Estabilidade Financeira* (November 2008), p. 134.

4 The Caixa Economica Federal (Federal Savings Bank)

1. La Porta, Lopez-de-Silanes and Schleifer, 'Government Ownership of Banks', Gurley and Shaw, 'Financial Aspects of Economic Development'.
2. Two exceptions: G. B. Silva, *Caixas Econômicas: A Questão da Função Social* (Rio de Janeiro: Forense, 2004) and H. A. Souza, 'O Crédito Imobiliário da CEF' (Rio de Janeiro: Masters Dissertation, EPGE, Fundação Getulio Vargas, 1992). Two legal and administrative histories of the Caixas remain, one from 1937 another from 1960: J. Henrique, *Estrutura e Conjuntura das Caixas Econômicas Federais* (Rio de Janeiro: Conselho Superior das Caixas Econômicas Federais, 1960) and O. J. De Placido e Silva, *As Caixas*

Economicas Federais: Sua História, Seu Conceito Jurídico, Sua Organização, Sua Adminis-tração e Operações Autorisadas (Curitiba: Empresa Gráfica Paranaense, 1937).

3. J. Mura (ed.), *History of European Savings Banks*, 2 vols (Stuttgart: Sparkassen Verlag, 1996–2000).

4. R. Price, *Proposal for Establishing Life Annuuities in Parished for the Benefit of the Indus-trial Poor* (London, 1773), J. Acland, *A Plan for Rendering the Poor Independent of Public Contributions* (Exeter, 1786), F. Eden, *Observations on Friendly Societies for the Mainte-nance of the Industrious Classes during Sickness, Old Age and other Exigencies* (London, 1801) and P. Coloquhoun, *A Treatise on Indigence* (London, 1806).

5. P. Gosden, *The Friendly Societies in England, 1815–1875* (Manchester: University of Manchester Press, 1961).

6. Mura (ed.), *History of European Savings Banks*.

7. In Austria, savings banks retain 17 per cent of assets, deposits and loans in the domestic banking market. In Germany, the Sparkasse system (and Landesbanks) sum to 35.5 per cent of assets, 38.7 per cent of bank deposits and 28.1 per cent of loans. The Spanish sav-ings banks, Cajas de Ahorro, retained 39.0 per cent of domestic bank assets, 50.0 per cent of deposits and 46.9 per cent of loans in the country (2005).

8. F. Scharpf, *Governing in Europe* (Oxford: Oxford University Press, 1995) and E. Ostrom, *Governing the Commons* (Cambridge: Cambridge University Press, 1990).

9. On postal savings banks in Asia, see: M. Sher and N. Yoshino (eds), *Small Savings Mobi-lization and Asian Economic Development: The Role of Postal Financial Services* (London: M. E. Sharpe, 2004).

10. J. F. Sigaud, *O Homem Benfazejo ou das Vantagens que Resultam da Fundação da Caixa Econômica dos Povos Civilizados* (Rio de Janeiro: Tipografia Imperial e Constitucional de Seignot-Plancher & Cia. Vol. XII Biblioteca Constitucional do Cidadão Brasileiro, 1832) and A. Rocha, *As Caixas Econômicas e o Crédito Agrícola* (Rio de Janeiro, 1905).

11. Currency during the Empire was the milréis ($1,000). A thousand milréis equalled one conto de réis, or conto written as 1:000$. At the 1846 fixed foreign exchange rate, one milréis = 27 pence: 1 pound sterling = 8$890 (8.890 contos) or 8.89 milréis.

12. Decree 2,723 January 1861, cited in De Placido e Silva, *As Caixas Economicas Federais*, p. 12.

13. Finance Ministry, *Relatório 1874*, Appendix.

14. 'Savings Banks, as beneficent establishments, will be managed without salary by directors nominated by the government: and the good services thereby rendered shall be consid-ered for any and all ends.' Law 1083, Article 1, paragraph 14, 1860.

15. On finance sources for war with Paraguay, see: L. C. Carreira, *Historia Financeira e Orçamentária do Império do Brasil* (Brasilia: Senado/Fundação Rui Barbosa, 1980), p. 469. Government bonds purchased by the Caixa after 1874 provided alternative source for funds amidst concern about government debt among creditors and the high cost of credit.

16. Finance Ministry, *Relatório, 1871*, p. 52.

17. F. T. Souza Reis, *A Dívida do Brasil: Estudo Retrospectivo* (São Paulo: Officinas Graphi-cas da '*Revista de Commercio e Industria*', 1917), p. 106–7.

18. De Placido e Silva, *As Caixas Economicas Federais*, p. 70.

19. Finance Ministry, *Relatório, 1902*, p. 691.

20. Repartição de Estatística e Archivo do Estado, *Annuario Estatístico de São Paulo* (São Paulo, 1920), p. 307.

21. *Annuario Estatístico de São Paulo*, 1920, p. 303.

22. Caixas in states able to accumulate reserves (patrimony fund) acquired autonomy, while others remained subordinate to Finance Ministry regional offices.
23. De Placido e Silva, *Caixas Econômicas Federais*, p. 232.
24. Ibid. p. 80.
25. Ibid. p. 82.
26. In 1934, Caixa branch offices existed in the states of Rio de Janeiro, São Paulo, Rio Grande do Sul, Parana, Pernambuco, Bahia and Minas Gerais. By 1945, branch offices had been opened in the Amazon, Ceará, Espirito Santo, Maranhão, Mato Grosso, Pará and Santa Catarina states. In 1946, branches were opened in Alagoas, Goias, Paraiba, Piaui, Rio Grande do Norte and Sergipe, followed by December 1956 in the territories of Acre, Amapa, Rondonia and Rio Branco. J. Henrique, *Estrutura e Conjuntura das Caixas Econômicas Federais*.
27. Conselho Superior das Caixas Econômicas Federais, *1959 Report*, p. 96.
28. Caixas Econômicas *Relatório, 1969*, pp. 38–9.
29. C. Lemgruber, *Uma Análise Quantitativa do Sistema Financeiro no Brasil*, p. 243.
30. F. Giambiagi and M. M. Moreira (eds), *A Economia Brasileira nos Anos 90* (Rio de Janeiro: BNDES, 1999), Parte 2, 'A Crise Fiscal'.
31. The Caixa was used to cover the difference, extending long term loans to state governments at 2.75 per cent per month, below the 8 per cent per month market rate for credit. This shift began when the Central Bank of Brazil capped lending to state governments against future budget receipts (Anticipação de Receitas Orçamentárias) from R$1.7 billion to R$900.0 million in 1997.
32. On 12 October 1995, the first conditional loans to states (total R$90.0 million) were signed with Alagoas, Minas Gerais and Piaui, with an additional R$40.0 planned for Sergipe and Maranhão. Subsequent conditional loans granted Santa Catarina (R$90.0 million), Rio de Janeiro (R$180.0 million), Pará (R$53.0 million), Rio Grande do Sul (R$150.0 million), Acre (R$27.0 million), Bahia (R$100.0 million), Alagoas (R$55.0 million) and Minas Gerais again (R$190.0 million).
33. Caixa Econômica Federal, *Relatórios de Administração*, 2005–8.
34. Ibid.
35. Central Bank of Brazil, 'Diagnóstico do Sistema de Pagamentos de Varejo do Brasil, Adendo Estatístico – 2007'(Brasilia: Central Bank of Brazil, 2007), p. 9 and Caixa *Annual Reports*, 2003–8.
36. Central Bank of Brazil and Caixa, *Relatórios de Administração*, 2003–8.

5 The Banco Nacional de Desenvolvimento Econômico e Social (National Bank for Economic and Social Development, BNDES)

1. A. C. Castro (ed.), *Desenvolvimento em debate* (Rio de Janeiro: BNDES, 2002), L. Sola, *Idéias Econômicas Decisões Políticas* (São Paulo, Edusp, 1998) and E. Gudin and R. Simonsen, *A Controvérsia do Planejamento na Economia Brasileira* (Rio de Janeiro: IPEA/INPES, 1978).
2. E. J. Willis, 'The State as Banker: The Expansion of the Public Sector in Brazil. '(Austin, TX: Ph. D. dissertation, University of Texas Department of Political Science, 1986) and L. Martins, *Pouvior et Développment Economique: Formation e Evolution de Structures Politiques au Brésil* (Paris: Anthropos, 1976).

3.   B. Aghion, 'Development Banking', *Journal of Development Economics*, 58 (1999), pp. 83–100 and Woo-Cummings, *The Developmentalist State*, K. Sikkink, *Ideas and Institutions: Developmentalism in Brazil and Argentina* (Ithaca, NY: Cornell University Press, 1991), A. O. Hirschman, 'Ideologies of Development in Latin America', *Latin American Issues: Essays and Comments* (New York: The Twentieth Century Fund, 1961), G. Arbix, et al. (eds), *Razões e Ficções do Desenvolvimento*. São Paulo: Unesp, 2001 and R. Bielschowsky, *Pensamento Econômico Brasileiro: O Ciclo Ideológico do Desenvolvimento* (Rio de Janeiro: Contraponto, 1998).

4.   'The existing commercial banks were unable to provide industry with long-term finance for two main reasons. First, they were unwilling to bear the inevitable risks associated with the financing of new enterprises. Second, they lacked the specialized skills required to deal with the higher risk long-term investments ...', Aghion, 'Development Banking', p. 3. Amman also argues that state finance in the capital goods sectors of developing countries are designed to provide: 'Enhanced protection, development of internal markets through government procurement, support for research and development, regulation of technology transfer, coordination and regulation of the development of new industrial capacity (capacity licensing) and the support of user-producer interaction.' E. Amann, *Economic Liberalization and Industrial Performance in Brazil* (Oxford: Oxford University Press, 2000), p. 31.

5.   'The logically sound basis for the presumption against long-term commitments is that it is much more difficult to estimate a borrower's creditworthiness 20 years ahead than 6 months ahead. The factors relevant to creditworthiness are substantially different over the longer period and the capacity and experience required in the bank manager are of an all together different order, an order it is not reasonable generally to expect unless he has specialized expert staff.' R. S. Sayers, *Central Banking After Baghot* (Oxford: Oxford University Press, 1957) cited in Aghion, 'Development Banking', p. 3.

6.   R. Sylla, 'The Role of Banks', in R. Sylla and G. Toniolo (eds), *Patterns of European Industrialization in the 19th Century* (London: Routledge, 1991), pp. 45–63. Aghion notes: 'The oldest government-sponsored institution for industrial development is the Societe General pour Favoriser l'Industrie National which was created in the Netherlands in 1822. However, it was in France that some of the most significant developments in long-term state-sponsored finance occurred. In this respect, the creation in 1848–1852 of institutions such as the Credit Foncier, the Comptoir d'Escompte and the Credit Mobilier, was particularly important', Aghion, 'Development Banking', p. 3.

7.   On development banks in Europe, see: C. Kindleberger, *A Financial History of Western Europe* (London: George Allen & Unwin, 1984) and R. E. Cameron, *Banking and Economic Development: Some Lessons of History* (New York: Oxford University Press, 1972). 'Of even greater importance than the outcome of the operations of the Credit Mobilier were the intangible benefits such as the imitated skills of the engineers and technicians which it sent abroad, the efficiency of its administrators and the organizational banking techniques which were so widely copied.' R. E. Cameron, 'The Credit Mobilier and the Economic Development of Europe', *Journal of Political Economy*, 53:6 (1953), p. 486 (cited in Aghion, 'Development Banking', p. 86). Compare Schneider: 'Many BNDE *técnicos* left the bank (they were often in great demand) and took its institutionalization, professionalization and developmental nationalism to other parts of the bureacracy', B. R. Schneider, *Politics within the State: Elite Bureaucrats & Industrial Policy in Authoritarian Brazil* (Pittsburgh, PA: University of Pittsburgh Press, 1991), p. 35.

8. W. Diamond, *Development Banks* (Baltimore, MD: Johns Hopkins University Press, 1957).

9. Aghion cites: Societe National de Credit a l'Industrie (Belgium, 1919), Credit National (France, 1919), 1928, National Bank, Poland, 1928), 1928, Industrial Mortgage Bank (Finland, 1928), Industrial Mortgage Institute (Hungary, 1928), 1933, Instituto Mobiliare Italiano (Italy, 1933), Instituto per la Reconstructione Industriale (Italy, 1933).

10. Diamond notes: 'Probably the aggregate resources provided by the development banks have been small, but the fact that there were made available at particular times for strategically important enterprises and industries gave them a significance far greater than the amounts involved suggest', Diamond, *Development Banks*, pp. 38–9. On import substitution industrialization in Brazil and Latin America, see: A. Fishlow, 'Origins and Consequences of Import Substitution in Brazil', in L. Di Marco (ed.), *International Economics and Development* (New York: Academic Press, 1972), pp. 339–56 and W. Baer, 'Import Substitution and Industrialization in Latin America: Experiences and Interpretations' (*Latin American Research Review*, 1972), pp. 95–122.

11. Johnson, *MITI and the Japanese Miracle*.

12. 'Since its foundation in 1952, this official bank had become an active center of investment and development planning for such strategic sectors of the economy as electric power, transportation and basic industry. The bank became the natural home for a group of economists who were convinced that economic development required various 'structural 'changes and needed to be firmly guided by the state, but by a new, managerial and efficient state rather than the old, clientelistic, parasitic 'Cartorial State'. A. O. Hirschman, *Journeys Toward Progress: Studies of Economic Policy-Making in Latin America* (New York: Norton, 1963), p. 73. The concept of Cartorial state comes from H. Jaguaribe, *O Nacionalismo na Atualidade Brasileira* (Rio de Janeiro: Instituto Superior de Estudos Brasileiros, 1958).

13. Woo, *Race to the Swift*.

14. Evans, *Embedded Autonomy: States and Industrial Transformation*.

15. Woo-Cumings (ed.), *The Developmental State*.

16. On competing explanations of the Asian financial crisis, see: R. Hall, 'The Discursive Demolition of the Asian Development Model', *International Studies Quarterly* 47:1 (2003), pp. 71–99.

17. Annual BNDES reports from 1952–60 review programme of 'reaparelhamento econômico. '

18. S. B. Viana, *A política econômica no segundo governo Vargas (1951–1954)* (Rio de Janeiro: BNDES, 1987), A. Cruz, A. M. A. , C. M. L. Costa, M. C. S. D'Araujo and S. B. da Silva, *Impasse na democracia Brasileira (1951–1955)* (Rio de Janeiro: FGV, 1983) and M. C. S. D'Araujo, *O Segundo Governo Vargas (1951–54): Democracia, Partidos e Crise Política* (Rio de Janeiro: Zahar, 1982).

19. On ECLA training of first generation BNDE officials, see: E. Willis, 'The State as Banker', pp. 220–2 and N. Leff, *Economic Policymaking and Development in Brazil, 1947–64* (New York: Wiley, 1968), Schneider, *Politics within the State*, Martins, *Pouvoir et Développment Economique* and reviews of BNDES history published by the bank in 2002.

20. BNDE-ECLA, 'Esboço de um Programa de Desenvolvimento para a Economia Brasileira no Período 1955–62' (Rio de Janeiro: BNDE, 1953).

21. To modernize the São Paulo-Rio de Janeiro railway.

22. Companhia Nacional de Álcalis (RJ): Usina Rio Bonito (ES): Fábrica Nacional de Motores (RJ): Viação Férrea do Rio Grande do Sul (RS): Superintendência das Empresas Incorporadas ao Patrimônio Nacional (Seipan) in Rio de Janeiro.

23. BNDE contracts from 1956–1960 are listed in J. L. Dias, 'O BNDE e o Plano de Metas. 1956/61' (Rio de Janeiro: BNDES, 1996).

24. Leff, *Economic Policymaking and Development in Brazil*, pp. 39–40.

25. The Conselho Nacional de Desenvolvimento (National Development Council, CND) was composed of federal government ministers, presidential staff (civil and military affairs) and the presidents of the Banco do Brasil and BNDE. For review of Kubitshek policies, see: Sikkink, *Ideas and Institutions*, M. V. Benevides, *O governo Kubitschek – desenvolvimento econômico e estabilidade política – 1956 for 1961* (Rio de Janeiro: Paz e Terra, 1979) and C. Faro and S. Quadros, 'A década de 50 e o programa de metas', in A. Gomes, *O Brasil de JK* (Rio de Janeiro: FGV-CPDOC, 1991).

26. Dias, 'O BNDE e o Plano de Metas', p. 81.

27. On foreign exchange regulations, see: D. Huddle, 'Disequilibrium, Foreign Exchange Systems and the Generation of Industrialization and Inflation in Brazil', *Economia Internazionale* (1972), pp. 35–71.

28. Dias, 'O BNDE e o Plano de Metas', p. 51.

29. Ibid. p. 107.

30. 'In 1956 managers instituted an entrance examination and over the years the BNDE codified rules for merit-based promotion (which was also on the whole rapid). The bank also instituted a range of technical courses, management training programmes and scholarships for outside study. Schneider, *Politics within the State*, p. 35.

31. Dias, 'O BNDES e o Plano de Metas'.

32. On auto production in Brazil, see: C. Addis, *Taking the Wheel: Auto Parts Firms and the Political Economy of Industrialization in Brazil* (University Park, PA: Penn State University Press, 1999) and H. Shapiro, *Engines of Growth: The State and Transnational Auto Companies in Brasil* (Cambridge, MA: Harvard University Press, 1994).

33. On reforms, see: Studart, *Investment Finance in Economic Development*, and J. Welch, *Capital Markets in the Development Process: The Case of Brazil* (Pittsburgh, PA: University of Pittsburgh Press, 1993).

34. On BNDES lending and national security policy, see: J. C. Oliveira, 'Em Busca de um Modelo de Segurança de Suprimento de Matérias-Primas Fundamentais' in D. C. Monteiro Filha and R. L. Modenesi (eds), *BNDES: Um Banco de Ideías: 50 anos refletindo o Brasil* (Rio de Janeiro: BNDES, 2002), pp. 47–62.

35. Fundo de Desenvolvimento Técnico e Científico (Technical and Scientific Development Fund, Funtec).

36. On BNDES technology transfer and incentive policies, see: D. J. Allen, 'Tecnologia: Suas Formas, a Legislação e o Apoio Institucional', in Monteiro Filha and Modenesi *BNDES: Um Banco de Ideías*, pp. 113–76 and H. Rattner (ed.), *Instituições financeiras e desenvolvimento tecnológico autônomo: o Banco Nacional de Desenvolvimento Econômico e Social* (São Paulo: IPE/USP, Fapesp, 1991).

37. In September 1966 (Decree 59.170), Finame was transformed into the Agência Especial de Financiamento Industrial (Industrial Development Agency) providing funds for technical and graduate education.

38. On industrial interest groups, see: P. Schmitter, *Interest Conflict and Political Change in Brazil* (Stanford, CA: Stanford University Press, 1971), E. Amman, *Economic Liberalization and Industrial Performance in Brazil*, F. S. Erber, 'Technological Development

and State Invervention: A Study of the Brazilian Capital Goods Industry' (Ph.D. dissertation, University of Sussex, 1978), B. R. Schneider, *Politics Within the State*, L. Payne, *Brazilian Industrialists and Democratic Change* (Baltimore, MD: Johns Hopkins University Press, 1994) and M. A. P. Leopoldi, *Política e Interesses na Industrialização Brasileira. As associações dos industriais, a política econômica e o Estado* (São Paulo: Paz e Terra, 2000).

39. In 1970, the Fundepro was replaced by the Fundo de Modernização e Reorganização Industrial (Industrial Modernization and Reorganization Fund, FMRI).

40. Programa Especial de Apoio Financeiro à Indústria Básica do Nordeste (Special Programme for Financial Assistance to Northeast Basic Industries), the Programa de Modernização e Reorganização da Comercialização (Modernization and Reorganization of Commerce Programme) and Programa Especial Bancos de Desenvolvimentos (Special Development Bank Programme).

41. In 1973, Cebrae was spun off from the BNDE as a private non-profit institution and renamed Sebrae.

42. M. C. Tavares, *Da Substituição de Importações ao Capitalismo Financeiro*, 7th edn (Rio de Janeiro: Zahar Editores, 1978).

43. L. G. M. Belluzzo and L. Coutinho (eds), *Desenvolvimento Capitalista no Brasil: Ensaios Sobre a Crise* (São Paulo: Brasiliense, 1983).

44. On public project finance in the early 1970s, see: E. Bacha, A. B. Araújo, M. Mata and R. Modenesi, 'Análise Governamental de Projetos de Investimento no Brasil. Procedimentos e Recomendações' (Relatório de Pesquisa, no 1. Rio de Janeiro: IPEA-INPES, 1972). Three credit lines were created for underdeveloped regions: The Programa Especial de Apoio Financeiro à Indústria Básica do Nordeste (Special Programme for Financial Assistance to Basic Industries in the Northeast, PIB-NE), the Programa de Modernização e Reorganização da Comercialização (Programme of Modernization of Commerce, PMRC) e o Programa Especial Bancos de Desenvolvimentos (Special Development Bank Program, PEB). These programmes proved important for development of agroindustry in the 1970s.

45. A. L. R. Carlos, et al., 'O BNDES e a Agroindústria', in Monteiro Filha and Modenesi, *BNDES: Um Banco de Ideías*, pp. 177–86.

46. R. Bonelli and A. C. Pinheiro, 'O Papel da poupança compulsória no financiamento do desenvolvimento: desafios para o BNDES', *Revista do BNDES*, 1:1 (1994), p. 27.

47. Welch, *Capital Markets in the Development Process*, p. 14.

48. On economic policies and growth during the 1970s, see: A. B. Castro and F. E. P. Souza, *A Economic Brasileira em Marcha Forçada* (São Paulo: Paz e Terra, 1985). On the BNDE and PND II, see: M. A. C. Pinto, 'O BNDES e o Sonho de Desenvolvimento: 30 Anos de Publicação do II PND', *Revista do BNDES*, 11:22 (2004).

49. W. Suzigan, 'Financiamento de projetos industriais no Brasil', *Relatórios de pesquisa IPEA*, 9, 1974, A. B. Araújo and R. L. Modenesi, 'Avaliação de Projetos no Brasil', in Monteiro Filha and Modenesi, *BNDES: Um Banco de Ideías*, pp. 63–91 and W. A. Magalhães, 'Comparação entre os Pressupostos do BNDES e da Análise de Custo-Benefício na Análise de Projetos', Monteiro Filha and Modenesi, *BNDES: Um Banco de Ideías*, pp. 187–208 and B. Frydman, et al., 'Metodologia de Análise de Projetos', Monteiro Filha and Modenesi, *BNDES: Um Banco de Ideías*, pp. 209–42.

50. L. Corrêa do Lago et al., *A Industria Brasileira de bens de Capital*.

51. Amman, *Economic Liberalization and Industrial Performance in Brazil*, ch. 4.

52. On military doctrine of national security and creation of BNDE subdivisions, see: J. C. Oliveira, 'Em Busca de um Modelo de Segurança de Suprimento de Matérias-Primas Fundamentais'.

53. On the political economy of ethanol policy, see: M. H. Castro Santos, *Política e Políticas de Uma Energia Alternativa: O Caso do Proálcool* (Rio de Janeiro: Anpocs/Notrya, 1993).

54. 'The Figueiredo government changed the BNDE drastically and deinstitutionalized one of the bastions of procedure and technical rationality within the Brazilian state. 'B. R. Schneider, *Politics within the State*, p. 190.

55. The Ministry of Industry and Commerce housed two secretariats: Secretaria de Tecnologia Industrial (Secretariat of Industrial Technology, STI) and Conselho de Desenvolvimento Industrial (Industrial Development Council, CDI).

56. On economic forecasting at the BNDE, see: E. Marques, 'Prospec: Modelo de Geração de Cenários em Planejamento Estratégico', in Monteiro Filha and Modenesi, *BNDES: Um Banco de Ideías*, pp. 291–330.

57. The 'S' for social in BNDES wasadded in 1982. Decree 1940 of 25 May 1982 created a Fundo de Investimento Social (Social Investment Fund, Finsocial) administered by the BNDES. The bulk of early BNDES social and environmental spending went to the computerization of prisons and the construction of urban recycling centers. See: M. Nardim (et al). 'Usinas de Reciclagem de Lixo: Aspectos Sociais e Viabilidade Econômica', in Monteiro Filha and Modenesi, *BNDES: Um Banco de Ideías*, pp. 271–90.

58. M. R. R. Pizzo, 'Participação do Setor Privado nas Áreas de Infra-Estrutura', in Monteiro Filha and Modenesi, *BNDES: Um Banco de Ideías*, pp. 331–344 and S. Najberg, 'Transformação do Sistema BNDES em Financiador do Setor Privado Nacional' (Memo, BNDES, 1989).

59. Bonelli and Pinheiro, 'O Papel da poupança compulsória no financiamento do desenvolvimento', pp. 29–31.

60. Companhia de Tecidos Nova América (junho de 1987), Máquinas Piratininga do Nordeste, Máquinas Piratininga SA, Caraíba Metais, Sibra, Celpag, Siderúrgica Nossa Senhora Aparecida.

61. On planning, BNDES, 'Plano de Ação do Sistema BNDES, 1978–80' (BNDES. On agricultural finance, C. A. L. Roque, J. M. A. Monteiro de Barros and H. Hermeto Filho 'BNDES e a Agroindústria', in Monteiro Filha and Modenesi, *BNDES: Um Banco de Ideías*, pp. 177–86. From 1985 to 1990, the BNDES published business plans that reveal the transition away from state-led strategies toward privatization, private sector lending and the modernization of internal administration and decision-making along lines of private investment and commercial banking. See: '1º Plano Estratégico do Sistema BNDES' (for 1985–7), '2º Plano Estratégico do Sistema BNDES' (for 1988–90). See: BNDES, 'Metodologia de Análise de Projetos' (Rio de Janeiro: BNDES, 1988).

62. E. Diniz (ed.), *Empresários e Modernização Econômica: Brasil anos 90* (Florianópolis, UFSC, 1993) and Giambiagi and Moreira (eds), *A Economia Brasileira nos Anos 90*.

63. The first large privatization was Usiminas, the Minas Gerais state government steel enterprise, despite opposition from Governor Itamar Franco.

64. Programa de Financiamento à Exportações de Máquinas e Equipamentos (Machine and Equipment Export Promotion Finance, Finamex).

65. CSN, Cosipa, Companhia Siderúrgica de Tubarão, Companhia Siderúrgica da Piratini, Companhia Siderúrgica da Acesita, Cosinor and Açominas.

66. Law 8.987, 1995.

67. Shares representing 28.3 per cent of Petrobras voting shares were sold.
68. On second generation reforms, see: A. Velasco and M. Tommasi, 'Where Are We in the Political Economy of Reform?' *Journal of Policy Reform*, 1:2 (1996), pp. 187–238, and M. Naim, 'Latin America: The Second Stage of Reform', *Journal of Democracy*, 5:4 (1994), pp. 32–48. On reforms and BNDES policy, see A. S. Barreto and R. Arkader, 'Novos Paradigmas de Competitividade: Implicações para a Atuação do Sistema BNDES', in Monteiro Filha and Modenesi, *BNDES: Um Banco de Ideías*, pp. 383–412.
69. On global strategies in Brazilian industry, see: M. Laplane and L. Coutinho, *Internacionalização da Indústria no Brasil* (São Paulo: Editora UNESP, 2003).
70. BNDES programmes to channel finance to small and medium enterprises, with little success, include: Programa de Capitalização de Empresas de Pequeno Porte (Small Enterprise Capitalization Programme, Contec), Investimento em Empresas Emergentes (Emerging Enterprise Investments) and Apoio às Novas Sociedades Anônimas (New Business Assistance).
71. The Fundo de Amparo ao Trabalhador (Worker Compensation Fund, FAT), created in 1970, is administered by the BNDES, remaining 17 per cent of deposits in 2008. FAT council mandates use of funds in productive investments and prohibits purchase of government bonds.
72. Source: BNDESpar, 'Financial Statements', 2008, pp. 33–4.
73. BNDESpar, 'Financial Statements', 2008, pp. 23.
74. BNDES, *Annual Reports*, 2002–6.

Conclusion

1. R. K. Merton, 'The Unanticipated Consequences of Purposive Social Action', *American Sociological Review*, 1 (1936), pp. 894–904.
2. A. A. Bearle Jr and G. Means, *The Modern Corporation and Private Property* (New York: Macmillan, 1932).
3. HM Treasury, 'Discussion Paper on Non-Bank Lending' (London: HM Treasury, 2010).
4. J. Rawls, *Political Liberalism* (New York: Columbia University Press, 1996).
5. R. A. Dahl, *Polyarchy* (New Haven, CT: Yale University Press, 1973), G. Sartori, Parties and Party Systems (New York: Cambridge University Press, 1976), C. Tilly (ed.), *The Formation of National States in Western Europe* (Princeton, NJ: Princeton University Press, 1975), S. Huntington, *Political Order in Changing Societies* (New Haven, CT: Yale University Press, 1968).
6. D. A. Gold, C. Lo and E O. Wright, 'Recent Developments in Marxist Theories of the Capitalist State', *Monthly Review*, 27:5 (1975), pp. 29–43.

WORKS CITED

Official Sources

Banco do Brasil., 'Annual Reports (1824–1949) and (2002–2009)'. 1824–1949 reports available on Centre for Research Libraries, Brazilian Government Document Digitalization Project, at http://brazil.crl.edu/bsd/bsd/hartness/fazend.html and, for 2002–8, online at http://www.bb.com.br [accessed 10 February 2010].

Bank for International Settlements (BIS)., 'Evolving banking systems in Latin America and the Caribbean: challenges and implications for monetary policy and financial stability'. *BIS Papers, No. 33*, Monetary and Economic Department (February 2007), at http://www.bis.org/publ/bppdf/bispap33.htm [accessed 10 February 2010].

—, 'The New Basel Accord: An explanatory note.' *Secretariat of the Basel Committee on Banking Supervision* (January 2001), at http://www.bis.org/publ/bcbsca01.pdf [accessed 10 February 2010].

—, 'Survey of Electronic Money Developments' *CPSS Publication No 38* (May 2000), at http://www.bis.org/publ/cpss38.pdf [accessed 10 February 2010].

—, 'Cycles and the Financial System' *Basel* (Switzerland: Annual Report 2002), at http://www.bis.org/press/p030630b.htm [accessed 10 February 2010].

BNDES, 'Annual Reports' (1998–2009), at http://www.bndes.gov.br [accessed 10 February 2010].

BNDES, '1º Plano Estratégico do Sistema BNDES' (Rio de Janeiro, BNDES, 1984).

BNDES, '2º Plano Estratégico do Sistema BNDES' (Rio de Janeiro, BNDES, 1987).

BNDES, 'Metodologia de Análise de Projetos' (Rio de Janeiro: BNDES, 1988).

Booz-Allen Hamilton / Fundação Instituto de Pesquisas Econômicas (USP)., 'Relatório de Alternativas para a Reorientação Estratégica do Conjunto das Instuições Financeiras Públicas Federais', at http://www.fazenda.gov.br [accessed 10 August 2000].

Caixa Econômica Federal., 'Annual Reports and Financial Statements'(1861–2008), available on Centre for Research Libraries, Brazilian Government Document Digitalisation Project (1860–1949), at http://brazil.crl.edu/bsd/bsd/hartness/fazend.html, and (2002–8) at http://www.caixa.gov.br [accessed 10 February 2010].

Caixas Econômicas Federais., *Revista das Caixas Econômicas*. (Rio de Janeiro, Caixas Econômicas Federais, 1949–64).

Central Bank of Brazil., 'Financial Stability Reports' (2002–8), at http://www.bcb.gov.br/ [accessed 10 February 2010].

—, 'Credit Time Series' (1988–2009), Sisbacen, at http://www.bcb.gov.br/?SERIESFN [accessed 10 February 2010].

—, 'Top 50 Banks', at www.bcb.gov.br/?50TOP [accessed 17 March 2010].

—, 'Trabalhos de Discussão' (2003–2009), at www.bcb.gov.br/?TRABDISC [accessed 10 February 2010].

—, 'Relatório de Economia Bancária e Crédito', Brasília (2006), at www.bcb.gov. br/?RELECON06 [accessed 10 February 2010].

—, 'Resolução n° 37, de 17/09/1999, do Senado Federal – art. 4°' *Departamento da Dívida Pública, Programa de Refinanciamento das Dívidas Públicas Municipais Relatório das Operações Realizadas,* Brasília (2000).

Cleofas, S. Jr. 'Bancos Estaduais: dos problemas crônicos ao PROES.' Central Bank of Brazil (2004), at http://www.bcb.gov.br/?BANEST [accessed 10 February 2010].

Conselho das Caixas Econômicas. *Revista das Caixas Econômicas,* Rio de Janeiro (1949– 1963).

BNDES, Annual Reports, 2003–8 (Rio de Janeior: BNDES, 2003–8). Available on http:// inter.bndes.gov.br/english/annual_report.asp [accessed 5 February 2010].

HM Treasury, 'Discussion paper on non-bank lending' (London: HM Treasury, 2010). Available on http://www.hm-treasury.gov.uk/d/non_bank_lending_discussionpaper.pdf [accessed 29 March 2010]

Instituto Brasileiro de Geografia e Estatística., 'Pesquisa Nacional de Amostra de Domicílios', Annual Editions (1995–2006), at http://www.ibge.gov.br/home/estatistica/.../default. shtm [accessed 10 February 2010].

Instituto Brasileiro de Geografia e Estatística., *Estatísticas do Século Vinte,* 2003, available at http://www.ibge.gov.br/seculoxx/default.shtm [accessed 20 March 2010].

Kumar, A., A. Parsons and E. Urdapilleta, 'Expanding Bank Outreach through Retail Partnerships: Correspondent Banking in Brazil', orld Bank Working Paper 85 (2006), at http://siteresources.worldbank.org/INTTOPCONF3/Resources/363980.pdf [accessed 10 February 2010].

Ministry of Finance, 'Annual Reports' (1821–1949), available on Centre for Research Libraries, Brazilian Government Document Digitalisation Project, at http://brazil.crl. edu/bsd/bsd/hartness/fazend.html [accessed 10 February 2010].

Ministry of Finance (Secretaria Executiva, Ministério da Fazenda), *Nota Técnica 020* (23 July 1995).

Ministry of Finance (Ministério da Fazenda, Secretaria do Tesouro Nacional), *Perfil e Evolução das Finanças Municipais 1998–2003* (Brasília, Agosto 2004).

Ministry of Finance, *Parecer da Commissão de Inquérito sobre as Caixas Econômicas e Montes de Socorro* (1892).

Ministry of Finance (and Conselho do Estado), *Parecer da Commissão sobre as Caixas Econômicas e Montes de Soccorro* (Rio de Janeiro, 1882).

Ministry of Finance, *Parecer da Commissão sobre as Caixas Econômicas e Montes de Soccorro* (Rio de Janeiro, 1875).

Monteiro Filha, D. C., and R. L. Modenesi (eds), *BNDES: Um Banco de Ideías; 50 anos refletindo o Brasil* (Rio de Janeiro: BNDES, 2002), at http://www.bndes.gov.br/SiteBNDES/export/sites/default/bndes_pt/Galerias/Arquivos/conhecimento/livro_ideias/livro-00.pdf [accessed 10 February 2010].

State Council and Finance Ministry (Conselho do Estado e Ministério da Fazenda), *Parecer da Commissão sobre as Caixas Econômicas e Montes de Soccorro* (Rio de Janeiro, 1882).

World Bank, International Finance Corporation, *1º Empréstimo de Ajustamento do Setor Financeiro*. Memorando de Iniciação (1988).

—, 'Brazil: The Industry Structure of Banking Services,' Brasília: June 2007.

World Trade Organisation, *Opening Markets in Financial Services and the Role of GATT* (1997) at http://www.wto.org/english/res_e/booksp_e/special_study_1_e.pdf [accessed 10 February 2010].

Secondary Sources

Abreu, M. P. (ed.), *Ordem do Progresso: Cem Anos de Política Econômica Republicana* (Rio de Janeiro: Campus, 1990).

Abrucio, F., *Os Barões da Federação* (São Paulo: Edusp, 1999).

Acland, J., *A Plan for Rendering the Poor Independent of Public Contributions* (Exeter, 1786).

Addis, C., *Taking the Wheel: Auto Parts Firms and the Political Economy of Industrialisation in Brazil* (University Park, PA: Penn State University Press, 1999).

Aghion, B., 'Development Banking', *Journal of Development Economics*, 58 (1999), pp. 83–100.

Allen, F., and D. Gale, *Comparing Financial Systems* (Cambridge, MA: MIT Press, 2000).

Altunbas, Y., L. Evans and P. Molyneux, 'Bank Ownership and Efficiency', *Journal of Money, Credit and Banking,* 33:4 (November 2001), pp. 926–54.

Amable, B., *The Diversity of Modern Capitalism* (Oxford: Oxford University Press, 2003).

Amann, E., *Economic Liberalisation and Industrial Performance in Brazil* (Oxford: Oxford University Press, 2000).

Amsden, A., 'Editorial: Bringing Production Back In: Understanding Government's Economic Role in Late Industrialisation', *World Development*, 25:4 (2003), pp. 469–80.

—, *The Rise of The Rest: Challenges to the West from Late-Industrializing Economies* (Oxford: Oxford University Press, 2001).

Aoki, M., and H. T. Patrick (eds), *The Japanese Main Bank System: its Relevance for Developing and Transforming Economies* (Oxford: Oxford University Press, 1994).

Aragão, J. M., *Sistema Financeiro da Habitação* (Curitiba: Juruá, 2006).

Arbix, G., M. Zilbovicius and R. Abramovay (eds), *Razões e Ficções do Desenvolvimento* (São Paulo: Unesp, 2001).

Arestis, P., P. Demitriadis and K. B. Luintel, 'Financial Development and Economic Growth: The Role of Stock Markets', *Journal of Money, Credit and Banking*, 33:1 (2001), pp. 16–41.

—, 'Financial Development and Economic Growth: Assessing the Evidence', *Economic Journal*, 107:442 (1997), pp. 783–99.

Arida, P., 'Prefácio', in A. C. Pinheiro and L. C. Oliveira Filho (eds), *Mercado de Capitais e Bancos Públicos* (Rio de Janeiro: Contra Capa-ANBID, 2007).

Armijo, L., P. Faucher and M. Dembinska., 'Compared to What? Assessing Brazil's Political Institutions', *Comparative Political Studies*, 39:6 (2006), pp. 759–86.

Ayadi, R., R. H. Schmidt and S. C. Valverde, *Investigating Diversity in the Banking Sector in Europe: The Performance and Role of Savings Banks* (Brussels: Centre for European Policy Studies, 2009).

Bacha, E., 'Do Consenso de Washington ao Dissenso de Cambridge', in A. C. Castro (ed.), *Desenvolvimento em debate: novos rumos do desenvolvimento no mundo* (Rio de Janeiro, BNDES, 2002).

Baer, W., 'Import Substitution and Industrialisation in Latin America: Experiences and Interpretations', *Latin American Research Review* (1972), pp. 95–122.

Baer, W., and N. Nazmi, 'Privatisation and Restructuring of Banks in Brazil', *Quarterly Review of Economics and Finance*, 40:1 (2000), pp. 3–24.

Baltensperger, E., 'Alternative Approaches to the Theory of the Banking Firm', *Journal of Monetary Economics*, 6 (January 1980), pp. 1–37.

Barros, J. R. M. and F. A. J. Mansueto, 'Análise do Ajuste do Sistema Financeiro no Brasil', *Política Comparada,* 1:2 (1997), pp. 89–132.

Bortolotti, B., and D. Siniscalco (eds), *The Challenges of Privatisation: An International Analysis* (Oxford: Oxford University Press, 2004).

Bearle Jr, A. A., and G. Means, *The Modern Corporation and Private Property* (New York: Macmillan, 1932).

Beck, T., and R. Levine, 'Industry Growth and Capital Allocation: Does Having a Market- or Bank-based System Matter?', *Journal of Financial Economics*, 64 (2002), pp. 147–80.

Beck, T., J. M. Crivelli and W. Summerhill, 'State Bank Transformation in Brazil: Choices and Consequences', *Journal of Banking and Finance*, 29:8–9 (2005), pp. 2223–57.

Beck, T., A. Demirgüç-Kunt and R. Levine, 'Finance, Inequality and the Poor', *Journal of Economic Growth*, 12:1 (2007), pp. 27–49.

Beck, T., R. Levine and E. Loayza, 'Finance and the Sources of Growth', *Journal of Financial Economics,* 58:1–2 (2000), pp. 261–300.

Belluzzo, L. G. M., and L. Coutinho (eds), *Desenvolvimento Capitalista no Brasil: Ensaios Sobre a Crise* (São Paulo: Brasiliense, 1983).

Benevides, M. V., *O Governo Kubitschek: Desenvolvimento Econômico e Estabilidade Política 1956–1961* (Rio de Janeiro: Paz e Terra, 1979).

Berger, A. N., and D. B. Humphrey, 'Efficiency of Financial Institutions: International Survey and Directions for Future Research', *European Journal of Operational Research*, 98 (1997), pp. 175–212.

Berger, S. (ed.), *Organizing interests in Western Europe* (Cambridge: Cambridge University Press, 1981).

Bielschowsky, R., *Pensamento Econômico Brasileiro: O Ciclo Ideológico do Desenvolvimento* (Rio de Janeiro: Contraponto, 1998).

Boeri, T., M. Castanheira, R. Faini, V. Galasso, G. B. Navaretti, C. Stéphane, J. Haskel, G. Nicoletti, E. Perotti, C. Scarpa, L. Tsyganok and C. Wey (eds), *Structural Reforms Without Prejudices* (Oxford: Oxford University Press, 2006).

Bonelli, R., and A. C. Pinheiro, 'O Papel da Poupança Compulsória no Financiamento do Desenvolvimento: Desafios para o BNDES', *Revista do BNDES*, 1:1 (1994).

Boudoukh, J., M. Richardson, R. Stanton and R. Whitelaw, 'MaxVaR: Long Horizon Value at Risk in a Mark-to-Market Environment', *Journal of Investment Management*, 2:3 (2004), pp. 14–19.

Boycko, M., A. Shleifer and R. W. Vishny, 'A Theory of Privatisation', *Economic Journal*, 106:435 (March 1996), pp. 309–19.

Brady, H., and D. Collier (eds), *Rethinking Social Inquiry: Diverse Tools, Shared Standards* (Lanham, MD: Rowman and Littlefield, 2004).

Bresser Pereira, L. C., *Globalization and Competition* (Cambridge: Cambridge University Press, 2010).

Bresser Pereira, L. C., and J. M. Rego (eds), *A Grande Esperança em Celso Furtado* (São Paulo: Editora 34, 2001).

Caldeira, J., *Mauá: Empresário do Império* (São Paulo: Companhia das Letras, 1995).

Calogeras, J. P., *La Politique Monétaire du Brésil* (Rio de Janeiro: Editora Nacional, 1910).

Calomiris, C., *The Postmodern Bank Safety Net: Lessons from Developed and Developing Countries* (Washington, DC: AEI Press, 1997).

Cameron, R. E., *Banking and Economic Development: Some Lessons of History* (New York: Oxford University Press, 1972).

Campbell, J. L., J. R. Hollingsworth and L. N. Lindberg., *Governance of the American Economy* (Cambridge: Cambridge University Press, 1991).

Carreira, L. C., *Historia Financeira e Orçamentária do Império do Brasil* (Brasília: Senado/ Fundação Rui Barbosa, 1980).

Castelo, A. M., 'Sistema Financeiro da Habitação' *Pesquisa e Debate*, 8:10 (1997), pp. 169–92.

Castro, A. B., and F. E. P. Souza, *A Economic Brasileira em Marcha Forçada* (São Paulo: Paz e Terra, 1985).

Castro, A. C. (ed.), *Desenvolvimento em Debate* (Rio de Janeiro: BNDES, 2002).

Castro Santos, M. H., *Política e Políticas de Uma Energia Alternativa: O Caso do Proálcool* (Rio de Janeiro: Anpocs/Notrya, 1993).

Chang, H. J., *Kicking Away the Ladder? Policies and Institutions for Economic Development in Historical Perspective* (London: Anthem Press, 2002).

Claessens, S., T. Glaessner and D. Klingebiel., 'Electronic Finance: Reshaping the Financial Landscape Around the World', *Journal of Financial Services Research*, 22 (2002), pp. 29–61.

Coleman, W., 'Policy Convergence in Banking: A Comparative Study', *Political Studies*, 42 (1994), pp. 274–92

Coloquhoun, P., *A Treatise on Indigence* (London, 1806).

Conaghan, C. M., and J. Malloy, *Unsettling Statecraft: Democracy and Neoliberalism in the Central Andes* (Pittsburgh, PA: University of Pittsburgh Press, 1994).

Costa, F. N., 'Por uma alternativa para a reorientação estratégica das instituições financeiras públicas federais: uma crítica construtiva ao Relatório Booz Allen and Hamilton – FIPE/ USP submetida à audiência pública' *Memo 2000*, Universidade de Campinas (2004).

Cruz, A. M. A., C. M. L. Costa, M. C. S. D'Araujo and S. B. da Silva., *Impasse na Democracia Brasileira (1951–1955)* (Rio de Janeiro: FGV, 1983).

Cysne, R. P., and P. C. C. Lisboa, 'Imposto Inflacionário e Transferências Inflacionárias no Brasil: 1947–2003', EPGE-FGV Ensaios Econômicos, no 539 (Rio de Janeiro, March 2004).

Dahl, R. A., *Polyarchy* (New Haven, CT: Yale University Press, 1971).

D'Araujo, M. C. S., *O Segundo Governo Vargas (1951–54): Democracia, Partidos e Crise Política* (Rio de Janeiro, Zahar, 1982).

Demirgüç-Kunt, A., and R. Levine (eds), *Financial Structure and Economic Growth: A Cross-Country Comparison of Banks, Markets and Development* (Cambridge, MA: MIT Press, 2004).

De Placido e Silva, O. J., *As Caixas Economicas Federais: Sua História, Seu Conceito Jurídico, Sua Organização, Sua Administração e Operações Autorisadas* (Curitiba: Empresa Gráfica Paranaense, 1937).

Dewatripont, M., and E. Maskin., 'Credit and Efficiency in Centralised and Decentralised Economies', *Review of Economic Studies,* 62:4 (1995), pp. 541–55.

Diamond, D., and R. G. Rajan., 'Liquidity Risk, Liquidity Creation and Financial Fragility: A Theory of Banking', *Journal of Political Economy*, 109:2 (2001), pp. 287–327.

—, 'A Theory of Bank Capital', *Journal of Finance*, 55:6 (December 2000), pp. 2431–65.

Diamond, W., *Development Banks* (Baltimore, MD: Johns Hopkins University Press, 1957).

Dias, J. L., 'O BNDES e o Plano de Metas. 1956/61', *BNDES* (Rio de Janeiro,1996).

Diniz, E., 'Correspondentes Bancários e Microcrédito no Brasil: Tecnologia Bancária e Ampliação dos Serviços Financeiros para a População de Baixa Renda', *GVpesquisa Report* (São Paulo: FGV-EAESP, 2007).

— (ed.), *Empresários e Modernização Econômica: Brasil anos 90* (Florianópolis, UFSC, 1993).

Dinç, S. I., 'Politicians and Banks: Political Influences on Government-Owned Banks in Emerging Markets', *Journal of Financial Economics*, 77 (2005), pp. 453–79.

Dore, R. P., *Flexible Rigidities: Industrial Policy and Structural Adjustment in the Japanese Economy, 1970–80* (Stanford, CA: Stanford University Press, 1986).

Dunlop, J. R., *Curso Forçado*, 2nd edn (Rio de Janeiro: Laemmert, 1888).

Dymski, G. A., 'Banking on Transformation: Financing Development, Overcoming Poverty', *Paper presented to UFRJ Economics Institute* (September 2003).

Eaton, K., and J. T. Dickovick., 'The Politics of Recentralisation in Argentina and Brazil', *Latin American Research Review*, 39:1 (2004), pp. 90–122.

Eden, F., *Observations on Friendly Societies for the Maintenance of the Industrious Classes during Sickness, Old Age and other Exigencies* (London, 1801).

Edquist, C., *Systems of Innovation: Technologies, Institutions and Organisations* (London: Pinter, 1997).

Ekkehard, E. C., *Financial Systems, Industrial Relations and Industry Specialisation: An Econometric Analysis of Institutional Complementarities* (Paris: OECD, 2002).

Erber, F. S., 'Technological Development and State Invervention: A Study of the Brazilian Capital Goods Industry' (Ph.D. dissertation, University of Sussex, 1978).

Evans, P., *Embedded Autonomy: States and Industrial Transformation* (Princeton, NJ: Princeton University Press, 1995).

Fama, E.F., 'Banking in the Theory of Finance', *Journal of Monetary Economics*, 6 (1980), pp.39–57.

Faro, C., *Vinte anos de BNH – a evolução dos planos básicos de financiamento para a aquisição da casa própria no bnh: 1964–84* (Niterói, RJ: EDUFF and Editora FGV, 1992).

Faro, C., and S. Quadros, 'A década de 50 e o programa de metas', in A. Gomes (ed.), *OBrasil de JK* (Rio de Janeiro: FGV-CPDOC, 1991), pp. 44–70.

FIPE-USP, *Sistema Financeiro Nacional: Diagnósticos e sugestões para reforma* (São Paulo: FIPE-USP, 1991).

Fishlow, A., 'Thirty years of combating inflation in Brazil: from the PAEG (1964) to the Plano Real (1994)', *Working Paper no. 68,* University of Oxford Centre for Brazilian Studies (2005).

—, 'Origins and Consequences of Import Substitution in Brazil,' in L. Di Marco (ed), *International Economics and Development* (New York: Academic Press, 1972), pp. 339–56.

Foxley, A., *Latin American Experiments in Neo-Conservative Economics* (Berkeley, CA: Univesity of California Press, 1983).

Gasques, J. G., and C. M. Villa Verde, 'Gastos Públicos na Agricultura, Evolução e Mudanças', *Discussion Paper n. 948* (Brasília: Ipea, 2003).

Giambiagi, F. and M. M. Moreira (eds), *A Economia Brasileira nos Anos 90* (Rio de Janeiro: BNDES, 1999).

Gold, D. A., C. Lo and E. O. Wright, 'Recent Developments in Marxist Theories of the Capitalist State, *Monthly Review*, 27:5 (1975), pp. 29–43.

Goldfajn, I., K. Hennings and H. Mori, 'Brazil's Financial System: Resilience to Shocks, no Currency Substitution, but Struggling to Promote Growth', Central Bank of Brazil Working Paper 75 (June 2003).

Goldsmith, R., *Premodern Financial Systems: A Historical Comparative Study* (Cambridge: Cambridge University Press, 1987).

Gosden, P. H. G. H., *The Friendly Societies in England, 1815–1875* (Manchester: University of Manchester Press, 1961).

Gourevitch, P., *Politics in Hard Times: Comparative Responses to International Economic Crises* (Ithaca, NY: Cornell University Press, 1986).

Gruben, W. C., and J. H. Welch, 'Banking and Currency Crisis Recovery: Brazil's Turnaround of 1999', *Economic and Financial Review* (4th Quarter 2001), pp. 12–23.

Gudin, E., and R. C. Simonsen, *A Controvérsia do Planejamento na Economia Brasileira* (Rio de Janeiro: IPEA/INPES, 1978).

Gurley, J., and E. Shaw, 'Financial Aspects of Economic Development', *American Economic Review*, 45:4 (1955), pp. 515–38.

Gruben, W. C., and J. H. Welch., 'Banking and Currency Crisis Recovery: Brazil's Turnaround of 1999', *Economic and Financial Review* (4th Quarter 2001), pp. 12–23.

Haggard, S., C. Lee and S. Maxfield (eds), *The Politics of Finance in Developing Countries* (Ithaca, NY: Cornell University Press, 1993).

Hall, P. A., and D. W. Soskice, *Varieties of Capitalism: The Institutional Foundations of Comparative Advantage* (Oxford: Oxford University Press, 2001).

Hall, R. B., 'The Discursive Demolition of the Asian Development Model', *International Studies Quarterly*, 47:1 (2003), pp. 71–99.

Hawkins, J., and M. Dubravko, 'The Banking Industry in the Emerging Market Economies: Competition, Consolidation and Systemic Stability – An Overview' (Basel: Bank for International Settlements, 2001).

Hellwig, M., 'On the Economics and Politics of Corporate Finance and Corporate Control', in X. Vives (ed.), *Corporate Governance* (Cambridge: Cambridge University Press, 2000), pp. 95–134.

Henrique, J., *Estrutura e Conjuntura das Caixas Econômicas Federais* (Rio de Janeiro: Conselho Superior das Caixas Econômicas Federais, 1960).

Hirschman, A. O., 'Ideologies of Development in Latin America', *Latin American Issues: Essays and Comments* (New York: The Twentieth Century Fund, 1961).

—, *Journeys Toward Progress: Studies of Economic Policy-Making in Latin America* (New York: Norton, 1963).

Hoffmann, S., *Politics and Banking: Ideas, Public Policy and the Creation of Financial Institutions* (Baltimore, MD: Johns Hopkins University Press, 2001).

Hoggarth, G., R. Reis and V. Saporta, 'Costs of Banking System Instability: Some Empirical Evidence' *Journal of Banking and Finance*, 26:5 (2002), pp. 825–55.

Hollingsworth, J. R., and R. Boyer, *Contemporary Capitalism: the Embeddedness of Institutions* (Cambridge: Cambridge University Press, 1997).

Hollingsworth, J. R., and L. N. Lindberg, *Governance of the American Economy* (Cambridge: Cambridge University Press, 1991).

Hoshi, T., 'Back to the Future: Universal Banking in Japan', in A. Saunders and I. Walter (eds), *Universal Banking: Financial System Design Reconsidered* (Chicago, IL: Richard Irwin, 1996), pp. 205–44.

—, *Corporate Finance and Governance in Japan* (Cambridge, MA: MIT Press, 2004).

Huddle, D., 'Disequilibrium, Foreign Exchange Systems and the Generation of Industrialisation and Inflation in Brazil', *Economia Internazionale* (1972), pp. 35–71.

Huntington, S. P., *Political Order in Changing Societies* (New Haven, CT: Yale University Press, 1968).

Jaguaribe, H., *O Nacionalismo na Atualidade Brasileira* (Rio de Janeiro: Instituto Superior de Estudos Brasileiros, 1958).

Johnson, C. A., *MITI and the Japanese Miracle: the Growth of Industrial Policy, 1925–1975* (Stanford, CA: Stanford University Press, 1982).

Kearney, C. A., 'The Comparative Influence of Neoliberal Ideas: Economic Culture and Stabilisation' (Doctoral Dissertation, Brown University Department of Political Science, 2001).

Kindleberger, C., *A Financial History of Western Europe* (London: George Allen and Unwin, 1984).

King, R. G., and R. Levine, 'Finance and Growth: Schumpeter Might be Right', *Quarterly Journal of Economics*, 108:3 (August 1993), pp. 717–737.

—, 'Finance, Entrepreneurship and Growth: Theory and Evidence', *Journal of Monetary Economics*, 32 (1993), pp. 513–42.

Kingstone, P., *Crafting Coalitions for Reform: Business Preferences, Political Insitutions and the Politics of Neoliberal Reform in Brazil* (University Park, PA: Pennsylvania State University Press, 1999).

Kirschner, J. (ed.), *Monetary Orders: Ambiguous Economics, Ubiquitous Politics* (Ithaca, NY: Cornell University Press, 2003).

Klein, M., 'A Theory of the Banking Firm', *Journal of Money, Credit and Banking*, 3 (1971), pp. 205–18.

Krahnen, J. P., and R. H. Schmidt (eds)., *The German Financial System* (Oxford: Oxford University Press, 2004).

Kugelmas, E., 'Difícil Hegemonia: Um Estudo sobre São Paulo na Primeira República' (Doctoral Dissertation, Universidade de São Paulo Department of Political Science, 1986).

Lago, L. A. C., 'A retomada do crescimento e as distorções do 'milagre': 1967–1973', in Abreu, Marcelo (ed.), *A ordem do progresso: cem anos de política econômica republicana. 1889–1989* (Rio de Janeiro: Campus, 1990), pp. 233–94.

Laplane, M., and L. Coutinho, *Internacionalização da Indústria no Brasil* (São Paulo: Editora UNESP, 2003).

La Porta, R., F. Lopez-de-Silanes and A. Schleifer, 'Government Ownership of Banks', *Journal of Finance,* 57:1 (2002), pp. 265–301.

Laurence, H., *Money Rules: The New Poltics of Finance in Britain and Japan* (Ithaca, NY: Cornell University Press, 2001).

Lavelle, K. C., *The Politics of Equity Finance in Emerging Markets* (Oxford University Press, 2004).

Lazonick, W., *Business Organization and the Myth of the Market Economy* (Cambridge: Cambridge University Press, 1991).

Lees, F. A., J. M. Botts and R. P. Cysne, *Banking and Financial Deepening in Brazil* (Basingstoke: Macmillan, 1990).

Leff, N., *Economic Policymaking and Development in Brazil, 1947–64* (New York: Wiley, 1968).

Lemgruber, C., *Uma Análise Quantitativa do Sistema Financeiro no Brasil* (Rio de Janeiro: IBMEC, 1978).

Lenin, V. I., *Selected Works* (Moscow, 2001).

Leopoldi, M. A. P., *Política e Interesses na Industrialização Brasileira. As associações dos industriais, a política econômica e o Estado* (São Paulo: Paz e Terra, 2000).

Levine, R., 'Law, Finance and Economic Growth', *Journal of Financial Intermediation*, 8:1–2 (1999), pp. 8–35.

—, 'Financial Development and Economic Growth: Views and Agenda', *Journal of Economic Literature*, 35: 2 (1997), pp. 688–726.

Lincoln, A., *The Writings of Abraham Lincoln* (Gutenberg Project Centennial Edition).

Lundberg, E., 'Bancos Oficiais: Problema de Finanças Públicas ou Sistema Financeiro', *Informações FIPE No. 148* (USP Fundação de Pesquisas Econômicas, January 1993).

Lyra Filho, J., *O Estado Monetário: Introdução à História das Caixas Econômicas Brasileiras* (Rio de Janeiro: Irmãos Pongetti, 1948).

—, H. M., 'Bank Privatisation in Brazil: is the End of Financial Federalism in Sight?', *Centre for Brazilian Studies Working Paper 8*, University of Oxford (1999).

Martins, L., *Pouvoir et Développment Economique: Formation e Evolution de Structures Politiques au Brésil* (Paris: Anthropos, 1976).

Maxfield, S., *Governing Capital: International Finance and Mexican Politics* (Ithaca, NY: Cornell University Press, 1990).

McKinnon, R., *Money and Capital in Economic Development* (Washington, DC: Brookings Institution, 1973).

McQuerry, E., 'Managed Care for Brazilian Banks', *Federal Reserve Bank of Atlanta Review*, 86:2 (2001), pp. 27–44.

Merton, R. K., 'The Unanticipated Consequences of Purposive Social Action', *American Sociological Review*, 1 (1936), pp. 894–904.

Ming, C., 'O Lucro do Banco do Brasil', *O Estado de S. Paulo*, 27 February 2010, B2

Moura, A. R., 'Bancos Públicos Estaduais e Políticas Macroeconômicas', in Pinheiro, A. C. and L. C. Oliveira Filho (eds), *Mercado de Capitais e Bancos Públicos: Análise e Experiências Comparadas* (Rio de Janeiro: Contra Capa-ANBID, 2007), pp. 305–18.

Mura, J. (ed.), *History of European Savings Banks*, 2 vols (Stuttgart: Sparkassen Verlag, 1996–2000).

Naim, M., 'Latin America: The Second Stage of Reform', *Journal of Democracy*, 5:4 (October 1994), pp. 32–48.

Nakane, M. I., and D. B. Weintraub, 'Bank Privatisation and Productivity: Evidence for Brazil', *Journal of Banking and Finance*, 29 (2005) pp. 2259–89.

Nelson, J. (ed.), *A Precarious Balance: Democracy and Economic Reforms in Latin America* (Washington, DC: Overseas Development Council, 1994).

Nelson, R. R., *National Innovation Systems: A Comparative Analysis* (Oxford: Oxford University Press, 1993).

Nobrega, M. and G. Loyola., 'The Long and Simultaneous Construction of Fiscal and Monetary Institutions', in L. Sola and L. Whitehead (eds), *Statecrafting Monetary Authority: Democracy and Financial Order in Brazil* (Oxford: Centre for Brazilian Studies, 2006), pp. 57–84.

Novaes Filho, W., and S. Werlang, 'Inflationary Bias and State Owned Financial Institutions', *Journal of Development Economics*, 47 (1995), pp. 135–54.

O'Donnell, G., 'Illusions about Consolidation', *Journal of Democracy*, 7:2 (1996), pp. 34–51.

—, *Modernisation and Bureaucratic Authoritarianism* (Berkeley, CA: University of California Institute for International Studies, 1973).

Offe, C., 'Political Economy: Sociological Perspectives', in R. E. Goodin and H.-D. Klingemann (eds), *A New Handbook of Political Science* (Oxford: Oxford University Press, 1998), pp. 675–90.

O'Hara, M., 'A Dynamic Theory of the Banking Firm', *Journal of Finance*, 38:1 (March 1983), pp. 127–40.

Ostrom, E., *Governing the Commons: The Evolution of Institutions for Collective Action, Political Economy of Institutions and Decisions* (Cambridge: Cambridge University Press, 1990).

Paes, J. P. P., 'Bancos Estaduais, "Criação" de Moeda e Ciclo Político' (Masters Dissertation, EAESP-FGV, São Paulo, 1996).

Pagano, M., and P. Volpin., 'The Political Economy of Finance', *Oxford Review of Economic Policy*, 17:4 (2001), pp. 502–19.

Payne, L., *Brazilian Industrialists and Democratic Change* (Baltimore, MD: Johns Hopkins University Press, 1994).

Peláez, C. M., and W. Suzigan., *História Monetária do Brasil* (Brasilia: UNB, 1981).

Pérez, S., *Banking on Privilege: The Politics of Spanish Financial Reform* (Ithaca, NY: Cornell University Press, 2003).

Pinheiro, A. C., and L. C. O. Filho, *Mercado de Capitais e Bancos Públicos: Análise e Experiências Comparadas* (Rio de Janeiro: Contra Capa-ANBID, 2007).

Pinto, M. A. C., 'O BNDES e o sonho de desenvolvimento: 30 anos de publicação do II PND', *Revista do BNDES*, Rio de Janeiro, 11:22 (2004).

Polanyi, K., *The Great Transformation* (New York: Farrar and Rinehart, 1944).

Price, R., *Proposal for Establishing Life Annuuities in Parishes for the Benefit of the Industrial Poor* (London, 1773).

Przeworski, A., *Social Democracy as a Historical Phenomenon* (Cambridge: Cambridge University Press, 1979).

Rajan, R., and L. Zingales, 'The Great Reversals: The Politics of Financial Development in the Twentieth Century', *Journal of Financial Economics*, 69:1 (2003), pp. 5–50.

—, 'Financial Dependence and Growth', *American Economic Review*, 88:3 (1998), pp. 559–86.

Rawls, J., *Political Liberalism*. (New York: Columbia University Press, 1996).

Roberts, R. and D. Kynaston., *The Bank of England: Money, Power and Influence, 1694–1994* (Oxford: Clarendon Press, 1995).

Rocha, A., *As Caixas Econômicas e o Crédito Agrícola* (Rio de Janeiro, 1905).

Rodrigues de Paula, L. F., *The Recent Wave of European Banks in Brazil: Determinants and Impacts* (Oxford: Centre for Brazilian Studies, 2001).

Samuels, D., 'Fiscal Straightjacket: The Political Economy of Macroeconomic Reform in Brazil, 1995–2002', *Journal of Latin American Studies,* 35 (2003), pp. 1–25.

Santomero, A. M., 'Modelling the Banking Firm', *Journal of Money, Credit and Banking*, 16:4 (November 1984), pp. 609–11.

Sartori, G., *Parties and Party Systems* (New York: Cambridge University Press, 1976).

Scharpf, F. W., *Governing in Europe* (Oxford: Oxford University Press, 1995).

Schmitter, P., 'Still the Century of Corporatism', *Review of Politics*, 36 (1974), pp. 85–131.

—, *Interest Conflict and Political Change in Brazil* (Stanford, CA: Stanford University Press, 1971).

Schmitter, P. C., and W. Streeck, *Private Interest Government: Beyond Market and State* (London: Sage, 1985).

Schneider, B. R., *Politics within the State: Elite Bureaucrats and Industrial Policy in Authoritarian Brazil* (Pittsburgh, PA: University of Pittsburgh Press, 1991).

Shapiro, H., *Engines of Growth: The State and Transnational Auto Companies in Brasil* (Cambridge, MA: Harvard University Press, 1994).

Shaw, E. S., *Financial Deepening in Economic Development* (New York: Oxford University Press, 1973).

Sher, M. J., and N. Yoshino (eds), *Small Savings Mobilisation and Asian Economic Development: The Role of Postal Financial Services* (London: M. E. Sharpe, 2004).

Shleifer, A., 'State versus Private Ownership', *Journal of Economic Perspectives*, 12:4 (1998), pp. 133–50.

Schleifer, A., and R. W. Vishney, *The Grabbing Hand: Government Pathologies and their Cures* (Cambridge, MA: Harvard University Press, 1998).

Shonfield, A., *Modern Capitalism: The Changing Balance of Public and Private Power* (Oxford: Oxford University Press, 1965).

Sigaud, J. F., *O Homem Benfazejo ou das Vantagens que Resultam da Fundação da Caixa Econômica dos Povos Civilizados* (Rio de Janeiro: Tipografia Imperial e Constitucional de Seignot-Plancher and Cia. Vol. XII Biblioteca Constitucional do Cidadão Brasileiro, 1832).

Sikkink, K., *Ideas and Institutions: Developmentalism in Brazil and Argentina* (Ithaca, NY: Cornell University Press, 1991).

Silva, G. B., *Caixas Econômicas: A Questão da Função Social* (Rio de Janeiro: Forense, 2004).

Skidmore, T., *Politics in Brazil, 1930–1964: An Experiment in Democracy* (New York: Oxford University Press, 1967).

Smith, A. *The Wealth of Nations* (New York: Modern Library, 2000).

Sola, L., *Idéias Econômicas Decisões Políticas* (São Paulo: Edusp, 1998).

Sola, L., and E. Kugelmas, 'Crafting Economic Stabilisation: Political Discretion and Technical Innovation in the Implementation of the Real Plan', in L. Sola and L. Whitehead (eds), *Statecrafting Monetary Authority: Democracy and Financial Order in Brazil* (Oxford: Centre for Brazilian Studies, 2006), pp. 85–116.

Sola, L., and L. Whitehead (eds), *Statecrafting Monetary Authority: Democracy and Financial Order in Brazil* (Oxford: Centre for Brazilian Studies, 2006).

Souza, C. A., *A Anarquia Monetária e suas Conseqüências* (São Paulo: Monteiro Lobato, 1924).

Souza Reis, F. T., *A Dívida do Brasil: Estudo Retrospectivo* (São Paulo: Officinas Graphicas da 'Revista de Commercio e Industria' 1917)

Stiglitz, J., and A. Weiss, 'Credit Rationing in Markets with Imperfect Information', *American Economic Review*, 71 (1981), pp. 353–76.

Studart, R., *Investment Finance in Economic Development* (London: Routledge, 1995).

Tavares, M. C., *Da substituição de Importações ao Capitalismo Financeiro: Ensaios sobre Economia Brasileira*, 7th edn (Rio de Janeiro: Zahar Editores, 1978).

—, 'O Sistema Financeiro Brasileiro e o Ciclo de Expansão Recente', in L. G. M. Belluzo and L. Coutinho (eds), *Desenvolvimento Capitalista no Brasil: Ensaios sobre a Crise* (São Paulo: Brasiliense, 1983).

—, 'O rombo do Banco do Brasil', *Correio Brasiliense* (14 April, 1996).

Tilly, C. (ed.), *The Formation of National States in Western Europe* (Princeton, NJ: Princeton University Press, 1975).

Tobin, J., 'The Commercial Banking Firm: A Simple Model', *Scandanavian Journal of Economics,* 84:4 (1982), pp. 10–28.

—, 'The Commercial Banks as Creators of 'Money', *Essays in Economics*, 3 vols (Cambridge, MA: MIT Press, 1982–7), vol. 1.

Topik, S., *The Political Economy of the Brazilian State, 1889–1930* (Austin, TX: University of Texas Press, 1987).

Triner, G. D., 'Banking, Economic Growth and Industrialisation: Brazil, 1906–30', *Revista Brasileira de Economia,* 50:1 (1996), pp. 135–53.

Velasco, A., and M. Tommasi, 'Where Are We in the Political Economy of Reform?', *Journal of Policy Reform*, 1:2 (1996), pp. 187–238.

Vidotto, C. A., 'Reforma dos Bancos Federais Brasileiros: Programa, Base Doutrinária e Afinidades Teóricas', *Economia e Sociedade*, 14:1 (2005), pp. 57–84.

Vieira, D. T., *A Evolução do Sistema Monetário Brasileiro* (São Paulo: IPE-USP, 1962).

Vilela, N. L. (ed.), *Idéias Econômicas de Joaquim Murtinho* (Brasília: Senado Federal/Fundação Rui Barbosa, 1980).

Villela, A. A., 'The Political Economy of Money and Banking in Imperial Brazil, 1850–1870' (Doctoral Dissertation, London School of Economics and Political Science, 1999).

Villela, A. V., and W. Suzigan., *Política do Governo e Crescimento da Economia Basileira, 1889–1945* (IPEA/INPES, 1973).

von Mettenheim, K., and L. Gonzalez, 'Government Ownership of Banks Revisited', *memo* (São Paulo: FGV-EAESP, 2007).

Weinstein, D., and Y. Yafeh, 'On the Costs of a Bank Centred Financial System: Evidence from the Changing Main Bank Relationships in Japan', *Journal of Finance*, 53 (1998), pp. 635–72.

Werlang, S., and A. Fraga, 'Os Bancos Estaduais e o Descontrole Fiscal: Alguns Aspectos', *Revista Brasileira de Economia*, 49:2 (1995), pp. 165–75

Whitley, R., *Divergent Capitalisms: The Social Structuring and Change of Business Systems* (Oxford: Oxford University Press, 1999).

Woo-Cummings, M. (ed.), *The Developmentalist State* (Ithaca, NY: Cornell University Press, 1999).

Woo, J., *Race to the Swift: State and Finance in Korean Industrialisation* (New York: Columbia University Press, 1991).

Zini Jr, A. A., 'Uma avaliação do setor financeiro no Brasil: da reforma de 1964/65 à crise dos anos 80' (Masters Dissertation, DEPE-UNICAMP, 1990).

Zysman, J., 'How Institutions Create Historically Rooted Trajectories of Growth', *Industrial and Corporate Change*, 3:1 (1994), pp. 243–83.

—, *Governments, Markets and Growth: Financial Systems and the Politics of Industrial Change* (Ithaca, NY: Cornell University Press, 1983).

INDEX

Abbink Mission review, 148
ABN-Amro, 7
administrative costs increase, Caixas, 121
Agricultural and Industrial Credit Scheme, 1937, 75
Agricultural/ Industrial Credit Facility, 75, 76
agriculture/ agro industry, loans, 86
  1995–2009, 42–3, 42–3*f*2.9–10
  Banco do Brazil and, 75, 76, 87
Allen, F., and A. Gale
  government banks and markets theory, 17–18
  government banks or markets theory, 16–17
Almeida, José F., 132
alternative energy development, BNDE and, 154
Amazonia Integration Programme, 159
Aranha, Oswald, 74, 79
assets over equity ratios, Caixa, 135
ATM citizenship cards, 3, 4, 11
  expansion, 49, 50
  Caixa and, 103, 138
  family grants, 24–5
Austria, savings banks development, 105
authoritarian regimes, transitions from, 25

bad credit, 7, 8–9, 9*f*1.1, 52–6
  credit, agriculture loans, 43*f*2.10
  business loans, 45*f*2.12
  consumer loans, 47, 47*f*2.14
  Finance Ministry asset management and, 34
  home loans, 41*f*2.8
  late loans/ provisions comparison, 54*t*2.1

loans control, 52–6
loans to Federal Government, 36*f*2.2
loans to industry, 39*f*2.6
loans to state/ municipal governments, 38*f*2.4
policies for, 130–1
Bahia Savings Bank, 110
Banco Brasileiro e Portuguez, 112
Banco Commerical de Rio de Janeiro (BCRJ), 65
Banco da República, 68–70
Banco do Brasil (first), 60, 61–5
  insolvency, 63–5
Banco do Brasil (second), 60–8
Banco do Brasil (present), 5, 7, 59–100
  and PT coalition, 89–90, 97
  as national bank, 1889–1930, 68–73
  balance sheet summaries, 2002–8, 91–3, 92*t*3.1
  comparison Itaú and Bradesco, 94*t*3.2
  reorganized, 1942, 75–6
  shares, market valuation, 96*f*3.1–2, 97
Banco Econômico, failure, 30–1
Banco Nacional
  Banco do Brasil, 1893 merger, 68
  failure, 30–1
Banco Popular do Brasil, Banco do Brazil and, 91
Banespa (São Paulo state bank), 7
  privatization, 159
bank accounts, popular
  increase, 23–4
  simplified, 50
Bank Mobilisation Fund, 1930s, 73, 74
Bank of England, origin, 61

Bank Stabilisation Account, Banco do
     Brazil, 77
bank-centred financial systems, 16
banking crises
     1864, effects, 111–12
     1900, 117
     inflows increase during, 27, 31
banking theory, competitive advantages,
     25–8
banks
     25 largest in Brazil, 6t1.1, 7
     and innovation, 17
     coalitions, Maxfield on, 13–14
     correspondents, 4, 11
     market shares, 7
     reforms, 1980s, 85
     returns, 7, 9t1.2, 10
     solidity, 52–6
     transactions, cost reduction, 27
     vs markets dichotomy, 3
Banque du France, origin, 61
Barbosa, Rui, 68–9
Barreto, Humberto, 124
Basel Accord
     guidelines, Banco do Brazil and, 90
     reserve requirement, 22t1.4n
Basel Indexes, 7
     bad loans, 52–3
     Caixa, 135
     minimum capitalization, Caixa, 133
     requirements, 52–3
     value-at-risk, 56
Basic Inputs (Fibase), 154
Bearle, Adolf, 178
Belgium, savings banks development, 105
Bernardes administration, 71
Berzioni, Ricardo, 89
Bisol, José Paulo, 87
BNDE *see* National Bank for Economic
     Development (BNDE)
BNDE-ECLA working group, 149
BNDES *see* National Bank for Economic
     and Social Development (BNDES)
BNDES-Exim, 158
BNDESpar, capital markets investment, 164
bonds, indexed, as alternative contracts cur-
     rency, 84
Booz Allen-Hamilton, reform alternatives
     report, 33–4

Boudoukh, J., et al., value-at-risk calcula-
     tions, 56
Bovespa, 2
     collapse, 50–1, 89
     Banco do Brasil and, 60, 88, 93–4
Bradesco, 7, 93–6, 121, 167
     comparison Itaú and Banco do Brasil,
          94t3.2
Braga, Cincinato, 71–2
branch offices
     Caixas, 121
     community presence, advantages, 47–50
     expansion during foreign debt crisis, 85
     increase, Banco do Brasil, 76
     mini-branches (PAB), 49
Brás, Venceslau, 117
Brazilian Democratic Movement (PMDB),
     90
Brazilian Investments (Ibrasa), 154
Brazilian Machinery (Embramec), 154
Brazilian System of Savings and Loans
     (SBPE), 126–7
Bresser-Pereira, Luiz Carlos, on developmen-
     talism, 19
Bretton Woods system, 77, 148
budget policies, national development plan,
     BNDES and, 159
Bulhoes, Otávio de, 70, 79, 122
Business Finance (Finem) Programme,
     BNDES, 162–3
businesses, non-financial, loans, 1995–2009,
     44–5, 44–5f2.11–12

Caixa de Conversão, 70–1
Caixa Econômica e Monte de Socorro, 102,
     110–11
Caixa Econômica Federal, 5, 7, 101–44
     created, 1970, 123
     ATM citizenship cards, 24–5, 103
     concession lottery shops, 49
     corporate governance modernization,
          131–2
     'IMF-like' conditional loans, 1, 103, 129,
          133
     simplified bank accounts, 50
Caixa Superior Council, 122, 143
Caixas, 1861–89, 110–15
     balances, 114t4.3
     centralization, 122–4

pawn services, 111
provincial, 113–14
regulation, 1860, 111
state, 102
Caixas Econômicas, 1889–1930, 116–17
Calliari, Alcir, 87
Calogeras, João Pandiá, 117
  on Banco do Brazil (first) insolvency, 63
  on Barbosa's regional banks, 68
Campos, Roberto
  on BNDE project criteria, 148–9
  on development banking, 23, 122
Canevalli, on savings banks, 109
capital
  flight from Brazil, 2001–2, 10
  flow direction, savings banks, 140–1
  starvation, public sector, 56
capital markets investment, BNDESpar,
    164–5
Capital Markets Programme, BNDES,
    162–3
capitalization
  Caixa, 2001–8, 133–8
  PROEF and, 33–4
Caravelli, on US/UK banks consolidation, 47
Cardoso, Fernando Henrique, administra-
    tion, 5, 159
  and Banco do Brazil, 86–9
  and Caixa, 132
  and private banking, 29
  federal banks and, 34, 182
  1993 Immediate Action Plan, 33
Carreira, Castro, on Banco do Brazil (first)
    insolvency, 63
Cartão do Cidadão (citizenship card), 24–5
Castelo Branco, Humberto de Alencar,
    administration, 83
Central Bank of Brazil, 122
  Banco do Brasil and, 59, 60
  replaces SUMOC, 82
Chang, H. J., on developmentalism, 19
civil war, Rio Grande do Sul, 72
coffee crisis, Banco do Brasil lending and,
    73–4
Collor, Fernando, 86, 87
  Collor Plan, 157–8
commanding heights approach, 18, 19
  BNDES, 146, 147, 150, 163
  providing depth, 2, 175, 177, 181

commercial banks, Banco do Brazil and, 78,
    79–80
competitive advantages, 25–8
  organizational structure, 47–50
competitive integration, Petrobrás/ BNDES
    report, 157
Congressional Finance Committee enquir-
    ies, 72
Constitution, and Banco do Brasil, 59
Constitutionalist revolt, defeat, 74
consumer loans, 1995–2009, 45–7,
    46–7f2.13–14
corporate governance modernization, Caixa,
    131–2
correspondent banking, 49–50
corruption, Banco do Brasil (first), 62–5
Coruja & Cia, failure, 113
cost reduction, bank transactions, 27
Costa e Silva, Artur da, 83
counter-cyclical credit/ finance, 1, 50–2
  2008 financial crisis, 146
  federal banks and, 23
  Lula administration, 35
Coutinho, Luciano, 160, 165
credit/ finance
  counter-cyclical, 1, 50–2
  during, 1980s, Banco do Brasil, 85
  leverage, 51
  policy, 1970s, Banco do Brasil, 83
Credit Mobilier, 146
crisis/ recovery cycles, 50–2
Cruzado Plan, 85–6
currency, indexed bonds as alternative, 84
currency boards
  1920s, 71–3, 74
  Caixa de Conversão, 70–1
  Carteira de Emissão e Redesconto, 71
currency emissions
  Banco do Brasil (first), 62, 63
  Banco do Brasil (second), 65–6, 67
  Banco do Brasil (third), 77–80
  banknotes, inflation, 64
  limits, 1920s, 71
  regional banks, 68–9
Cutolo, Sergio, 129
Cysne, Roberto, on GDP transfer, 86

Dahl, Robert, 181
Dahrendorf, Ralf, on planned vs market
    economies, 20t1.3

data aggregation fallacy, 15
de Castro, Danilo, 132
debit cards, citizenship cards as, 24–5
debt crises
    BNDES and, 155–7
    Banco do Brasil and, 73–5, 88
    Banco do Brasil (second) and, 66–7
Defoe, Daniel, 101, 104
Demirgüç-Kunt, A. and R. Levine, govern-
    ment banks and markets theory, 18
democratization, effects, 182
Denmark, savings banks development, 105
Deodoro da Fonseca, President, 68, 69
deposits/ withdrawals, Caixas, 1862–89,
    111–13, 112*t*4.1, 113*t*4.2
development banking
    BNDES, 145–71
    Caixa, 103
    Campos and, 23, 122
    history, 146–8
developmentalism, 18–19
    Caixas and, 120–2
    Kubitschek administration, 80–1
    vs liberalism, 1945–64, Banco do Brasil,
        76–80
Diamond, D., and R. G. Rajan, on bank
    safety, 27
disequilibria, Caixas, 120–2
Dom Pedro I, and Banco do Brasil (first),
    63–5
Dom Pedro II, and Banco do Brasil (sec-
    ond), 65–7
Dore, Ronald, market- vs organization-ori-
    ented systems, 20*t*1.3
downsizing proposals, Banco do Brasil, 87,
    88
Dutra, Eurico Gaspar, 77

economic adjustment, policies for, 130–1
Economic Development Council (CDE),
    153–4
Econômico, 130
efficiency comparisons, 21–2
electric energy, BNDE and, 148–50
Eletrobras, 150
Emerging Tech Firm Fund, 159
Empresa Gestora de Ativos (Emgea), 34
    and BNH portfolio, 41
    Caixa non-performing assets sold to, 133
equity markets, BNDES and, 155

Estado Novo, Banco do Brasil and, 75–6
ethanol production, 168
Europe
    banking cooperation, 109–10
    savings banks development, 104, 105–9
Evans, Peter, on developmentalism, 19
Exchange Rate Portfolio, Banco do Brasil,
    75, 78
Eximbank (US), and US–Brazilian agree-
    ment, 148
export/ import finance
    Banco do Brasil, 75, 79
    BNDES, 162–3
    BNDES-Exim, 158

Fama, E. F., on Modigliani-Miller theorem,
    26
family grants, 4
    ATM cards, 24–5
federal banks capitalization, 5, 7, 34
    compared state government banks, 11
    privatization alternatives development,
        33
Federal Government, loans to, 1995–2009,
    35–8, 35–6*f*2.1–2
FGTS payroll surcharge pension fund, 102,
    122, 126, 127
Filho, Café, 80, 81
Finance Programme for Small and Medium
    Enterprises (Fipeme), 151–2, 154
financial reforms, and BNDE, 151–3
financial sector growth, 1955–75, 2–3, 83
Financial Operations Tax (IOF), 152
Fiocca, Damion, 160
fiscal deficits, BNDES and, 156–7
fiscal management, Treasury, 59
Fiscal and Inspection Council, Caixas, 111
Fiscal Responsibility Law, 2000, 129, 130
fixed assets to equity ratios, 7
foreign accounts deterioration, 1950s, 79
foreign debt, BNDES and, 155–7
foreign exchange
    shortages, 79
    trading, Banco do Brasil, 75, 78, 79
foreign/ private bank lending, 1995–2009,
    34–47
    as GDP percentage, 7–8, 8*f*1.1
Foreign Commerce Account (Cacex), 82
Fortunati, José, accountability proposals, 33
Fraga, Arminio, 5, 33

France
  bank-centred system, 16
  savings banks development, 105–6
Franco, Itamar, 87, 127, 132
Franco, Souza, 67
Freire, Anibal, 72
Fund for Agroindustrial Conversion
  (Funar), 152
Fundo Amazonia, BNDES and, 168
Furlan, Luiz Fernando, 160
Furtado, Celso, Three Year Plan, 81

General Credit Portfolio, Banco do Brazil,
  75
Germany
  bank-centred system, 16
  savings banks development, 106
Gerschenkron, Alexandre, 2
  on development banks, 147
  on political economy, 10
  on rapid industrialization, 7
Gide, Charles, 101, 104
Goldfajn, I., K. Henning and H. Mori, on
  bank expansion, 30
Goldman Sachs, on federal banks privatization, 33
Gomes, Ciro, 87
Gosden, P., on UK friendly societies, 104
Goulart, João, 81
government bank accounts, 85
government bank lending, 1995–2009,
  34–47
  as GDP percentage, 7–8, 8*f*1.1
government banking
  and markets theory, 17–18
  change theories, 14–19, 15*f*1.3
  disagreements about, 11
  liberal economists and, 173–7
  or markets theory, 15*f*1.3, 16–17
  savings banks role, 101–2
government bonds, Caixa purchase, 113
government budget deficits, and inflation, 77
government control
  Banco do Brasil (first), 61–3
  Banco do Brasil (second), 65
  national banking, 69–73
Government Plan of Economic Action,
  1965 (PAEG), 82
Grameen Bank, 4
Great Britain *see* United Kingdom

Greece, savings banks development, 106
Gros, Francisco, 159
Guarantee Fund for Competitivity Promo-
  tion (FGPC), 158
Gudin, Eugênio, 80
Gurley, Shaw, on banks as intermediating
  institutions, 26
Gushiken, Luiz, 89

Hall, P. A. and D. Soskice
  on case studies, 180
  on coordinated market economies, 19,
    20*t*1.3
  on European cooperation in banking,
    109
  varieties of capitalism, 3
Hellwig, M., on innovation, 17
Hirschman, O., on development banks, 147
home/ construction loans
  1995–2009, 40–2, 40*f*2.7, 41*f*2.8
  Caixa and, 126–8, 133–5
  Caixas, 121–2
  middle classes, 102, 103, 121–2, 124, 131
Home Construction Fund for Low Income
  Populations (FAHBRE), 126
Home Finance System (SFH), 40–1, 126–7
Home Finance System (SFI), 127, 143
Home Finance System, 1966, 122
Homem, Sales Torres, 67
Huntington, Samuel, 181
hypothetical shocks comparison, 56–7

IMF
  exchange rates accord, 79
  federal banks support, 56–7, 81–2
  money supply control, 84
  on federal banks privatization, 33
import substitution, BNDE and, 153–6
indexed bonds, as alternative contracts currency, 84
industrial change, 1
Industrial Bank of India, 146
Industrial Bank of Japan, 146
Industrial Finance Agency, BNDE, 151
industrialization, BNDE and, 150, 153–6
industry, loans to, 1995–2009, 38–40,
  39*f*2.5–6
Industry and Commerce Ministry, BNDE
  and, 155
inflation
  1950s, 79–80
  1980s, 85–6

and government budget deficits, 77
banknotes, 64
effects, 124–5
inflows increase, during banking crisis, 27, 31
insolvency, Banco do Brasil (first), 63–5
Inter-American Development Bank, BNDE and, 151
interbank lending, BNDES and, 161, 161t5.1
interest rates, and shocks, 56–7
investor confidence recovery, 89
Ireland, savings banks development, 106–7
Italy, savings banks development, 107
Itaú, 7
    comparison Banco do Brasil and Bradesco, 93–7, 94t3.2
    Unibanco merger, 7, 89, 91

Jackson, Andrew, and First Bank of the US, 63
Jackson, Henry, 5
Jafet, Ricardo, 79
Japan, bank-centred system, 16
Japan Development Bank, 146
Johnson, Chalmers Ashby, on liberal vs coordinated/ developmental, 19, 20t1.3, 147
Jorge, José, 87
Jorge, Miguel, and the Caixa, 103
Jornal do Comercio, on, 1900 Banco do Brasil, 70
JP Morgan
    Emerging Market Bond Index, 50
    value-at-risk calculations, 56

Kelly, George, rule-governed vs purpose-governed state, 20t1.3
Kennedy administration, and Furtado Three Year Plan, 81
Keynes, John Maynard, on uncertainty and liquidity, 27
King, R. G., and R. Levine, on banks and information, 17
Kirschner, J., politics determines policy, 13
Klein, M., organizational conception of banks, 26
Kreditanstalt fur Weidaraufbau, 146
Kubitschek de Oliveira, Juscelino
    administration, and BNDE, 149–51
    developmentalism, 80–1

La Porta, R., Lopez-de-Silanes and Schleifer
    government banks AND markets theory, 18
    modernization theories, 14–15
Labour Party (UK) Clause IV, 7
Lafer, Celso, 78
Latin American debt crisis, BNDES and, 155–7
Laurence, H., on politics and financial reforms, 13
leadership, political, Banco do Brazil, 89–90
Leme, Paulo, on federal banks privatization, 33
lending
    and coffee crisis, 73–4
    as GDP percentage, 7–8, 8f1.1
    Caixa market share, 125–6, 125f4.1
    comparisons, 1995–2009, 34–47
    government, cost advantages, 21–3, 22t1.4
    interbank/ non-bank, BNDES, 1995–2008, 161t5.1
    loan approvals by programme, BNDES, 162t5.2
    of last resort, 66–7, 74, 160
    trends, 7, 8f1.1, 8–9
    see also bad credit; debt crises
Leninist theories, 2, 12, 175
Lessa, Carlos, 160
letters of credit, Caixa, 128
Lewis, Arthur, 2
    on development banks, 147
    on rapid industrialization, 7
liberal markets
    economic theory, 2, 3
    and government banking, 173–7
    vs coordinated/ developmental markets, 19–21, 20t1.3
    vs developmentalism, 1945–64, Banco do Brazil, 76–80
liberalization/ privatization, interaction, 173–9
Lima, Cassio Casseb, 89–90
Lima Neto, Antonio Francisco de, 90
Lincoln, Abraham, 5
Lindblom, Charles Edward, on muddling through, 4, 12
Lipset, Seymour Martin, 181
loans *see* bad credit; debt crises; lending

long-term funding, BNDES and, 145–71, 156–9, 163

Lopes, Lucas, Finance Minister, 81

Loyola, Gustavo, 87

Lucena, Baron, 69

Lula da Silva, Luis Inácio, administration, 3
    Banco do Brazil and, 89–97
    BNDES and, 159, 160–70
    countercyclical strategies, 35
    federal banks and, 182
    neo-developmentalist policies, 159

Lundberg, Eduardo, on development roles, 33

Malan, Pedro, 5, 33, 129

management assistance, BNDES, 168

Management Committee of Federal Public Financial Institutions (COMIF), 33

Mantega, Guido, 95, 160

Mariani, Clemente, 81

market share
    Caixa, 125–6, 125f4.1
    comparisons, 1995–2009, 34–47
    during Cruzado Plan, Banco do Brazil, 85

market-centred economies, 16

Marshall Plan, 148

Mattoso, Jorge, 134

Mauá, Baron, and Banco do Brasil (second), 65

Maxfield, S., on banker's coalitions, 13–14

Means, Gardiner, 178

Meirelles, Henrique de Campos, Central Bank President, 95

Mendes, Odorico, on Banco do Brasil (first) insolvency, 64

Meridional bank, 130

Mexican debt crisis
    BNDES and, 155–7
    effects, 84–6

middle class, and Caixa, 102, 103, 121–2, 124, 131

military government, effects, 10
    BNDE, 151–3
    Banco do Brasil, 60, 82–3
    Caixas, 122–4

modernization
    Caixa, 124–6
    during foreign debt crisis, 85
    theories, 14–16

Modigliani-Miller theorem, 26

monetary policies
    1920s, 71–3
    Banco do Brasil and, 82–3
    SUMOC, 59

monopolies, Banco do Brasil (first), 61

movement account, zeroed Treasury obligations, Banco do Brazil, 83

multiplier effect, government loans, 21–3, 22t1.4

municipal governments
    BNDES lending, 168–9
    Caixa loans to, 129–30

Murtinho, Joaquim, 69, 70

Myrdal, Gunnar, 2
    on rapid industrialization, 7
    on development banks, 147

Nassif, Luis, on competitive integration, 157

national banking
    Banco do Brasil, 1889–1930, 68–73
    government control, 69–73

national development plan, BNDES and, 159

national populism, Caixas Econômicas and, 119–20

National Bank for Economic Development (BNDE), 145, 148–56
    project criteria, 148–9

National Bank for Economic and Social Development (BNDES), 5–6, 7, 145–6, 154–71
    compulsory reserves exempt, 53
    financial results, 2002–6, 164t5.3
    long-term finance, 33–4
    structure, 48–9
    total assets, 2007, 165

National Coffee Department (DNC), 74

National Household Survey, 2006, 24

National Housing Bank (BNH), 40–1, 122, 126, 153

National Monetary Council (CMN), replaces SUMOC, 82

National Popular Housing Plan (PAN-HAP), 126

National Sanitation Plan (PLANASA), 126

neo-developmentalist policies, BNDES and, 159, 160–70

Netherlands, savings banks development, 107
Norway, savings banks development, 107
Nossa Caixa, 7
    Banco do Brasil and, 91, 94

O'Hara, M., organizational conception of banks, 26
Official Pension Fund (FGTS), 102, 122, 126, 127
oil shocks, 16, 155
organizational structure, competitive advantages, 47–50
Ostrom, E., on European cooperation in banking, 109

Pais de Almeida, Sebastião, 81
PAREFE, 1995 (Programme of Assistance for State Fiscal Adjustment), 31
Parente, on reform, 33
pawn services, Caixas, 111, 113
payroll taxes, for worker retirement, 102, 152–3
Peixoto, Floriano, 69
Pena, Afonso, 70
Pérez, S., on domestic groups and financial reforms, 13, 14
performance
    comparisons, 1995–2009, 34–47
    indicators, Caixa, 2005–8, 135–8, 136t4.6, 138t4.7
    since capitalization, Caixa, 133–8, 134t4.5
Petrobrás, 157, 159, 168
petroleum production
    BNDES and, 167–8
    deep sea, 160
Pinto, Rossano Maranhão, 90
PIS-Pasep fund, 165
Polanyi, Karl, *The Great Transformation*, 1, 3, 10, 12, 13, 179
policies
    since capitalization, Caixa, 133–8
    disputes, Banco do Brasil and, 90–1
Policy for Production Development, BNDES and, 168
political economy, 10
    and government banking, 177–8
political elites, federal banks support, 57
political history, Banco do Brasil, 59–100

politicization
    Banco do Brasil, 89–90
    Caixa, 123–4
Portuguese monarchy, and Banco do Brasil (first), 61–2
postal agencies, Caixas, 113, 121
poverty alleviation, and banking services access, 24
price stability, Banco do Brasil and, 86–9
private equity/ investment funds, BNDES and, 166
private/ foreign bank lending
    1995–2009, 34–47
    as GDP percentage, 7–8, 8f1.1
private sector lending increase, Banco do Brasil, 77
privatization
    alternatives development, 33
    opposition to, 57
    PROES, 31–3
    proposals, Banco do Brasil, 87
    state enterprises, BNDES and, 156–9
    UK savings banks, 104
Pro-Home Programme, 128
PROEF, 1999–2001 (Federal Programme to Strengthen Federal Financial Institutions), 30
    capitalization and reform, 33–4
PROER, 1995–7 (Programme to Stimulate Restructuring and Strengthening of National Financial System), 30
    and national bank strengthening, 31
    Caixa and, 130
PROES, 1996–9 (Incentive Programme for Reduction of State Public Sector in Banking Activity), 30
    privatizations, 31–3
Programa Centro-Oeste, 159
Programa Reconversul, 159
Programme for Formation of Public Servant Patrimony (Pasep), 152–3
Programme for Social Integration (PIS), 123, 152–3
Programme for Stimulation of Capital Market Development (Procap), 154
Programme of Immediate Action (PAI), 1994, 87
Programme of Joint Operations (POC), 154
Przeworski, A., on Chile, 25
PSDB reforms, Banco do Brasil and, 86–9

PT coalition (Workers' Party), 3, 43, 50, 57, 89–90, 97, 159, 160, 170–1, 174
Banco do Brazil and, 89–90, 97
public policy, government banks and, 11–12, 21–3
public sector
  capital starvation, 56
  finance projects, Caixa, 128–30
  loans to, 1995–2009, 35–8, 35*f*2.1
  modernization, 1

Quadros, Jânio da Silva, 81

Rajan, R., on innovation, 17
Ramos, Maria Fernanda, 134
Rawls, John, *Political Liberalism*, 180
Real (private bank), 7
Real Plan, 10, 29, 85, 88, 124
Rede Ferroviária Federal S.A., 151, 158
Rediscount Facility, Banco do Brazil, 74–7
reforms
  Caixa Econômica Federal, 102–3
  PROEF and, 33–4
  veto coalition against, 60
regional banks, acquisition, Banco do Brasil (second), 65–6
Regional Emerging Entreprise Funds, 159
Regional Industrial Modernization and Reorganization Fund (FMRI), 152
regulations exemption, Banco do Brazil, 76–7
reorientation, Caixa, 2001–8, 133–8
reporting standards, Caixa, 135
reserves, 52–6
  requirements, Basel II Accord, 22*t*1.4*n*
  requirements exemption, Banco do Brazil, 76–7
returns on assets, 7, 9*t*1.2, 10
Revista das Caixas Econômicas, 122, 123
revolution, Banco do Brasil (first) and, 63–5, 73–6
Rio Branco, Viscount, 111, 113
Rio de Janeiro Caixa, runs on, 113
Rio de Janeiro Savings Bank, 110
risk analysis, municipal governments, 169
Rokkan, Stein, 181
rural debt crisis, 1995, 88
Russia, foreign debt moratorium, 56

Salary Variation Compensation Fund (FCVS), 127
Santander (bank), 7
Santomero, A. M., on returns maximizing, 26
São Paulo Caixa, 117–19, 118*t*4.4
Sartori, Giovanni, 181
savings and loan bankruptcies, USA, 108
savings banks
  Brazil, 1861–89, 110–15
  Europe, comparisons, 101, 104–10
  in former colonies, 110
  legislation, 142–4
  state government, 117–19
savings
  deposits increases, Caixas, 120
  indexation, 102
  official, Caixa and, 123, 124
Scharpf, F., and Ostrom, on European cooperation in banking, 109
Schneider, Ben R., 145
science and technology development fund, BNDE, 151
Second National Development Plan, PND II, 153–4
Serra, João Duarte Lisboa, 65
Setubal, Olavo, 95
shareholdings, BNDES, 166–7
shocks, hypothetical, comparison, 56–7
Shonfield, A., *Modern Capitalism*, 10, 12–13, 179
SICREDI, branches, 48
Siderbrás, liquidation, 158
Smith, Adam, 173
social economies, development, 2
social inclusion, 1, 4, 23–5, 182
social policies
  Caixa Econômica Federal and, 102, 103
  competitive advantages, 139–40
Social Assistance Fund (FAS), 123
Social Development Council, 123
Souto bank, collapse, effects, 67, 111
Spain, savings banks development, 107–8
stabilization
  Caixas, 114–15
  policies for, 130–1
start-ups, BNDES and, 160
state enterprises, privatization, 156–9

state governments
    banks, Banco do Brasil acquisition, 93, 94
    BNDES lending, 168–9
    Caixa loans to, 129–30
    loans to, 1995–2009, 36–8, 37–8*f*2.3–4
    savings bank creation, 117–19
    state-centred banking policies, 124
state-led import substitution industrialization, BNDE and, 153–6
Studart, Rogerio, on banks and finance supply, 27
Sturz, J. J., on Banco do Brasil (first), 62, 63
Sturz, on Rio de Janeiro Savings Bank, 110
Superintendence of Money and Credit (SUMOC), 59, 76–7, 78, 79–80, 82
Sweden, savings banks development, 108
Swedish Riksbank, origin, 61
Switzerland, savings banks development, 108

Taubaté accord, 70
Technical and Scientific Development Fund (Funtec), 151
Telebrás, 158–9
Tilly, Charles, 181
Tobin, J., on banks behaviour impact, 26
Torres, Joaquim José Rodrigues, 65, 101
transportation, BNDE and, 148–50
Treasury bonds, holding/ trading, 51
Treasury, fiscal management, 59
Treasury funds, access, Banco do Brasil and, 60
Treasury obligations zeroed, Banco do Brazil, 83

Unibanco, 7
UNICRED, branches, 48
United Kingdom
    market-centred economy, 16
    savings banks development, 104, 106
United Nations Economic Commission on Latin America (ECLA), 149
United States
    and federal banks, 5
    market-centred economy, 16
    US–Brazilian Joint Commissions, 146, 148
    USAID, BNDE and, 151

University of São Paulo Foundation for Economic Research, 34

value-at-risk calculations, 56
Vargas, Getulio, 60, 73, 80
    and BNDE, 148–9
    and currency boards, 72–3
    and savings banks, 119–20
    economic policies, 78, 79
    Estado Novo, 75–6
Vasconcelos, Bernardo, on Banco do Brasil (first), 64
Vidotto, Carlos Augusto, on privatization alternatives development, 33
Vieira, D.T.
    on Banco do Brasil (first) currency issues, 62
    on political change, 74–5
Vilella, A., on Banco do Brasil (second), 67
Vision, 2005 BNDES strategic plan, 159
Votorantim Bank, 7
    Banco do Brazil and, 91, 95

Weber, Max, on planned vs market economies, 20*t*1.3
Weinstein E., and Y. Yafeh, on innovation, 17
Werlang, S., on banking coordination, 33
Whitaker, Finance Minister, 72, 74
Woo-Cummings, M.
    on development banks, 147
    on government banking, 155
    on politics and financial reforms, 13, 14
Workers' Assistance Fund (FAT), 159, 163
Workers' Party (PT) coalition, 3, 43, 50, 57, 89–90, 97, 159, 160, 170–1, 174
working people, and São Paulo Caixa, 119
World Bank
    and US–Brazilian agreement, 148
    on federal banks privatization, 33
    on poverty alleviation, and banking services access, 24

Ximenes, Paulo César, 87

Yunus, Muhammad, 4

Zini, A. A., on financial sector growth, 1955–75, 83
Zysman, John, 10, 178

For Product Safety Concerns and Information please contact our EU
representative GPSR@taylorandfrancis.com
Taylor & Francis Verlag GmbH, Kaufingerstraße 24, 80331 München, Germany

www.ingramcontent.com/pod-product-compliance
Ingram Content Group UK Ltd.
Pitfield, Milton Keynes, MK11 3LW, UK
UKHW021614240425
457818UK00018B/557